Wide Awake
The Miracle of
Spiritual Breakthrough

Interviews on Enlightenment
Compiled by

Quidam Green Meyers

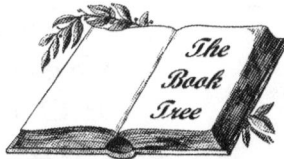

The Book Tree
San Diego, CA

ISBN 1-885395-37-X

First Edition: 2002

Cover design: Lerentia Basson

Layout and design: Lee Berube

Printed on Acid-Free Paper

Published by
The Book Tree
P O Box 16476
San Diego, CA 92176

We provide fascinating and educational products to help awaken the public to new ideas and information that would not be available otherwise.
Call 1 (800) 700-8733 for our *FREE BOOK TREE CATALOG*.

Dedication

To the One Divine Spirit, the true Self of all in which everyone and everything arises. It is from this One that the many voices have appeared on these pages.

To my beloved Diana—the ground of my being. In her total sacrifice to Truth, she lovingly provided the time and the support which allowed this book to become real. My gratitude and love for you are infinite.

To Mom and Dad, Jesse, Lynn and Elizabeth, John and Dave whose love has sustained me.

To Andy for ongoing love, faith and support.

To Saniel, Isaac, Catherine, Wayne, Surya, Nadeen, Arjuna, Dasarath, Alan, Antonio, Akash, Raphael, Neelam, Michael and Matthew for daring to give voice to That which cannot be spoken.

To Brooke, Paul and Vicki for helping to bring the words to life.

...and to the Divine Muse whose endless Dance is all that exists

Table of Contents

About Capitalization

It is traditional for us to capitalize words relating to God—delineating, for example, that the Divine Nature is not afforded the same literal meaning as the "world of nature." In this text, however, we approach this topic from a more expansive perspective.

To begin with, I do not accept the traditional view that the Divine Being is in any way "out there" or separate from myself or is some thing or condition to be attained at some time in the future. The contemporary Awakened posture is that the Divine is the very "field" in which "I" arises—that every thing which exists appears within the vast, infinite, eternal Divine Being.

Therefore, it seems illogical for us to simply carry on with a traditional use of capitalization for terms relating to God. Yet, to date, there is not a universally agreed upon standard for such capitalization.

In this text, then, each interview bears the capitalization desired by the speaker. In this way, the book remains true to each speaker's views on this issue, some of whom are quite definitive in their opinion on the topic.

The same holds true for my words. In the Introduction, Epilogue, questions and any other portions of the book which represent my words, I have chosen to capitalize when I wish for delineation other than ordinary usage. So the word "Presence" should be read to mean the "Divine Presence", as opposed to, "Your presence at the meeting was appreciated." In this way, I hope to serve as yet another voice seeking clarity of meaning while hoping for an eventual standard of capitalization.

— Quidam

Introduction

"I recently bought a new tea kettle. The first time I used it, I noticed that when the water boiled I enjoyed the whistling sound of this new kettle much more than the whistle of the former kettle. But, when I sipped my tea that morning, did it taste better? Had the water somehow boiled <u>more</u> or <u>better</u>? Did this new kettle produce a superior cup of tea?

No. Each kettle just sings at its own unique pitch while performing the basic function of boiling water. And my relative enjoyment of the sound was simply an act of being aware and having a preference. In other words, I was noticing the content of one moment and comparing it to the content of another moment. We notice that moments arise, have content of some kind, and then slip away. And this Awareness is who we are at the core of our Being."

—Quidam, from a live talk Nov. 11, 1999
Sydney, Australia

A popular magazine recently conducted a poll of both scientists and lay readers, asking the question, "What is the most significant technological development in history?" At first, I was a little surprised to see that the Gutenberg printing press topped the 100-place chart. But, on reflection, it does seem reasonable that a process allowing the printed word to be mass-produced (and therefore widely shared) could win an honor at least near to the top. And further developments allowing Gutenberg's process to move into the computer age have been at least as stunning as was the original invention.

Yes, this truly is an amazing age. Technological developments in the last decade alone have surpassed those of many previous lifetimes combined. We've been to the moon and back and now have our sights set on manned landings in deeper space. Life expectancy in the West has expanded to a level undreamed of by our grandparents. It's clearly a time of unprecedented change and growth.

Yet, amid this stunning explosion of logic, science and communication, there are children going hungry in my very own neighborhood. As our labs solve the mysteries of DNA cloning, our fellow travelers on this planet—the animals—are *still* being eradicated at a pace both steady and alarming. The fact that two of the best-selling prescription medications of this "New Age" are Prozac and Viagra speaks volumes about our sense of serenity and security. Indeed, most of us have felt at one time or another that inner peace may seem to be missing (or at least concealed) during the fiery moment-to-moment activities of our busy lives.

In some of us, this very dissatisfaction has led to a more intense interest in religion and spirituality. We find that here, too, recent developments have shown dramatic patterns of shift and growth. The ecumenical movement which was once felt to be profoundly new and progressive now just seems to

7

be basic common sense to most of us. Clergy from all faiths freely intermingle and cooperatively share ideas and teaching methods. Yes, some very significant changes have happened. But these more obvious shifts amount to mere window-dressing compared to some of the developments on the frontiers of radical self-realization.

For much of known history, many of the most profound spiritual teachings—those involving deeply transcendent (life-changing) practices—were kept secret from the masses. Until very recently, for example, the Hindu non-dualistic path of *advaita vedanta* carried a very strict prohibition against the dissemination of certain teachings and practices to the unprepared or casual student. Only senior monks and nuns were initiated into these deep secrets—and then only after years in a cloistered environment where they had proven proficiency in advanced levels of meditative and devotional practice. This was also the case in the study of *dzogchen*, in the Buddhist tradition. Years of successful preliminary work with a zen master would be required before the aspirant would even be considered a candidate for the more transcendent practices of *dzogchen*.

So, for most ordinary seekers, a consideration such as spiritual Awakening in this lifetime appeared to be an impossibility. A very small percentage in any age were able to jump the gap from a self-centered existence to that rare jewel known as Awakening or Enlightenment. It seemed only to happen to others and precious few of them, at that! Because of the rarity of such men and women, it was said in the East that the simple sighting (*darshan*) of the physical body of an Enlightened being bestowed great blessing on the seeker. The possibility that such a presumably lofty state might be true of one such as you or me was assumed to be in a realm comparable to science fiction.

Yet, this is exactly what seems to be taking place all over the Western world. So-called "ordinary" men and women are noticing a longing for something not often found in even the most successful worldly life. In unusually large numbers, people are seeking (and finding) something transcendent, something lasting. And, somehow, many seem to be more easily slipping into a recognition that they *are* (and have always been) that very condition of Awakening that was said to be almost unattainable just a generation ago.

It is from a sincere desire to serve this new vision in human awareness that this book springs.

How This Book Came To Be

One day in the fall of 1999, my friend Arjuna Nick Ardagh and I met for lunch in a cozy little restaurant in Nevada City, CA. At that time, my wife Diana and I were participants in Arjuna's ministry program, and he and I had worked closely together on a number of projects. During the meal, we spoke about this recent phenomenon of a more accessible truth. It seems that we both knew close friends who had seemingly "fallen Awake" and were living relatively ordinary modern lives from that perspective.

And some of these men and women were choosing to openly teach others, spreading the word about how to live from Awareness in one capacity or another.

So, the topic of the "dinner party" came up. Diana and I had often thought that it would be fun to rent a large suite in a nice hotel and host a dinner party for the twenty or more friends on our imaginary guest list of spiritual teachers.

Arjuna wisely commented, "But you know, even if you could arrange such a party, only those in attendance could enjoy it. Why not have the conversations at the 'party' be a book where lots more people can participate?"

I loved the idea. A book would, indeed, allow many more spiritual seekers to be "flies on the wall" at an event that I had long thought would be most fascinating. After all, if these notable men and women were, in fact, Awakened or Enlightened (or even in *any* way interesting!), just to be able to hang out with them and ask them some questions might be most enjoyable. Right?

So, the process of planning this book began. One of the first tasks at hand was the assembling of a "wish list" of teachers/writers—the "guests"—to be interviewed. Version I of that list was written on a few paper bar napkins we grabbed while having lunch that day.

I had decided from the very beginning that since this book would be read primarily by Westerners, those interviewed should be from the West as well. (The title *Wide Awake* would come much later. For quite some time, the working title was *Wide Awake in the West*, which was scrapped when another excellent interviews book entitled *The Awakening West* appeared on the market. And, if memory serves me correctly, one of the other titles we considered early on was *An Ordinary Buddha*.)

A few weeks after our lunch, on a flight to Santa Fe, Arjuna and I worked on the major "plot line" of the book: the questions. Our first challenge was to make this collection unique in some way. It dawned on us that the most interesting variation on the theme would be to ask each guest *exactly the same questions*. It would be months later, when this book was more than halfway completed, that I recognized how important this particular twist would be.

In these early stages, I had a rather simplistic view of the process. Each conversation was to be guided toward a uniform unfolding of information, with the interviewer (me) being essentially invisible. If that was to be the case, we realized that the questions themselves would become the all-important factor. So, during a few more discussions over the next few weeks, we settled on the series of questions found in this book.

The Methodology

From the outset, I knew that I did *not* want to ask our guests a bunch of deeply-philosophical, theoretical questions. To begin with, there are literally thousands of very good books written by qualified researchers that discuss this topic from a detached, scholarly point of view and many, many more which offer traditional simplified, story-book abstractions of truth. I felt no need to go there. Our interest was in uncovering a more experiential, participatory understanding.

What I recognized was that I was about to have the privilege of spending a few moments speaking directly with some of the West's best-known spiritual teachers. At that point, I recalled a story once told to me by a friend who had accidentally found himself alone in a Washington, D.C. elevator with then-Secretary of State Dr. Henry Kissinger. The chance meeting took place during the Vietnam war, when Kissinger was one of the world's most powerful political figures. My friend realized that he had a minute or two, at best—just enough time to ask *one* question. He took a deep breath. "Dr. Kissinger, since it's just you and me here, could I ask your *honest* opinion on the state of the world?" he stammered. Peering back at my friend through those famous black-rimmed glasses, Kissinger—ever the consummate politician—replied in his heavy German accent, "I think it's going to be all right."

I recognized that I was about to be "alone in an elevator" with a number of men and women who are actively *living* this condition of spiritual freedom in their moment-to-moment existence. These are the human guinea pigs whose deep yearning for freedom has led them to immerse themselves in some form of a living *process of Awareness*. They are the front-line troops, stationed on the leading edge of modern consciousness exploration. They live in, talk about, work with and teach *Awareness*.

So, what we asked them would be all-important. We chose questions that we felt might reveal a deep level of reality about them and their life-activities. We wanted to delve into the actual nitty-gritty of *living* spiritual liberation in the 21st century. Does such a reality exist, and if so, what is it like (or not like)?

We wanted to ask what they actually practiced and what they teach others to practice. I wanted to know how they deal with money, sex, relationships, and other pragmatic issues. How does one live an ordinary, integrated life in the world while animating full Truth of Being? Thus, the questions were born.

Once we knew *what* to ask, I came up with a sort of preliminary structure for *how* to ask. In other words, I put together a logical framework for the interview process itself. In this original interview plan, I naively assumed that I would simply ask the questions verbatim, in the same order as written, in each and every interview. There would be three groups of questions. We'd open with a series of questions regarding the big picture, exploring the reality or unreality of the *concept* of Awakening. Then I would make a few inquiries into how this plays out in the life of the guest. I wanted to offer the reader a practical look into their day-to-day activities, a peek at how he or she adapted a normal human existence to a life lived in spiritual freedom. Then, to close, I planned to ask the guest to speak directly to the reader. This all seemed perfectly logical in this early stage. I honestly expected to just ask/shut up, ask/shut up.

And I tried. I really did.

But once the interviews were under way, this plan proved to be a rather impractical methodology. For example, in one of the very first interviews, I learned that it was simply *impossible* to keep the attention of the subject if I used words like "you". It seemed that in his Awakened condition, his spiritu-al "style" simply didn't recognize an "I" or a "you" enough to keep such per-sonal pronouns from raising red flags in the interview process.

So, gradually, the idea of a totally structured questioning process shifted into a more relaxed, conversational interviewing style. What I realized was that while my sincere intent was to collect a uniform set of data, asking the questions *using exactly the same words* in each conversation was very often not effective. At times this actually proved to be counterproductive. As the interviews progressed, I became more sensitive to the wisdom of asking the questions more naturally, more conversationally.

Similarly, I began to be more flexible about the order in which the ques-tions were asked. I began to let the questions "invite themselves" into the dis-cussion by *feel*, basically just making sure that each of the predetermined points was touched upon in some appropriate form. (Please see the Wayne Liquorman interview for a humorous example of how, in one case, even *that* simple detail could not be met.)

If the natural course of the chat led past the so-called "next" question on the list, I let it go there. I just made it a point to get back to the skipped ques-tion later in the interview. Incorporating these small changes seemed to help the conversations be more, well, conversational.

Another useful tool that was developed along the way involved a self-imposed discipline against casual chitchat before the interview began. Anyone who knows me personally will tell you that I love to talk. And let's face it—here I was with a brief period of complete access to men and women whose work I had long admired. While the personal tendency to indulge in spurious conversation was great, I realized that the process would be best served by getting the tape machine rolling as quickly as possible. The guests had not been given access to the questions beforehand because I wanted their words to be fresh and unprepared. So an opening routine was devised where I would begin the meeting by asking them to forgive me for seeming abrupt. Then, I'd just begin asking the questions.

After the interview was complete, I would take some time to engage in casual chat with the guest, but explained that I would leave the tape deck rolling. In more than one instance, some very important information came from these post-interview segments and these were blended back into the body of the transcript.

Another area that seems important to mention is editing. One of the pur-poses of this book is to reveal to the reader the diverse ways in which men and women live lives of spiritual freedom. As such, we didn't want to in any way look like we favored one guest over another, nor give the editorial impression that one guest is somehow more right than another. So I decided that the guests would appear in the book according to the chronological date of the interview. For that same reason, we chose to ask each guest to supply their own biography, which was printed verbatim.

We did not edit the chapters to create uniform length. Some guests chose to speak at great length, while others offered concise statements of Truth. So even though some interviews were quite short and others fairly long, they come to you as they were offered. In allowing the words to stand as stated, the text honors the fact that what you are about to read is what the speaker intended to communicate.

Obviously, sometimes the spoken word doesn't smoothly translate onto the page. So what sparse editing we did choose to do was for the sake of conversationality. By basically leaving the content in original form, we hoped to retain the integrity of each interview (and of the collection as a whole). Like whistles on teakettles, each sings at a different pitch, yet all express Truth equally.

And, in fact, as the completed interviews were collected, it became clear to me *why* honoring the speaker's intent had seemed so important during the process itself. It turned out that by preserving the integrity of the initial words, both the similarities *and* the differences in the collected interviews could be more easily recognized.

Gathered together, these discussions seem to point to a mysterious, unstated, shared Place. It may be that this space is different for each reader—at least we hope so. You see, it's in the silence *prior* to the words and in the vastness *between* the concepts where you may find your own place in this circle.

So, the kettle is boiling, my friend. Care to join me and my guests for tea? Bring the book with you...

Quidam Green Meyers
Los Angeles, California, USA

Saniel Bonder

Interviewed in San Raphael, California
May 6, 2000

We were quite excited. We were beginning a new project and the first interview was with someone I already knew. Saniel Bonder had been a close acquaintance of mine for quite a while in the Da Free John (Adi Da Samraj) community a couple of decades earlier. We had even worked together for a summer setting up a regional office for Master Da in New York City, but I hadn't spoken to him for a number of years. So in December of 1996 when I heard that he had "fallen Awake" I couldn't resist phoning him.

The result of that call was that Diana and I travelled to Northern California a few times to sit with Saniel and his growing community there. I consider Saniel to be one of a few spiritual "midwives" who directly served my own first recognition of Awakening (or "decentralization" as I like to call it) in March of 1997.

So, it was with great joy and anticipation that we found ourselves zipping up a very steep (and very narrow) mountain road in Marin County on a cloudy Saturday morning. At the top of the hill, we pulled into the driveway of the attractive home that Saniel shares with his wife Linda. It was Linda— a beautiful woman whose bright smile practically shouts her Blessed Nature to any fortunate enough to meet her—who ushered us in.

After some hugs and a cup of tea, Saniel arrived, fresh from a workout at a local gym. He's a handsome man whose deep, piercing eyes immediately communicate an intensity and compassion which can captivate you in a heartbeat. Yet, like the Siberian tigers he so dearly loves, Saniel has the fierce heart of a true warrior. And this, too, clearly shines forth.

His thirty years on the front lines of the turbulent battle to share Truth have not dulled his playfulness nor his energetic presence. While clearly growing into his role as one of the great Awakeners of our time, Saniel remains a serious student *of this Way as well.*

13

As he spoke, I found myself falling in love—again—with his sincerity and unwavering commitment to freedom. His eyes flashed fire at times, then they would close and a deep stillness would seem to fill the room. The intensity built as the interview progressed. His delivery was that of a master musician layering a solo toward a burning crescendo. But Saniel's interview ended in a way that was far more moving than we ever could have expected.

During his response to the last question ("What would you say to those readers interested in this Awakening?"), tears rolled freely down his cheeks as he urged people to not give up, to have courage even in the dark days of the search. We watched—amazed and deeply moved—as he totally gave himself over to this plea for steadfastness.

And, as we slipped back down the mountain, all we could feel was gratitude that he is here and that he makes himself available to human hearts. We're also glad to be able to call him our friend.

Q - In your experience, is there such a reality as Awakening, Enlightenment, Liberation or spiritual freedom?

SB - [Chuckle] What a great first question!

Q - Thank you!

SB - Ahhhh.....yes! That's my answer! [Laughter] We could call it by any of those names, any other name. We could call it by no name at all. Something has occurred that has amounted to a radical shift in my whole existence, and I use terms like those to describe it. And I sometimes try to come up with others, but you're reminding me just in your wording of the question of one of our forebears in all of this. U. G. Krishnamurti used to refer to it as "the catastrophe". Whatever it was in his case (and of course that's part of the question), yes, in my experience there is such an event possible because such an event has actually occurred for me.

Q - Have you experienced or attained anything distinct from so-called "ordinary" or "normal" human experience?

SB - Yes. This Awakening or Realization that has taken place—the prepositions get awkward—"for me", "in me", "to me", "as me"—I don't know...it's not an objective event which happened that I experienced per se, it's a shift in the subject Itself that I am. And, yes, it has so dramatically distinguished the life post that event from what was previous to it that it's a kind of a great divide in my history as a human being. So, yes.

Q - Did this seem to happen at a particular moment or event, or did it seem to gradually evolve?

SB - In doing my work, I've noticed that for some people it's more during a period of time whereas others can point to an instant. I'm kind of a curious combination of the two. In my case there were two major aspects to what was going on in my—to use the Indian term, *sadhana*—spiritual practice or quest for such an Awakening.

After many years with especially one guru and a couple of decades of work in general, a point came where I was very intensely involved in the exploration of consciousness directly. And, there was also a very mysterious and magical encountering of and embrace of—and I'm trying to word this carefully—a presence, a spirit, a life, a vortex of energies that I recognized. And the language that came naturally to me was "this is the Goddess"—which I had not been looking for.

But She (so to speak) appeared, and so there was a particular period of a couple of days of an actual sexual initiation with a woman who I felt was manifesting or animating this tremendous spiritual energy or presence. And it was mysterious to both of us. Because of my training and background I could put words on it, but because she had no such training, she had no words for it. Yet it was obvious to both of us that something was happening in a big way, not only for me but for her.

And during the time that we became lovers this to me became a tantric sexual initiation as well a tantric initiation in more general terms of entering a more expansive understanding of existence. And so, after the second of our first two evenings together, in this very wonderful and delightful way (it was also falling in love that was going on), I went to a local restaurant.

While I was sitting there that morning, I looked out the window and suddenly there was this instantaneous recognition that there was no difference between "my consciousness" and the consciousness that simply Is. The word that came to me was "seamless". And later, I came up with the term "Onlyness" to put some kind of word to it that would suggest the nature of this event.

So, I went on for a couple of years under the assumption that the transition had really occurred during this ecstatic embrace of a woman who was animating the living spirit of the Divine Female, as I was the Divine Male and vice versa. I see men and women as both—I'm not going to put sexist labels on this! But, for a couple of years, I was in the habit of saying, "Well, the awakening occurred during that tantric embrace, probably that second night we were together."

But, I think in 1995 as I was writing my first book *The White-Hot Yoga of the Heart*, it occurred to me that really I should identify the moment of awakening as that instant of recognition, looking out the window from the chair in the restaurant.

The feeling I had was a sense that it had already happened, but that it took my body and my mind, especially, until that instant to make the singular recognition. So, that's my sort of "both/and" answer to that question.

Now, some of the people whom I've had the privilege and blessing to serve in their own autonomous replication of this have later said, "Well, I can't really identify a moment. Somewhere during such-and-such a period a shift occurred and I recognized later that this was already the case." Others like Linda, my partner, can speak of a very precise incident. In her case, we've even got it on tape. It was during a meditation and she was sitting there grinning ear-to-ear. She very energetically described the condition of consciousness recognizing Itself as such—with no further need for work for that to be so.

So, over the years there have been quite a number of people who could point to that moment. But quite a number can't and it appears to make no difference whatsoever.

Q - Do you have an experience of growing, maturing, or evolving in this process?

SB - Yes, and I want to qualify my response.

[Long pause] The basic radical shift simply is so. And, I have come to refer to it as a "second birth." And more and more over the years, I recognize that it's really a useful analogy. But, I feel that it's not *just* an analogy, that there's a biological as well as a spiritual logic to this that is closely linked into the circumstances that produce our birth into human form [slaps his leg several times] to begin with. So, calling it a "second birth" is not just a metaphor.

One of the things I like about using that particular phrase is that if we look at an infant, and then at what happens afterward, there are tremendous changes. But, the condition of being a born human being stays the same. Likewise, in this shift that has occurred there is something about the essential nature of it that's just a given now. It's the given of my life now as being born into infancy was the given of my life fifty years ago.

In that given—from that platform, on that foundation—*endless* changes are happening and the work, pretty much, is keeping up with the changes. What appears as the mind is kind of like your dumb kid brother, you know? The living body and the conscious nature are cooking, cooking, cooking, and the mind has to kind of grope and huff and puff sometimes to clarify. "Oh, this is what's happening, here's how I need to move with this, gotta zig when I thought I was needing to zag." That kind of thing.

And the changes are happening on every level of my existence. It's as if at the moment of Awakening booster rockets were fired and it took my transformation process into an ongoing warp speed. And it's more or less continued that way.

Sometimes Linda and I joke about "do we ever get a break from the parade of changes that we have to adapt to?"

Q - What is your experience of thought and emotion?

SB - Thought and emotion are natural functions of this living organism that I am. So, they are me. I have thoughts, I have emotions. There are patterns of thought and emotion that are very characteristic to Saniel Bonder, some of which can get real aggravating to me, as well as to others, at times. And I work with them. My motivation to change patterns of thought and emotion, where there is that motivation, often springs from a desire to live more harmoniously with people, to make changes in my life that feel important to me.

But, in this business of awakenings and how people relate to thought and emotion from that perspective, I don't feel thought and emotion are problems in any sense. I don't find that any thought or emotion has *any capacity whatsoever* to compromise the fundamental awakeness and freedom of being.

And so, I give myself permission to experience them all. And they always have things to show me. Every now and again, in an investigation of certain patterns I recognize, "Well, gee, I've really been down this pike before and I don't need to keep going here." But I don't like to foreclose on that investigation before it has really revealed what it can. So, as an example, in the early period after my awakening there were these kind of fits of self-doubt that would come over me. And, because very early on I was prompted in a variety of ways to work with others to help them duplicate this, because I knew I was going into that kind of teaching role and would have some kind of visibility in doing so, I really wanted to make sure that if there was something that needed to be doubted—something that was missing—I wanted to know! So, I would go into it completely and suffer a great deal over a few hours or a couple of days or however long it would be until there would be a kind of a burning through, almost like a drill bit getting through a piece of wood, you know? Zzzzzzzz-pop! And it would be like, "Oh, that was mind!" The mind contracts and expands, and when it's in a particularly contracted or uptight condition, one of its qualities is doubt. It has no more effect on my whole-being awakeness than clouds do on sunshine.

So, after many such events and coming at it from many different angles, I saw pretty clearly, "There's nothing in this for me. And, there's also nothing in it for others who are relying on my confidence in Being as they develop theirs!" And that was a great teaching. A woman who was working with me on her own Awakening at one point said to me when I mentioned something about my passages through self-doubt, "Could you burn that bridge behind you? Because every time you go back to that playground, I feel like I'm cut adrift." And I said, "Well, since you said it that way, I think I'll burn the playground, too."

In real terms, what did that mean? Did it mean that doubt never, ever arose in my mind again? No. It has from time to time, but I know what I'm going to find at the end of that tunnel and so I can simply not take that route of investigation.

So, that's just an example. We could talk about anger, we could talk about love. We could talk about times when my mind is racing and we could talk about times when it's relatively calm. To me, all of that is the ebb and flow or flux of the phenomenal dimension of my being. Thankfully, I'm happy to have gone through the stages of significant self-doubt—and this is my life!

You know, it takes a conversation like this to actually remember that there was actually something before, you know? This is just me! Which is a good point! From moment to moment, I don't especially feel "Awakened"! It's just the way it is now.

Q - Do you have a sense of anything that might be called evil or negative energies within life?

SB - Yes. I feel a lot of emotion around this. I don't feel that evil is intrinsic to Being such that it's untransformable, but I do feel that evil is a force in the world—one of the forces in the world—that we would do well to take very seriously. [Saniel's voice softens; he's visibly overcome] I'm really glad you asked this. It's a very important question.

[Long pause]

It, it's...you know I'm sitting here contemplating, looking for words. It's complex. I guess one way that I can get into it is to say that I feel we are living in, and are the products of, a very psychological age. The Twentieth Century was really...well, I think as humanity gets further and further away then looks back, one of its great characteristics was that it was the age of psychology. It was the age when psychological understanding of human nature—starting especially with Freud, I mean, he really kicked open the door and then it just proliferated, it blossomed, it grew like a wild vine—that kind of understanding developed.

And as many people have pointed out, Martin Buber being one of my favorites, we run a great risk in reducing all human phenomena to psychological components.

So, to me then, the question of evil is one that needs to be addressed that way. I'm planning to write a book about it, actually. The working title is *Can We Outgrow Hatred, Violence, and Evil?* With that being the question, rather than a set-up for my self-assured answer it seems to me that it's possible, but woweeee, have we got a job to do!

And I'm hopeful that as more men and women do relax into a non-separate, Awakened participation in reality, we will more and more be able to counter human evil in all of its forms without reducing it, or minimizing it as just some form of pathology within the psyche of the individual.

I do believe that there are forces which may be outside the human species as we mostly know ourselves to be that prey on us and, for whatever reasons, are not very wise and compassionate presences or intelligences. And, my study of these things suggests to me that as more and more of us do awaken, this question is going to come more front and center. Because I do feel that an awakening into non-separate consciousness doesn't prevent human beings from doing some really rotten things—things that, depending on what criteria you are using, you might be able to evaluate and say, *"Wow, there's evil there!"* Or find such a profound degree of misguidedness or subjective isolation, or self-aggrandizement, or whatever, that you can't just sit back and say, "Well, it's all Divine Play," when discussing the effects that human beings, including spiritual teachers, can have on one another.

One of the things that I love about what you are doing with this book, and about the general mood or at least the impulse of cooperation among our generation of awakeners and realizers and teachers, is that it's like the finger is on the pulse here. Looking back at our forebears, whoa, I don't want to risk winding up like some of those guys did. I don't want to do that to people. I mean, you probably had a similar experience to mine which is that I had to do a lot of cleaning up *after*. And also, I know that other people have cleaned up after me—have done work to, you know, curb the excesses and, basically, just try to take everything into account. And in that sense, I don't blame anybody, but I'm quite disturbed.

I guess I'm winding this around from a sort of abstract potential of evil to the things that even spiritually awakened men and women can do that, while they are not *intending* to be evil, wind up having a very much less-than-benign effect on others.

I mean, there are people whose souls have been *devastated* by their encountering of an awakened teacher. They have no confidence left in themselves, much less in God, Spirit, all of that. You know they are like walking palls of themselves. It's a real stretch to assign that kind of impact on someone to "Divine Grace", "crazy wisdom", and so on. And I have had that experience very frequently, encountering that kind of lost or devastated soul.

It would be an interesting roundtable discussion to begin to get groups of us awakeners into a room or into a tree house or someplace to discuss this. And in a way we are doing that, by virtue of projects like this book you are doing. I want to thank you for that. I feel that sharing in this way is a first step toward getting together on some kind of a different basis than meeting as representatives of traditions. I think that part of what characterizes a lot of awakeners is that we are just ourselves and you can see in us traces of this path and that path, this teacher, that teaching, and so on.

But we're not *required* to stand up and represent this or that variant of something. I think that openly discussing questions like this is...boy oh boy, it's really a big deal.

I'm not preaching from on high here, but I can say with confidence that I have always tried my best to clean up after myself where I could. I'm sobered by how hard it is to do *anything* in service to people without activating all of the projections we carry. So, one of our friends—one of the first teachers who emerged with my help—has a great phrase, "If I'm just being myself, somebody's going to get hurt."

To which I added that if we all just keep being ourselves and keep communicating, maybe more and more of us can get healed, and we can learn how to live together. But, I really do feel that the more we can cooperate, the more we can acknowledge that we have our finger on the pulse of this process. But we also have to keep coming to back to the point of that great two-word question: "Who knows?"

Q - Do you teach?

SB - Yes.

Q - What do you teach?

SB - Whoooo. I'm going to resist labelling it, and see if I can actually describe it. I teach the most direct approach that I can take responsibility for at any given time that will help others duplicate this, we could say "condition of awakeness" or quality of integration and wholeness; non-difference between the human and transcendental divine dimensions of being. And I also teach my best sense of the most integrated, balanced, sane, and natural way to live beyond that transition, not only for the individual, but also for us cooperatively, so I make a big emphasis on mutuality.

I've defined this "mutuality" as being as true as you possibly can to your own self or being, in all of the testing moments of life, while cooperating with others who are really doing the same, consciously so, at whatever stage of awakeness or integration they might be. That's a pretty good summary.

Q - Do you have a Teacher?

SB - No, I don't, but I have many teachers. I had two great Master/ Initiators—Ramana Maharshi and Adi Da. There were other great enlightened or awakened beings who influenced particularly my early *sadhana*. One of them, Neem Karoli Baba came back around later as very helpful to me when I was extricating myself from the work I had been in for almost two decades, the Adi Da work.

So, each of those and other great spiritual masters have had great influence on me, as have men and women who wouldn't be characterized as such. Martin Buber, for example. Even though I only briefly looked into his work in my early twenties, more and more as I matured, his work has been an anchor for me, particularly his emphasis on "I-thou" dialog or mutuality, his word for something similar.

There were men and women who were my teachers when I was young ...my parents, many other people who have been important for me. And as my work developed, I got more and more clarity that I was (and am) bringing in a new expression and it can't be beholden to any previous expression. However, that doesn't—I hope—put blinders on my eyes so that I won't receive. So I feel I've been instructed by many, many beings, human and otherwise.

Linda and I were looking at homes recently and we happened to go up on a hill on the other side of San Rafael to look at a house that had absolutely *stunning* views of Mount Tamalpais and the East Bay, then all the way out west toward Fairfax. The vision of the mountain was just *awesome*. And, as I mentioned in *The White-Hot Yoga of the Heart*, I have a special connection with Mt. Tam. It's not easy to have a special connection with something that's other than a human being. But when we were at that house it blew me away! I can't get technical here. It just blew my heart wide open to be seeing this form that, to me, is a super-transmitter of radiant presence—and is, therefore, a teacher—prior to words.

This image of the Goddess that I have here, Chinnamasta [Saniel points to a beautiful wall-hanging], to me is not just an image, but is a manifestation of an archetype which has arrived for me, is not only objective to me, but is somehow part of my own Being as well. And, I learn from other humans all the time.

So, I have to give a more complete answer to that question because to just say that I don't have a teacher is kind of misleading. I don't have a single, primary teacher. My wife Linda is a constant teacher to me. Our cat is a constant teacher to me.

Q - Some people feel that we as a species are on the brink of a significant shift in consciousness, and that such a shift may even be necessary for our survival on the planet. Could you comment on this?

SB - Let me see how I can get into this....
[Very long pause. Saniel sits with eyes closed, then opens them to answer]

I see human history as a continually quickening evolutionary process. That's one of the reasons why I have tremendous respect for many traditions.

I'm not partial to the view that there is *an* absolute truth, at least in words, that always was so and always will be so. There are qualities of existence that appear to be very fundamental to our nature and to the nature of reality. The human species is itself an evolving *science*, not just *scientists*.

We are part of an event which is unfolding. And from that sort of large-view perspective, I do see that we appear to be in a time when a quickening is intensifying. The acceleration is accelerating. And, as you said, many people have a similar view.

So, yes, I feel that it's critical for survival. However, I like Duane Elgin's approach in his book *Awakening Earth*. He's the guy who wrote *Voluntary Simplicity* some years ago. Duane charted out the various ages through the Industrial Revolution and now into the Information Age, or as he calls it the Communication Revolution. He then projects on toward more and more species-wide transitions on ethical levels and onward in terms of awakenings and transformations and so forth. In due course, we would be somewhere that from *here* would look superhuman.

He winds up saying that it's going to take us at least five hundred years, even with all the enormous advances that are happening, and we're going to have to go through some severe, wild motions on the sine-curve of motions up and down globally to get there. And there are no guarantees. We could really screw it up royally. There are plenty of indications that as a species we have a tremendous tendency to do that.

But, I do feel it's critical for our survival that as many people as possible not only Awaken but also, to use my phrase, "wake down." This means to come to earth in their Awakeness, so that they're not just living in sort of abstract, transcendental "bubbles" of "nothing really matters." [Saniel takes a sip of his drink] Like, is this a beer or is it really a V8? [Laughter] *Editor's Note: It was a V8.*

At any rate, our accessibility and accountability to one another is one of our really big lifelines to the optimal survival of not only the human species but the biosphere. I remember when I was contemplating this quite a few years ago and I was thinking about the mountain here, "Gee, Mt. Tam is going to be around a long, long, long time if the earth goes the way it usually goes." I mean, mountains don't just disappear. It'll be here a lot longer than it's going to take to neutralize the nuclear waste that's deep-sixed in the Farrallon Islands near here.

Now, that's a very long time—but mountains and great rivers and tectonic plates are working on a time span that's very different from us creatures here on this relatively thin strip of biosphere.

So, there are perspectives that could take a very, very big-picture look and perhaps suppose that what happens to human life and life on earth doesn't matter. But I'm not of that orientation, and I do feel that humanity is crazed for lack of a grounded, integrated Awakeness. I teach that the problem is the "core wound." And I define this as the feeling that "there must be more than this." Our finiteness (which is so obvious) over against this sense of our Infiniteness (which for most of us is *not* so obvious) produces all these struggles and from the other species' standpoints must make us look very crazy and violent and bizarrely rapidly changing.

I don't see it as our problem; I see it as our evolutionary advantage. But, at this stage of human evolution, there is an enormous need for these bodies to become integrally conscious as rapidly as can be done.

And of course, it's one by one. There isn't a mass shift. If a mass shift occurred without people also doing the work to take responsibility, it would unravel people psychologically. We're already having plenty of that anyway. So, I feel that doing the work is crucial.

Another perspective on it is that, from the dissociated stance of the scientific and technical mind, we have punched right through to the inner sanctum of life. We are decoding the human genome. I've been wondering about this possibility for years. I just saw a television program last night about the Tasmanian tiger. The last Tasmanian tiger died in 1936. And they have now pulled out a fully-functional chunk of DNA and they feel that they will be able to clone this thing and bring that species back to life. So, I feel that the necessity for a morally and ethically grounding deepening of this kind of awakening couldn't be more important. Because we are going to implant chips and grow new organs and live to be 200 *within our generation!* Or if not, then damn soon thereafter.

It dawned on me a few months ago that if I live in relatively decent health until the age of 70, I will probably have the means available—many of us will—to live in relatively decent health and youthful vitality to 100. And, if we get to 100, we will probably be able to keep on going from there significantly. This very well may be the generation that takes the lid off the longevity question! So, all the issues facing us are just *screaming* for us to get Awake and grounded and be able to look each other in the eye and say, "Yes, I know my Godness, but *don't bow to me!*" Let's bow to <u>*one another*</u>, and let's bow to all of the other creatures on the earth.

Q - Do you have personal spiritual practice?

SB - Not in the sense of an identifiable routine that I do every day. But to be honest, no one has ever quite asked me this question before, so let me take a second.

[Long pause]

My practice is to identify the leading edge impulses that are coming up for me in my life; to question and test them, and then to see how everything stacks up. Then to determine the priorities of what are the most auspicious and the most necessary things to do; auspicious and necessary for me, yes, but also for everybody, for the totality. We need to do those things and to keep on seeing, investigating, looking into, expressing more, daring more often. Daring, recognizing and persevering is one of the triads that I've come up with—ways to characterize the daily ongoing practice that I feel is important.

It's an "incarnation yoga." It's getting here more and more fully. Which doesn't mean cutting myself off from other dimensions, qualities of experience other than what are normally considered earthly. But, it appears to me that this quality of awakened life is constantly pushing the envelope with respect to what's acceptable and what's okay, both in terms of my own conditioning and influences and residual belief systems, and those of my fellow human beings in this time and place. So, I'm always finding out where I am in relation to that envelope.

Q - There will be some readers of this book who may sense some form of Awakening in their lives, or at least have a great degree of interest in the topic. What would you like to say to them?

SB - [Long pause, then Saniel takes a deep breath, his eyes filling with tears] Oh...have courage. Persevere.

So many of my brothers and sisters are struggling so hard. There are so many of our generation who have lost hope, and despaired to the point of giving up. So that's my first recommendation—have hope. And even when you don't have hope, persist and endure. Persevere. Try not to shut down on the possibility that you, too, can awaken. If you do shut down, try to be as easy on yourself as possible.

If awakening is something that you feel desperate for in this lifetime, and you haven't been able to find it through more traditional sources, please consider checking out other sources. It may well be that you need to extricate yourself from the mind of what is, in effect, a childhood container of spiritual beliefs. That may be, as it was for me, one of the most important motions of self-liberation.

And, no matter how much help you get from anybody, no matter how profound anyone's transmission to you, or blessing of you, or radiating of spiritual energy, and good wisdom and instruction and counsel, my experience and observation is that when it all comes down, you have to somehow dare. Take the leap. Find your own way. The groping is self-empowering as is the despair all through the experience.

So, this book that you, Quidam, are putting together is, in my opinion, a great gift. You'll have at least a dozen people speaking all together, many of whom are functioning as teachers. Some arrive with a tradition, others not, all oriented to helping others find their way. What I can say to your readers is, check us all out. Read about us. Come see the ones who "talk" to you the most. And don't give up. *Don't give up.* If you can possibly help it, don't give up. If you have to give up, well, go ahead and give up for a while. But remember that Quidam and Diana and Linda and I and a whole bunch of other people are sitting here holding a Place in Being for you. We're a kind of a proxy, confident that you can do it, until you *do*.

[Long pause, then Saniel leans forward, eyes bright with both love and tears]

I guess that's really my, uh....I'm sure that everyone in the book is going to have some good things to say. That's the most important thing I can add.

Biography

Born in 1950 in New York, Saniel Bonder grew up in a Jewish family. He considers the influence of his parents and his teachers at a small prep school in Tennessee every bit as crucial to his development as that of his later spiritual teachers. He graduated from Harvard in 1972, having written for the *Crimson* and participated in the emerging anti-Vietnam war and "counterculture" movements.

At 20 he embarked upon his sacred journey of Self-realization. Early influences included the Beat poets, Martin Buber's *I and Thou* and *Legends of the Hasidim*, and several great Hindu yogis, especially the renowned sage Ramana Maharshi. During nearly two decades with his principal spiritual teacher, Adi Da (formerly Da Free John), he served as a writer, editor, educator, and speaker. There he also made extensive comparative studies of traditional and contemporary paths of transformation.

In August 1992, Saniel Bonder formally relinquished his relationship with Adi Da and left that community. Once freed of his teacher's regimen, he was amazed to experience spontaneous tantric initiation and to enter his own transcendental awakening. A few months later, in early December, he completed the awakening into Conscious Embodiment that had eluded him all those years.

Ever since, he has worked full time to help dozens of others achieve the same freedom, and to grow beyond it together in what he calls "the White-Hot Way of Mutuality." Many of his students have gone on to develop their own creative service. One of them, Linda Groves-Bonder, has become his wife and principal partner in his work. The work is growing now across the U.S. and in other countries, with primary centers in Colorado, the Northwest, the Washington, D.C., area, Los Angeles, and the San Francisco Bay Area. For more information, or to order free copies of Saniel's introductory audiotape, *White-Hot Freedom*, and a short documentary video on him and his work, *Saniel Bonder—Waking Down*, see www.sanielbonder.com or (in the U.S.) call toll-free at 888-741-5000.

Saniel has thus far published several books of teachings: *The White-Hot Yoga of the Heart* (1995), *Waking Down: Beyond Hypermasculine Dharmas* (1998), *While Jesus Weeps: Conversations in the Garden of Gethsemane-A Novel* (1998), *The Conscious Principle* (1999), and *The Incarnation of Mutuality, Volume One* (2000). His audiotapes include an unabridged audio book version of *Waking Down*.

Saniel and Linda reside in Marin County, California, near the mountain that is most sacred to him, Mt. Tamalpais. He loves playing flutes and is an avid golfer. The Bonders are developing a new, more public expression of their work called "Matter Magic." Its premise is to provide specific blessings "empowering your optimal health, wealth, and happiness--by helping you materialize what really matters to YOU." The website for this blessing activity will be www.mattermagic.com. They hope you'll come visit!

You can reach Saniel on his website at: www.sanielbonder.com

or by phone at: 888-741-5000 (toll free)

Isaac Shapiro

Interviewed by phone from Amsterdam
May 27, 2000

In the process of conducting these interviews, we had decided early on to meet personally with the guest whenever possible. Obviously, it is far preferable to sit face-to-face with another human being in any moment of true communication rather than talk by phone. And all the more so when information of such a critical nature as Truth of Being is to be discussed. But I quickly learned that this was just not possible in every case.

This was so in my interview with Isaac Shapiro. We had exchanged a few e-mails in April, finally settling on a "phoner" to be conducted the following month. Since Isaac was on a satsang tour in Europe, I arranged to phone him in Amsterdam—which due to the time difference meant a 5 a.m. call from my home in California.

So it was, then, that I found myself sitting in my office in the pre-dawn stillness—hot tea in hand—listening as a phone rang several thousand miles away. Clearing my head as Isaac answered, I offered the most heartfelt "good morning" that I could muster at such an hour. "Well, it's afternoon here," came the response. I could hear the smile in Isaac's voice.

I quickly found Isaac Shapiro to be an immensely likable man. He has a soft-yet-rich voice tinged with an attractive European accent whose origin I was unable to determine. There was an immediate sense of comfort and ease in speaking with him and I was lulled into relaxing and enjoying listening to him when an interesting twist in the interview process nudged me from my early-morning reverie, pressing me back to the job at hand.

I had been noticing early in our chat that Isaac's responses to the questions seemed somewhat measured or carefully constructed. Yet, there was no indication that this was the guarded, strategic tone of a man being cautious or reserved. Rather, it had seemed to me that he was playfully pondering the process of being asked and then answering.

27

But after the third or fourth question, he asked to go "off-the-record" for a moment, one of only a few such deliberate "edits" in this series of talks. I could still feel him smiling through the phone as he asked if I recognized the paradoxical nature of such a line of questioning. When I admitted that I did, he chuckled and explained that he was struggling with the questions because words are inadequate to express the profundity of such issues. He just wanted to be sure that it was all making sense.

I explained, with empathy, that some of the questions were being posed this way exactly because *we felt that such paradox arises for most spiritual seekers. Part of our methodology, I explained, was that we were hoping that the way that each of our guests dealt with this quandary would be instructive to the reader. He replied that he understood, and that he could see that great care had been taken in preparing the questions. He said he would do his best with them. I turned the tape deck back on.*

I was struck with the simple honesty of this man. His sincere wish was to communicate fully and to the very best of his ability, and he was even willing to admit freely any sense of inability *to do so! This is a man who speaks on this topic all over the world, and is considered by many to be among the very best advaitin teachers alive. How easy it would have been for him to just keep plowing through the interview, saving face, playing the "expert" in his field! And how totally refreshing and instructive was his simple bowing to Truth. The integrity shown in this simple act was clearly one of the high points for me in this series of interviews.*

So after a few moments of laughing together at the incomprehensibility of life's mysteries, we eased back into the questions. From that point on, the conversation took on a simple joy and remarkable sense of ease.

When I hung up the phone dawn was just breaking. The sun was coming up through the trees in my yard. My tea was still warm.

Q - In your experience, is there such a reality as Enlightenment, Awakening, Liberation or spiritual freedom?

IS - My experience is that it even jumps out of the realm of experience. There's just a seeing that what is Awake has always been Awake and until you know that there's just a sense of life that was asleep, although you did-n't know it was asleep. And it's so simple when you recognize it. You recognize that you've always known it. [Pause] That's about it.

Q - Have you experienced or realized anything that might seem distinct from what is called average or normal human experience?

IS - Yes. What's considered normal is a sense of separation. It's funny because you can't really call it an experience but it's a recognition in which all experience is seen to be just the filter that gets looked through. Yet there's no one looking and there's no filter.

But, in the sense of being somebody that knows something or that is something, that is an entity even...it doesn't seem so any more.

Q - When this was noticed, did it happen at a particular moment or during a particular event? Or did it happen gradually?

IS - The Truth is that it only happens now, and the whole idea of gradually or suddenly just is now. They're both just ideas that don't have any validity. So, if you want to speak in terms of time, it's an ongoing deepening of recognition of That.

Q - So, is there a sense of evolving, maturing or growing?

IS - Ahh, yes, you know, all these questions are kind of tricky to answer because there's the absolute level where nothing is happening, or what you could call Shiva, and then there's the play of energy, called Shakti or consciousness and in this play of energy, somehow Consciousness is revealing Itself to Itself. There are patterns seen which are not personal in any way. Somehow there's a sense of deepening, but there's no one that's deepening ...Consciousness is having a play with itself.

Q - What is your experience of thought and emotion?

IS - Thoughts and emotions come up. They're impersonal. There's nobody that's thinking them, they are happening by themselves. If anyone thinks that they're in control of thinking, all they need to do to prove that it's not them doing the thinking is to try to *stop* thinking. They will see really clearly that there's no thinker, or anybody that's doing it. It's just that the *activity* of thinking produces the *sense* of a thinker.

So thoughts and emotions come that are not personal. You could say that they're patterns in consciousness and ultimately get seen by consciousness.

And so, thoughts and feelings come and at moments they can look personal; at moments they can look serious; at moments they can seem solid. But, there's the recognition that they're really nothing.

Q - Do you have any sense of negative or evil energy in life?

IS - That can happen in a moment, but it's clearly just a projection of thought. There's no such thing. It's just a pattern, you could say, in consciousness, of thinking something should be different and really believing it for a moment. But ultimately, there's no such thing.

Q - Do you teach? And if so, what is it that you teach?

IS - [Laugh] Hmm...what is it that I do? [Pause] I show up!

Q - Maybe we'll get into that one from another direction. Did you or do you have a teacher?

IS - I'd say all of life, ultimately! [Pause] Yes, all of life—every moment. It's so funny because I understand the difficulty of asking the questions, because when you say, "Do you have a teacher?" it's like all of a sudden I have to become, like, someone who *had* something.

You know what's funny about this is that I met Papaji and, yes, he pointed me at myself and I could say that he was the manifestation of myself. And at the same time, you know, what limits does Consciousness have? It's just everything. It's like, I've really been playing with this one, because it almost feels too narrow to say that I have something like a lineage. This will be fun for some of the people stuck on lineage.

Q - So, when you "just show up" to teach, what is it that you do?

IS - I can say that there's a Resting as the Essence that we all are. And there are a few ways that this plays out, but mostly what happens is that a person will ask a question and, as I'm simply being That in them Which they are already, suddenly they see it from that perspective. And they see the question from the other way around, or they see it from There. And usually there's laughter or whatever happens.

And, of course there are times when someone is asking something from another level and I can just respond from experience at the time. But mostly, it's this play of recognizing what's true in someone—in everyone, actually— in every moment. And just enjoying that together.

Q - When people come with questions regarding the practicalities of life: money, sexuality, relationships, what sorts of suggestions might you make?

IS - You know it's really very moment by moment because life plays with me like it plays with anyone else and in different moments different things seem useful. So I guess it depends on what book I've just read or how things seem at that particular moment.

But it's so funny because a week later I might hear what I say and cringe. I guess, you know, there's the willingness to be naked and honest, as honest as I know how, anyway. And, usually when people see that what they are speaking about isn't as personal as they thought, that takes a huge bite out of it right there. There's a recognition that it's universal—whatever they're dealing with, I'm dealing with too. I think that's more important than what I actually ever say.

Q - Is there a particular practice that you engage in your daily life?

IS - Usually I watch a video every day...one of the latest releases. [Huge laughter] I've recently come out of a three-week period where I tried to practice... but it's kind of fallen in on itself again. I think that mostly it's just the enjoyment of being...and there's such an interest in it. And because of my life being what it is, being available to satsang, people seem to keep wanting to talk to me about it. If anything is my practice, it's just being available to that interest and serving that interest. So that's probably the strongest practice.

Q - It's said by some people that we as a species are in the midst of a shift in Consciousness. Some even say that such a shift is very significant in the evolution of mankind. What's your sense of that?

IS - It seems that way to me at times but at other times it doesn't seem like *anything* is happening. It's a funny play, you know? It's like when you really look at it, you can't describe this instant *at all*. And so, if you can't describe it, all you can do is live it. You can't really say if it's evolving or whatever the hell is happening.

So, it's like—in anybody's experience—all we can really describe is what we put a frame around. We can't ever describe the moment, it's just this funny play of thinking that we know what's going on which gives us time and space and all the rest of the funny stuff.

Q - For people who are reading this book and sense that they may be in the midst of some type of Awakening, or at least have some interest in this, what would your basic suggestion to them be?

IS - I would say for most people it's useful to be around somebody that they can sense their own Being with. Because this is a big assistance, to get that recognition clear in yourself. And then once that's happened, there's just a natural process that starts to go on and your attention gets interested in it in a conscious way, you could say. Then there's the usual thing of being around people with like interests. Yes, it's a funny thing because in one sense, there's the total recognition that what is needed will manifest no matter what you tell anybody. It's just like it's happening by itself. Whatever Intelligence there is that's taking care will guide them to the right place, the right person and the right circumstance for them to see.

Biography

At the age of nineteen, Isaac had a first experience of unconditional love. He realized that his way of life until then had been a mere shadow, and he became aware that what he desired most was freedom. The next day he resigned from studying medicine. He then spent a number of years investigating the functioning of the mind and developing a way to communicate his insights to others.

He started to work with people, pointing out to them how they were using their attention. This work was powerful, and successful to a degree, but for Isaac something was still missing.

Disillusioned with what he had experienced with Gurus and teachers, he was not interested in finding a Master. Then he heard about Poonjaji (also called Papaji) from a friend whom he could see had blossomed in Truth. After seeing this beauty, he had to meet Papaji for himself. He first met Papaji in Lucknow, India in October 1991. On their second meeting the following year, Papaji told Isaac that he had found the Diamond and to assist seekers from all around the world.

Since then, Isaac has been traveling worldwide, inviting all of us who are interested in Truth and Freedom, to the *direct experience* of who we are. Isaac teaches that our entire life, including all our beliefs, likes, dislikes and all our endeavours, is based on something that has never been consciously examined. We imagine there to be a personal "I" to whom all experience is happening. Upon examination *right here and now*, we find the foundation on which we have built everything to be non-existent. Everything just is, and we are surrounded by freedom—we are freedom itself.

You can contact Isaac through his website at:

http://www.geocities.com/Athens/Thebes/2689/home.html

Catherine Ingram

Interviewed by phone from Portland, Oregon
May 29, 2000

As I noted in the Introduction to this book, one of the interviewing tech-niques I employed involved not chitchatting casually with the guest before the interview itself. I wanted to be very careful to not in any way taint the Q&A process with casual pre-interview conversation. I am convinced that this procedure allowed us to get the freshest, most spontaneous comments possible on tape and in the book. However, there also seemed to be a down-side to this strategy, one which I believe surfaced briefly in this interview with Catherine Ingram.

There was a particular concern that I carried with me into this conversa-tion. While I was an admirer of her work as a spiritual teacher, I also knew that Catherine had been a journalist and had actually conducted many inter-views with major spiritual figures from all over the world. Frankly, this somewhat intimidated me, since I was about to attempt exactly the third interview of my life! So, I wanted to do my best to put her at ease and allow her to be comfortable on the other side of the interview process.

I phoned her near the end of May and (as I did with all of our guests) briefly went over the methodology of the interview, offering my standard apology for such an abrupt beginning. I was first struck with Catherine's beautiful command of the language. Her diction is lovely and her sense of the logic of the process struck me as exemplary. Yet, the abrupt startup of the interview seemed to be having an inhibitory effect on her. After all, most good interviewers take time to warm up their subject before beginning, and I had not allowed myself this luxury. It dawned on me that in Catherine's case, my "get it on tape immediately" technique may have put me at a slight disad-vantage. But here we were and the die was cast.

Fortunately, as the first few questions and answers unrolled, I felt her loosen up quite a bit. Where just moment before she had been picking care-fully among words, seemingly searching for the "best" response, her lan-

guaging and nuance started to shift into a more inspired, poetic mode. By the time we started talking about thought and emotion, Catherine had clearly overcome the liability I had naively placed in front of her, and Presence was pouring forth.

How instructed I was by this! Clearly, this conversation represented a metaphor for living, a microcosmic example of the larger issues being discussed! Life presents us with situations that often feel far less-than-optimal, yet spirit and good will can prevail if given a fertile field of energy and attention within which to grow.

A few months later, we learned that Catherine was staying for a while just a short drive from where we live, so Diana and I invited her to join us for lunch at a favorite restaurant of ours in Malibu. We had a marvelous time together and found a sense of kindred spirit that seems to be a hallmark of the men and women we were destined to meet through this book.

Q - In your experience, is there such a reality as Awakening, Enlightenment, Liberation or spiritual freedom?

CI - [Soft laugh] My experience, what I most deeply sense, has no words, no description. It's so utterly implicit and everything is so completely drenched in it that *any* word is reductionistic. I find that words such as enlightenment are so loaded that they are misleading to use for the most part. As soon as you say a word about it, all kinds of ideas and pictures arise. And this is contraindicated to the direct experience of the living presence that we can only know in our direct, silent immersion.

Q - Have you experienced or attained anything distinct from so-called "ordinary" or "normal" human experience?

CI - Well, you see, what is often called "normal" human experience is really an obsession with illusion. What I would call the experience of direct presence is the lack of obsession with the illusory thoughts and the mental formations that arise mostly in imagination. So, from my point of view, "normal" consciousness, as we might understand it on a planetary level, is very *ab*normal. It's a form of mental confusion whereby people are just transfixed like a deer caught in headlights by their images of an entity called "me". I often refer to it as "The Me Project." People are working in their minds on a sense of this somebody wandering around.

So, this is a kind of a collective hallucination in madness. What I always say in Dharma Dialogues is that the so-called "awakened condition" is no big deal. It's no big deal. It's just natural relaxation. It's when you are no longer obsessed with what is untrue.

Q - So, did this understanding seem to happen at a particular moment or event, or did it seem to gradually evolve?

CI - You know, it's a deepening that is ongoing. And all that's happening is that there's a greater and greater consistency in this noticing or in this ongoing recognition. And in this deepening there's a greater and greater appreciation for the nuances in form and in whatever is powering the form...whatever the power source is. There's just a kind of wonder about all of those nuances.

It was very much triggered by meeting Poonjaji, of course, in that the recognition came upon me as something that felt very familiar. I had just never quite honored it as such. In his presence I really just felt how simple the whole thing was and also knew that it was reverberating in my being all along. Something in the awareness had always known pure presence, but I'd been busy, being lost in my own madness, you know?

So, again, this recognition is really much more the absence of the drama, the fixation, the contraction, the story. In that absence the reality just shines through on its own. You don't have to go looking for it.

Q - So, my next question would have been..."Do you have an experience of growing, maturing, or evolving in this process?" Perhaps you've already covered that.

CI - Yes, but I'll answer it further. Definitely, this blaze of whatever this is—consciousness, whatever we want to call it—we can't really name it—is ongoing. It's always new, fresh. So, yes, there's always an ongoing deepening, always another moment to embrace. And, it has nothing to do with goal. It's a "journey without goal", as Trungpa Rinpoche called it. I once asked Poonjaji, "Is this ongoing for you?" And he said, "All the time. Every moment, even this moment."

Q - What is your experience of thought and emotion?

CI - Well, in my own perspective of this, you know, everything is absolutely welcome and has its own play. It has its own place, you could say. I am very allergic to too much leaning toward the absolute perspective. I don't ever have any use for that whole fiction, frankly, between absolute and relative. So, the arising of thought comes and it has its own place, its own usefulness or lack thereof. A discriminating awareness will know the difference. And with the arising of emotion, same thing. Emotions are generally born of thought. Thought precedes emotion generally, so some emotions have their usefulness and some don't. Playing with some thoughts is like chewing on old bones. But in any case a discerning awareness will know the difference.

And in this resting in clear presence, discernment deepens. You know, you asked about deepening. There are many aspects of this that are maturing on their own without any effort. And in that quiet presence, there is greater and greater love, greater and greater kindness. There's sensitivity to beings, so-called others. There's greater empathy, of course. And there's greater self-awareness, in terms of what aspect of what is arising in one's own organism is skillful or not skillful, etc. Does that answer that question?

Q - Very much so. Thank you. Do you have a sense of anything that might be called evil or negative energies within life?

CI - No, I call it ignorance. I don't have any sense of what is called evil whatsoever. I just see that there are different types of densities and that when one is very, very asleep to their own nature of clear, clear pristine presence, then pain ensues and that pain can instigate very, very painful acts, acts of suffering. But, even when I see mass murderers interviewed on television, they too are seen as manifestations of beingness, only very densely cloaked. That is not to say, however, that we shouldn't lock them up.

Q - You mentioned Poonjaji. Did you or do you have teachers other than Poonjaji?

CI - Oh yes, I do, and probably will continue to. I studied Buddhism for seventeen years prior to meeting Poonjaji and in addition I worked as a journalist specializing in issues of consciousness and activism. So, I interviewed every major teacher that I knew of. I studied over many years with many, many renowned Buddhist teachers, too many to list. And in addition, I sought out many teachers to interview. So I had a lot of one-on-one time with some of the real greats—Krishnamurti, Trungpa Rinpoche, the Dalai Lama and many others who weren't my personal teachers, but were great influences.

But the way that I approach life is that everyone and every circumstance kind of ends up being one's teacher. People who call me teacher are wonderful teachers to me and I feel so honored and privileged to know them. We just had a week-long retreat in northern California and I pretty much said everything that I had to say after the first day or two. After that, the silence does all the work. People begin speaking mystical poetry. It's not that they are being poetic. They are being descriptive. They are describing reality and it sounds like mystical poetry, like Rumi or Hafiz speaking.

So, I feel a sense of sitting there kind of awestruck by this universal intelligence speaking through so many people over time, crossing so many ages and cultures. The sense of the "soaking" going on is just more and more pronounced and I sense it...well, I can't say every moment, in all honesty. There are times when there is a dullness present or certain circumstances that just feel banal. But, even that is its own teaching.

Q - Do you teach? What do you teach?

CI - Well, I have held regular sessions called *Dharma Dialogues* over the last eight years in the U.S. and Europe. I could describe these sessions as a sharing. I could say that this instrument called Catherine is being played by some mysterious musician. And that we're all together in concert at *Dharma Dialogues.*

People call me their teacher, but the way I think of myself has nothing to do with any of that. I don't really even have much of a reference for myself as a teacher or even as a human being. [Laughs pensively] It's more a sense of...hmmm.......let me see...how *do* I see myself?

You know it's such a flow of phenomena happening all the time. So let's say that in one moment I have on a hat that represents sharing, as in *Dharma Dialogues*, and in another moment I'm schmoozing with my friend on the phone or I'm being a sister—dealing with my brother who has AIDS. A number of my friends are going through cancer treatments and I try to comfort them in that. You know, I don't feel a particular role but I feel that this expression, this manifestation basically gives itself away. That's all it seems to be doing, in different ways and in different roles: teacher, friend, sister, daughter, whatever.

Q - Do you have a personal spiritual practice?

CI - No. I did at one point. I used to go from retreat to retreat [Laughs] but I never liked the idea of a practice, and I never liked practicing. I was not one of those people who enjoyed having a daily meditation practice. I would do it as a form of discipline—kind of a drudgery. But, I notice now that I love the sitting, the quiet, because I'm not doing anything! You know, it's just total relaxation. I don't in any formal way practice meditation because for the most part I live a very quiet life. My life itself is very meditative. It has that quality of relaxed, present awareness very effortlessly. It doesn't require sitting in a particular position.

I also should say for those people who really love having a particular time of day of just sitting quietly, well and good. Just as someone might have a time of day that they like to walk or eat, some people love having such a schedule. I would simply recommend that they not have the idea that they are sitting with a particular goal in mind. Rather, they should just sit because they enjoy sitting at that particular time of day. I don't see it as somehow meritorious that they are doing so. [Laughs]

Q - When people ask you questions regarding practical issues such as money, sexuality, relationships, etc. what suggestions do you give?

CI - Well, again, I suggest to people that they be natural—be very natural. So, if what is naturally arising feels good and wholesome and celebratory is to be in partnership, hallelujah! I always recommend to be in partnership in freedom rather than having the sense that there are two halves becoming a whole, or matching up as soul-mates. I don't have much resonance with those ideas and I don't find them very useful. But if two people are celebrating in trust, in deep love (including a deep friendship-love) in partnership, then that's great, that's really a blessing.

And, if partnership is not arising in life, I see no problem with that whatsoever. There's a great intimacy available for anyone resting in presence. There's a delicate, beautiful intimacy of love and inter-beingness that doesn't require a formal, so-called spousal relationship.

With regard to sensuality, yes, sensuality comes very naturally as well. For anyone who is quiet there is a sensitivity which can be conducive to sensuality. And again, with all of these things, discernment is very important. People can justify everything with spiritual platitudes and beliefs. So, with sensuality there is a recognition in wakefulness that one doesn't just indulge every sensual desire inappropriately. There's appropriate behavior that does not cause confusion and suffering and huge tsunami waves of drama.

The Buddha taught what is called *sila* or ethics as a way to deepen concentration because he understood that if your behavior is not appropriate, not skillful, you cannot have a quiet mind. Unless you are a sociopath, inappropriate behavior gives rise to feelings of remorse, regret, re-living the pictures of the act. And as we get more and more soft and quiet, a very heightened sensitivity comes, greater than any ethical system that I know of. The slightest word or even a hurtful glance feels like a stab in one's heart, if you're the perpetrator of that. There arises what I call "healthy remorse."

Back to the subject of sensuality, it's very beautiful to experience it in freedom, in clarity. And I'm not just speaking of sexuality, although that's included. I mean in any domain, if freedom and clarity and basic goodness are not in conjunction with one's expression of sensuality, then it's better for one to refrain. It's better to just be restrained in certain circumstances. I think that this is a mark of someone who is mature because, in maturity, you don't need anything. You don't need something to be a certain way. You don't have to indulge anything, you're fine. You're on your mountainseat of freedom.

It's also not to deny anything or to say that there isn't plenty out there to celebrate with in form. You're just not desperate for it. It's not going to define you and it's certainly not going to make the difference between having happiness and not.

Now, with regard to money, this is a really interesting subject. You know, here we are in the West where money is god. We live in a milieu where we like to have a certain standard of living. All of us like that. So then it gets down to, "How much is enough?" At what point does need move into greed. And with regard to people who are so-called dharma teachers it's very, very delicate. From my point of view I have no problem with anyone, including dharma teachers making a living. I think that we can jettison a lot of the Asian disdain for money that we have inherited. That perspective is kind of antiquated.

I mean, everyone loves the idea that someone is sharing the dharma and doesn't charge money. But usually, if you look very closely, they are getting money somehow or another from another source or from a bunch of followers who have built them an ashram or something. It's all just an exchange of different forms of energy. So, we don't have to make money this horribly dirty thing.

On the other hand, at what point is enough? There are certain displays of use of money that just seem egregious. They are grotesque displays of greed. And again, our discernment knows the difference. When something is in balance, we see one teacher doing what they do with a kind of elegance and appropriateness and we know they are not going around in Rolls Royces and flying first class everywhere they go. They are doing things in a moderate manner and they are well taken care of and that feels fine. On the other hand, if it doesn't seem in harmony, we know that as well.

The other thing I would say on this subject is that I have a very strong love of this earth and an appreciation for the scarcity of our resources. I'm aware that there are very few places left that are wild, beautiful, unspoiled nature. Very few. Actually there are even few places left that one can even think of living in. Huge sections of our planet have been desecrated entirely, are turning into poisoned desert. And there are masses of populations—millions and millions of people—living in the most degraded circumstances, in filth and disease. To not have that in our awareness as we are consuming is a huge denial. And I have no use for any spiritual system that just says, "Oh, it's all just fine. It's just a dream that those people are having"...and so on, whatever the justification is. Usually the people who are making that justification are in very comfortable circumstances. So, I feel that is another aspect of grounding this question, "What is basic need, and where does it move into greed?"

It is important to have an awareness that we do live in a privileged situation here in America in particular. We are in the courtyard of the kingdom. Given that, let's be considerate, let's make our lives worthy of this incredible privilege and not abuse it and not take too much.

Q - Some people feel that we as a species are on the brink of a significant shift in consciousness, and that such a shift may even be necessary for our survival on the planet. Could you comment on this?

CI - Well, I have no idea whether or not we are in a shift. From one perspective it might look that way, especially in the satsang circles. There are certainly a lot of people interested in this. But then, you look at the world, you look at the huge populations in China and the Middle East and Africa and you might not get the sense that there's really so much shifting there. But, of course, it can happen fast. Who knows?

I find that I just don't have much interest in future speculation. Given that we simply cannot know. So much of what I used to think was going to happen didn't happen, and things I thought wouldn't happen did. Just watching the unfolding is enough. It takes up the whole screen, and prevents putting in any future picture.

Q - There will be some readers of this book who may sense some form of Awakening in their lives, or at least have a great degree of interest in the topic. What would you like to say to them?

CI - Well, given the sample of people who will be in this book, I think that any resonance that the reader might have with any of us (or any branches or teachers or books that those people may recommend) is a very useful place to start. It's helpful in the beginning to have a teacher, for want of another word, a person, a living presence within whom you can sense both their humanity and their divinity so easily. So, it's very, very helpful and inspiring. And, there's a worldwide *sangha* of fantastic people, not just the teachers but all of the people interested in this, who you immediately plug into when you begin studying this journey. All of that is very helpful and rich.

So for people who don't have access to that community, I would say, "Find it." Because, I know so many people who felt alone until they found *sangha*. Then they saw that there is an entire community speaking the heart-language, people who may have gone their whole lives, maybe even married with children, yet who still felt desperately alone, until they found family in *sangha*.

This is not to deny one's biological family at all. There's just a relaxation that comes when you are in the company of people with whom there is that heart understanding that needs nothing.

Biography

Catherine Ingram is an internationally known dharma teacher with communities serving several thousand students in a dozen cities in the U.S. and Europe. Since 1992 she has led *Dharma Dialogues*, which are public events of inquiry into the nature of awareness and the possibility of living in awakened intelligence. Catherine also leads numerous silent retreats each year in conjunction with *Dharma Dialogues*. She is president of *Living Dharma*, an educational non-profit organization dedicated to inquiry and service based in Portland, Oregon.

In 1999, The Irish Independent listed Catherine among the *Who's Who of the New Gurus*. She has been the subject of numerous print and radio interviews and is included in three anthologies about awakened teachers in the West: *The Awakening West*, by Lynn Marie Lumiere (Clear Visions Publications, 2000), *Like a Memory Lost*, by Paula Marvelly (due out in London in 2001), and this volume, *Wide Awake*, by Quidam Green Meyers (2002).

A former journalist specializing in issues of consciousness and activism, Catherine Ingram is the author of *In the Footsteps of Gandhi: Conversations with Spiritual/Social Activists* (Parallax Press, 1990). Over a fifteen-year period beginning in 1982, she published approximately 100 articles and served on the editorial staffs of New Age Journal, East West Journal (in house editor) and Yoga Journal (contributing editor).

For the past twenty-five years, Catherine has helped organize and direct institutions dedicated to awareness and service. She is a co-founder of Insight Meditation Society in Barre, Massachusetts (1976), widely considered the most prestigious Buddhist meditation center in the West. She is also a co-founder of Unrepresented Nations and Peoples Organization (UNPO) in The Hague, Netherlands (1991). This organization represents dispossessed nations and groups who are not recognized by the U.N. in international forums throughout the world. For six years (1988-1994), Catherine also served as a board director for The Burma Project, dedicated to raising international awareness about the struggle for democracy in Burma.

Catherine Ingram leads Dharma Dialogues and retreats throughout the U.S. and Europe. For schedules and other information or to purchase audio and video tapes please visit her website at www.dharmadialogues.org or contact her foundation at:

Living Dharma
P.O. Box 10431
Portland, OR 97201
PH: 503.246.4235

Wayne Liquorman

Interviewed in Hermosa Beach, California
June 1, 2000

In the early morning hours of the first day of June, Diana and I left Los Angeles and drove south along the Pacific. Having lived in the mountainous areas up north for some time, it felt good to breathe the salt air again and to just enjoy that special sense of grounding that close proximity to the ocean offers.

We parked our rented car on a quiet street in a sleepy little seaside town. We were early, so we powered the windows down and sat back to rest until the time for the interview. Relaxing into the reclined seat, I felt my eyes start to close.

Just a few minutes later, Diana nudged me asking, "What does Wayne look like?" Looking up, I saw a tall, bearded man outside the house about three doors down. It was Wayne Liquorman, the man that the great Indian sage Ramesh Balsekar calls his "spiritual son." He travels the world giving talks and seminars. And here he was carrying his trash to the recycling cans on the street! We knew this was going to be an interesting assignment!

Laughing at the total absurdity of life, we chatted a while more, giving him a few minutes to put the cans away. Then we gathered our things and walked to the house. Wayne's office assistant Donna answered the door and greeted us with a huge smile. We walked through a lovely (and wonderfully sparse) downstairs area, with a gorgeous Japanese-style koi pond visible through the French doors leading to the back deck. Donna led us upstairs to the large, pleasantly-decorated living room.

Wayne stood to greet us, a towering man with the face of a mischievous boy. We all shook hands warmly and sat for tea. Diana and I made ourselves comfortable on a long sofa, while Wayne took a seat in a chair to our left, his long legs dangling over the armrest.

He's a remarkably animated man with huge, dark eyes that twinkled wildly with a kind of mad humor. He has the look of a man who knows the punch

43

line to some cosmic joke. His long fingers flutter and gesture as he talks, as if he's conducting a symphony of words. But, as you'll see, he actually spoke very little. What he did say, however, was voiced with the conviction and passion of one who clearly lives what he teaches.

*This intensity of response actually influenced the interview, at one point. After a series of powerful answers (*stunning *might be a better word, actually), I checked my notes and found that the next question was to be about the existence of evil in the world. So taken was I with the simple strength of his previous comments that I just <u>could not</u> ask him that question! The result was one of many moments of hilarious laughter, as can be seen in the pages ahead.*

Without a doubt, this interview yielded more laughs-per-minute than could be humanly expected. At times, all three of us were out of our chairs and on the floor shrieking with delight. But there was also an incredible depth of spiritual understanding and an extremely high degree of sincerity in what Wayne shared.

Prepare yourself to visit with a man who offers a most profound view of Truth, wrapped up in a most unconventional and interesting package.

Q - In your experience, is there such a reality as Awakening, Enlightenment, Liberation or spiritual freedom?

WL - There is an event that happens through an organism, a body-mind mechanism that is called Awakening, or Enlightenment or whatever. And what constitutes this Enlightenment or Awakening is that a false notion—a belief in a sense of personal doership, a sense that "I am the center of the universe...I am the one who is doing"—that false notion falls away.

Now, the falling away of a false notion does not change anything. [Loudly] *Everything that was before continues to be!* And so, the notion of someone *being* enlightened is the questionable issue, not whether there is such a thing an event called Enlightenment. Because what really happens with this event of Enlightenment is that the one who would be enlightened, the one who is seeking liberation, freedom, etc. dissolves.

And what is left is Presence. What is left is what has been all along!

The Enlightened Being is only enlightened to someone else, not to himself. I think this is what prompted Robert Adams to say "We should have a '*Jnani* Convention'—a convention for enlightened people. And anybody who shows up will be immediately disqualified!" [All of us erupt into laughter]

Q - This event—in your case—did it happen at a particular moment? Or was it a gradual unfolding?

WL - *Every* event happens at a particular moment [Laughter] by its very nature! And it can be notionally linked to preceding events. That's what minds do—they take an event and then connect it to a bunch of other events that happened before and say "this is the process!" But—which events do you connect it to? I mean, it's an arbitrary process. Do you connect it to being dropped out of your crib at age two? Or do you connect it to meditating for twelve years? Both are events that preceded that one, but which one is causative? This notion of process has to do with causation—what causes the subsequent event? And the understanding is that *everything* causes the subsequent event! Nothing is independent.

Q - Is your experience of this in any way distinct or different from what might be called "ordinary" human experience?

WL - The experience that happens through this organism is a product of its nature. Its capacity for experience is determined by its senses—its ability to experience touch, smell, taste, sight and hearing. In the absence of any one of those senses, experience is different.

Now, what is absent in the sage is this false sense of an authoring of the "me". And, I liken that to the experience of walking around without a stone in your shoe. You walk around all day long without a stone in your shoe.

What is that like—to walk around all day without a stone in your shoe? Isn't it *wonderful* that you don't have a stone in your shoe? [Laughs] *Aren't you astounded at every moment...that you're walking around without the stone in your shoe?*

Exactly. There is no experience of *not* having a stone in your shoe except when you <u>do</u> have a stone in your shoe and the stone is removed! Then there's the experience of the *absence* of the stone in your shoe. This is the experience of Enlightenment—the experience in the moment of the absence of something.

Something happened, some event happened but there's no subsequent involvement in it after that. Therefore, there is no experience by the sage of Enlightenment. There is simply Understanding or Enlightenment there.

Q - Is there a sense that you are still evolving, growing, deepening?

WL - So, is there a deepening of the experience of not having a stone in your shoe?

Q - Uhhh—yes, that's the question.

WL - Yes...that is the question. *There is no experience of not having a stone in your shoe!* Therefore, there can't be a deepening of the experience of not having a stone in your shoe! When there is the experience of enlightenment, it's not Enlightenment! The experience of the deepening of Enlightenment is the experience of the deepening of spiritual experience! Now, this has been recast in today's spiritual milieu as Awakening.

I mean, you have a spiritual experience, you experience the Oneness—which virtually every seeker does—and then you meet other seekers who have been told, "That's Enlightenment—now go out and teach." And when you mention that your state is transitory, that it seems to come and go, you are told, "The reason you keep going into and out of this state is that you're maturing, you're deepening into it, you're blossoming into it, you're stabilizing in it, etc., etc. and...don't worry about it! Just go out and spread the word."

It's like a pyramid marketing scheme, you go out and enlighten two more, and they go out and enlighten two more... But that's not Awakening—that's spiritual experience! And that's what deepens!

The only thing that can deepen is experience. You mature. You develop with it. All of that is part of the spiritual process—of spiritual seeking, the ripening of the seed. And that happens. And it's well-documented—it's been happening for millennia! They just didn't used to call it Enlightenment! That's the only difference!

Q - What is your experience of thought and emotion?

WL - Thought and emotion arise. The full range of thought and emotion arise, and are expressed in accordance with the nature of the organism, and they pass. And then new ones arise. But the experience of it is only by an identified individual. In the absence of an identified individual, there is no subsequent experience of what is happening. *There is simply what is happening!*

Q - Did you (or do you) have a teacher?

WL - I do have a guru—Ramesh Balsekar in Bombay.

Q - What is your relationship to him?

WL - I love him more than life itself.
[Long pause]

Q - Do you teach?

WL - Yes.

Q - What do you teach?

WL - I teach *nothing*! In a most profound sense, what I teach is nothing. And...the nothing that I teach is that which is also everything. I have no doctrine or dogma or techniques associated with teaching, so calling it a "teaching" might be begging the question. Because normally, when you think of a teaching we ask, "What is it that you're teaching? What is it that you're trying to tell people?" And in my case I'm not trying to tell anybody *anything*! When people come—that's...when I teach. I mean if people don't come... [Everyone laughing]...no teaching.

I mean, I didn't even want to teach; that was not my intention. I was a businessman. There were a number of years after this event happened when I was quite content to operate my business and take care of my family and publish Ramesh's books and organize his tours. But the business disappeared, overnight. It was a full-fledged, quite substantial business in which I was the middleman. I got "un-middled", and the business evaporated.

That left me with some time, and I was finally able to go to India for Guru Purnima. And at the end of the Guru Purnima talk, Ramesh said, "You should all come back tomorrow. Tomorrow Wayne's giving the talk." And I was astounded because this was not at all in my plans. So I said, "Well, Ramesh, thank you very much but really, uhhh, you're doing a masterful job in this teaching deal. It would be presumptuous of me to talk about this stuff while you're still doing it." And he said, "Nonsense. If they come, talk to them." I said, "Fine. I think I'll be safe." But, people came and so I talked and answered some questions, and that was it.

And I thought that would be the end of it. But I got back to the States, and a few weeks later I got a phone call from somebody who said, "We have a small group in Atlanta, we hear you are talking, would you come talk to us?" And Ramesh had said, "If they come, talk to them," so I did. And the phone has been ringing since then. Now my schedule is quite full with traveling around the world because people call and say, "Come talk!" So what I do is I come and I sit down and see what happens. Each time it's a little different. Sometimes people love it, become *completely* enthralled, mesmerized, it's the most astounding thing they've ever heard. And most people leave at the break! *There's just nothing to do, you know?* They're like, "Man, this is the most *worthless* of teachings." And it *is* an absolutely worthless teaching—there's nothing there! So, it takes a particularly foolish kind of disciple to be interested in this *nothing*! But those are the ones that I delight in being with and talking to. Because in the absence of wanting to get something, the world shakes.

Q - Do you have a personal practice?

WL - [Long pause...then Wayne shakes his head]

Q - [Laughter] For the transcriber...that's a "no".

Q - So, when people "just show up", as you say, if they have practical questions about money, sexuality, relationships, diet, etc. What do you tell them?

WL - Make as much money as you possibly can. F--k as many people as you possibly can. Eat as much as you can. Live as long as you possibly can. And enjoy life! What's so difficult about that? [At this point we are *all* out of our chairs laughing].

Q - Wayne, I hesitate to ask you this question, but, it's kind of my job. Some people claim that there is a sort of a shift toward Consciousness taking place in mankind. Some even claim that such a shift is necessary for the survival of the race. Could you comment on that?

WL - [Belly laugh] I think that it's a delightful notion. And, it'll certainly draw people in! I mean, *everyone* wants to be part of the *Big Shift*! You'd hate to be left out of this *big cosmic occurrence*. I mean if you don't catch the wave it's like not getting into the rising stock market!

But what I see is that there is a growing interest in spirituality among rich people. I have a book business here and you can track where the books are going. And you can see who's interested in this stuff. And there are interested people on both coasts of the United States and a couple of major cities in between. And there is Germany, the Netherlands, England...But when you get further south into Spain, Greece, Italy where it's a little poorer, there's not a tenth of the interest! I mean it's in the more affluent countries—like Sweden—that's where the interest is.

So, certainly, amongst people who have taken materialism as far as it can go, have ridden that train as far as it'll go, then they're at the end of that line looking around for the next thing to get. Because that hasn't worked—it hasn't fulfilled the promise of satisfaction, peace and happiness that is was supposed to.

It's like you got all the great stuff, you got all the toys and you're still miserable! So, at the station where you get off that train there's a bunch of touts there pitching *their* resorts. It's like they're saying, "Come here, and you're *going* to get happiness and you're *going* to get wealth and you're *going* to get peace and you're *going* to get harmony and you're *going* to get that inner oneness that you're seeking." So, off you go. *And you may get it!* I'm not saying that this never happens. I'm just saying that it's certainly not guaranteed.

Q - There will be some readers of this book who may sense some form of Awakening in their lives, or at least have a great degree of interest in the topic. What would you like to say to them?

WL - I wouldn't say anything! But, if they come to me with some question...if they are drawn to me for some reason, then we can sit together. And we'll see what happens. That's all. It's part of this incredibly diverse dreamland, *leela* as they call it in the scriptures. So we're all playing our part. This organism [pointing to himself] gets to play the "guru part" in this regard, at least in reference to these people. Certainly to the check-out clerk at the supermarket I'm just a customer. I'm another guy in line, you know, with some cash! She's not going like, "Whoa. Do you feel the *shakti*?" [By now, we all are *shrieking* with laughter]

Yet, sometimes in the most unexpected places...like one time I was on a plane and the flight attendant is going down the aisle and I looked up and our eyes met. And she got a blast that just about buckled her knees! She didn't know what had happened. She had no clue what had just happened. She was stunned for a minute, and then she went on serving the others. Later she came back and knelt down in the aisle next to my seat and just looked at me. She said, "I just want to thank you for being here." And she had no context in which to put any of that. But the resonance —this connection—was there.

In terms of this book and its readers, all I can say is that different people are attracted to different teachers. They're at different stages of their spiritual development. For some, they will be attracted to a teacher who has a *plan*! They'll say, "Just tell me what to do! I'm so sick of trying to figure this shit out. Just tell me what to do—I'll do it! Okay? " [Laughter] Monasteries and ashrams are full of people like that: "Just f--king *tell* me!"

This teaching, as it has come to me from Ramesh, is one in which there are no prescriptions. It just continually points back to what is. Most seekers keep trying to get *there*, but "there" is <u>here</u>!

It doesn't get any better than this. I mean it'll change in the next moment but *this is it! This is what you've got! This is what is!*

And *this* is the touch-point for God. Right here!

Biography

Wayne Liquorman was born 1951 in Los Angeles, California where he lived in the suburbs until going to the University of Hawaii where he studied Creative Writing. After graduating with a BA he returned to the beach area of Southern California, married, started an import/export business and had two children. A nineteen-year bout with alcoholism and drug addiction ended spontaneously in 1985 leaving him sober and a spiritual seeker. He met his guru, Ramesh S. Balsekar after 16 months of intense seeking and soon began publishing Ramesh's books and arranging Ramesh's speaking tours in the U.S. The final Understanding occurred in April of 1989 soon after which, the book *NO WAY...for the Spiritually Advanced* was written under the pen name Ram Tzu.

Wayne has been talking publicly since 1996 after being told by Ramesh, "If they come, talk to them." His second book, *Acceptance of What IS...a Book About Nothing* was published in 2000.

You can contact Wayne, get his schedule of Talks (including Live Internet broadcasts), and further information at:

www.advaita.org

Lama Surya Das

Interviewed by phone from Boston, Massachusetts
June 7, 2000 and January 16, 2001

When I was told that Lama Surya Das had agreed to be interviewed, I recall looking forward to meeting him. After all, this man has quite an amazing reputation. His past teachers include "heavyweights" from both the Buddhist and Hindu traditions, including Neem Karoli Baba, the mysterious "jungle saddhu" who I first learned about in the pages of Ram Dass's remarkable book Be Here Now. I had long been attracted to Neem Karoli Baba, and Surya Das would be the first person I had ever talked with who had known Baba personally.

Surya has also served and studied with several luminaries in the world of Buddhism, including Dilgo Khyentse Rinpoche and Nyoshul Kenpo Rinpoche. This wide background of study with (and service to) such special teachers clearly added to my anticipation of the meeting.

However, circumstances moved our talk into "phone chat" mode. So, on the morning of June 7 I found myself dialing his number in Boston

Lama Surya Das is a very animated man. He speaks in an unmistakable New York accent, with the rapid-fire tempo of a man who has so much to say that the words are practically bursting to get out. In fact, his delivery was so forceful that the full impact of the words did not hit me during the initial interview. It was actually during the transcription of the interview that I began to realize the vast importance of what was said (and what is presented here). His humble yet powerful discourse spans a wide range of understanding, covering many areas of spiritual significance. And, as you'll see, Surya also weaves some very important views on global responsibility into his talk.

At the end of our conversation, Surya told me that he would be appearing at a book-signing in San Francisco on a date that happened to correspond to when Diana would be there. So we went to the event with great anticipation.

When we arrived, we found a cozy third-floor wing of the bookstore filled with attendees—perhaps 50 or more. We took what looked like the only available places—two lean-against-the-back-wall spots—and settled in for his talk.

Surya is a stocky, intense man who punctuates that quick New York delivery with a continuous array of emphatic hand gestures. He speaks with the authority of one who has been there and back again, and clearly captivated most of this audience with his talk. He deftly interwove a powerful thesis on compassion, surrender and love with fascinating information about his latest book. He spoke passionately about living one's Buddha-nature while engaging an ordinary Western life. All in all, he delivered a fine talk.

But it was his response to the few naysayers in the crowd that struck me as the measure of the man. One audience member clearly had the capacity (and intention) to consume the entire question-and-answer portion of the program with an endless supply of flat, self-absorbed inquiries and statements, eliciting more than a few audible murmurs from the attendees. With an impressive patience, Surya listened quietly and responded calmly to the first few statements from the man. Then, when the fellow tried to continue, the Lama compassionately but abruptly cut him off and moved directly to another questioner. This happened so quickly and with such grace that the transition was over almost before it happened, leaving many in the audience smiling.

During this whole time, Diana and I had been noticing a little man standing to our left who seemed to be pacing in place. He continually shifted his weight from one foot to the other, his hand raised to ask a question. This fellow's body language practically screamed *impatience. And sure enough, when called on, he proceeded to ask Surya a rather personal question—one that had absolutely nothing to do with the book or the talk. It was a query that was clearly designed to embarrass the Lama. A tangible chill could be felt moving through the assemblage and the room fell dead silent.*

For the first time in the talk, Surya's body movements stopped completely as he softly gazed at the little guy who had suddenly begun to stand stock still. For an instant it felt as if time and space were suspended in our little wing of the bookstore. Then, in a voice as soft as his glance, Lama Surya Das spoke to the man with a gentle ferocity that unglued the question without in any way diminishing or embarrassing the questioner. The whole room could be felt to move and breathe again, and without blinking an eye, Surya moved on to the next raised hand.

There was never a microsecond where Surya lost it. It was an awesome and humble display of the power of Truth and Presence, exercised by a man unafraid to face public criticism. It seemed to me that the way Surya Das had handled himself in the clinches was at least as important as the words that were said during his talk.

After the event had concluded and the books had all been autographed, we introduced ourselves to Surya and chatted with him for a while. Then, hand in hand, Diana and I walked out into Market Street to find a place to have lunch.

Q - In your experience, is there such a reality as Awakening, Enlightenment, Liberation or spiritual freedom?

LSD - Yes, absolutely. In fact, some wisdom masters say that it's the only reality, but that's a little too idealistic, I think. Enlightenment is definitely possible. Wisdom is within us. We only have to realize the truth of who and what we are—reality.

That's why there's a spiritual path—so we can get there. It's not just something to believe in, that somebody two thousand years ago might have gotten enlightened or become the only son of God or become an enlightened Buddha. Anybody can do it if they follow an authentic spiritual path.

Q - In this sense of liberation, have you experienced or attained anything distinct from so-called "ordinary" or "normal" human experience?

LSD - I think that human experience includes the Divine. So, no, I wouldn't make any special claims for myself. I could say that I'm the same as you and everyone else and that I know that. Not everyone does.

I certainly found what I was looking for in terms of inner peace and the goal of spiritual life. If I were to die today I'd die a happy man. And I wish that for everyone. The spiritual path is not an elitist path for saints and mystics only. Anybody can do it. That's my message. And that's the message of the Buddha. Anybody can become enlightened, as wise, unloving, unselfish as the Buddha himself. Anybody can wake up—old or young, male or female, learned or illiterate—by following the path of the Buddha or following any other authentic path.

Q - Did this seem to happen at a particular moment or event, or did it seem to gradually evolve?

LSD - Buddhists have been debating this for a couple of centuries, "Is enlightenment sudden or gradual?" One of my masters said that it's about suddenly awakening and then gradually cultivating, maturing and developing it and ironing out what we've realized or glimpsed. In general, a spiritual path is a pilgrim's journey. We make progress, we develop. We first turn ourselves toward spirit, toward the *dharma*. Then we start to learn about it, to dedicate more time and energy to it. We get some knowledge. Then we get some experiences, then insights and realizations. And ultimately, this knowledge and understanding develops into wisdom, into self-realization, illumination and full enlightenment. So, that's the kind of gradual path.

But, of course, the true mystical experience happens in a timeless time. It's in the moment. It's beyond linear time, beyond past, present and future. That's what we call in our Tibetan *dzogchen* tradition "the fourth time" or the "timeless time." It's the eternal now. And that's a sudden awakening. It's a moment of total nowness.

Q - Do you have an experience of growing, maturing, or evolving in this process?

LSD - Yes, I think so. I don't think there's any static state. If it's just a state then it's not the real thing, it's not the natural state or how things actually are, which is a little more mysterious or a little more flowing than fixed. There is a deepening, a depth. According to Buddhism, the fully enlightened, completely awakened Buddha—who's not just somebody who has had an Awakening or *satori* experience but somebody who has fully completed the spiritual journey over many lifetimes—is said to be beyond deepening. But for most of us, I think that that's not the case, although there is a part of us that is beyond deepening. That is true, because that's our true nature.

But our experience of it, our realization of it does seem to deepen. And those two sort of parallel lines do converge in the far horizon of duality. Even though in the realm of duality they are parallel lines which can never meet [Laughs].

Q - What is your experience of thought and emotion?

LSD - [Chuckle] I like to think a lot and I'd rather not feel anything. [We both laugh]. Look, I'm a guy! And an intellectual New Yorker, to boot! What can I say?

But I think that the body-mind/heart-mind split is a bit arbitrary. You know, in Buddhist philosophy the three poisons or afflictions—greed, hatred and delusion—sort of include thoughts and emotions. In other words, delusion is an emotion as much as greed or anger or hatred or lust or avarice. So, I think that the body-mind/heart-mind split is not that separate.

We're finding today in body-mind medicine what the yogis have known for millennia and more. Thoughts and intentions create our world and they create our emotional experience and our feeling world, too. This is not just an intellectual intention.

And I think that when we practice spirituality we do need to not just talk about things only from the eyebrows up—like clear vision, meditation, mindfulness, consciousness, awareness, realization, self-inquiry and all this. We need to bring it to the heart, to the feeling, the visceral levels, the energetic levels.

We need to open the energetic blockages and the kinks in our psyche, in our *nadis*, in our *chakras* and so on. All that is very valid spiritual practice and makes us a more well-rounded, luminous spiritual sun, rather than just being on sort of a one-way upwardly-directed street.

Spirituality is not unidirectional.

Q - Do you have a sense of anything that might be called evil or negative energies within life?

LSD - I don't think there's a devil or really any absolute good or bad. I think that these are relative notions. Of course, there is negativity and harmfulness and unwholesomeness in the world, and corruption and so on. That's for sure. There's plenty of oppression, injustice and greed and cruelty and meanness. But the shadows are also nothing but light. There's no such thing as absolute darkness. Even a serial killer or a Hitler has some spark of the Divine or Buddha-nature in him or her.

I also don't think there's any perfectly unmitigated good. We need to recognize that even a saint has some part of the dark still in their psyche, as well, even though it is well-integrated. And that's not to say that I fall prey to the current cultural relativism where people are afraid to stand up for any kind of values or ethics because everything seems so relative. I think there are universal values. No one wants to be harmed or killed or have their loved ones harmed or maimed or killed and so on. So values like non-violence, unselfishness, love, compassion, empathy, patience, forbearance and forgiveness are universal values. I think we need to look more deeply into cultivating and incubating those in ourselves and in the young ones in our society as well. We should not be afraid to take a stand about things that we see clearly.

Therefore, I don't have much patience for what I call "zen zippies" or those doing the "*vedanta* shuffle", as if *dzogchen* makes you drunk or something. People tell me, "I hear that *dzogchen* is beyond karma since everything is non-dual. There's no good or bad." And I answer, "But that's not where we live. Unless you don't mind which side of the street you drive on! Then, you can talk to me about non-duality! But I do notice that you drive on the correct side of the street and you do have a survival instinct intact."

So, in the realm of duality, long live wide discrimination and discernment between good and evil, helping and harming, wholesome and unwholesome, skillful and unskillful, virtue and vice. We need to make those discernments for ourselves for the benefit of one and all.

Q - Did you or do you have a teacher?

LSD - Yes, I've had many teachers. I had a guru, a root guru, the late Tibetan master Karmapa and others like His Holiness Dilgo Khyentse Rinpoche and Kalu Rinpoche. These are my root gurus.

My first guru was Neem Karoli Baba who gave me my name Surya Das. He is always with me. They are all always with me. They have made a big difference to me. All of them transmitted lineages to me, empowered me as a lama and so on, specifically my dzoghen master who died this past summer. I was his translator and attendant and assistant and closest Western disciple and lineage-holder. He really made a big difference to me. He inspired me, taught me a lot and transmitted his Crazy Wisdom directly to me in a way that study and other things can't really provide. I'm just beginning to understand it myself ten years later.

Q - And following through with that, do you teach? And if so, what do you teach?

LSD - Yes, I teach. I teach the dharma. I teach American Buddhism. I teach *dzogchen*. I teach meditation, chanting, Tibetan energy yoga, self-inquiry, ethical and compassionate action, *seva*. That's what I teach, all based in the *Mahayana* Buddhist tradition and the *dzogchen* lineage.

Q - Do you have a personal spiritual practice?

LSD - Yes, I practice daily meditation, chanting and some yoga, prayer and some of the Tibetan rites and rituals. Also, I consider service an important practice. I consider my teaching or pastoral work, spreading and preserving the *dharma*, bringing teachers from the East to the West, building monasteries and meditation centers here, interfaith work all as spiritual activism. They are kind of my *bodhisattva* mission, my spiritual practice, my own growth in the work.

Q - Some people feel that we as a species are on the brink of a significant shift in consciousness, and that such a shift may even be necessary for our survival on the planet. Could you comment on this?

LSD - Yes, I think that there is a shift happening. And I think that even political leaders and people from the most diverse walks of life from many countries are really calling for a spiritual revolution. We're realizing that we do have enough resources, but they are inequitably distributed. There's enough knowledge to live together harmoniously, but we are not meeting on a common ground and we need to do so.

I think that the millennium has made people think about this. The number of wars happening worldwide, the threat of nuclear holocaust, the AIDS epidemic in Africa, threats to the ozone layer and the environment, pollution, overpopulation—these have all made people think about this. It's making people realize that we have to pull together; we have to be a community. We have to consider other species and the flora and fauna of this planet and be guardians and caretakers of the whole and not just think about our own self, about personal and national profit.

These concerns are starting to make a contribution in this right direction. Of course, some of this is not explicitly described. We need to see that people don't fall into sectarianism, but it's more like what I call "stealth *dharma*." [Laughter] It's sort of insinuated into the system.

There are plenty of environmentalists, people who are very environmentally aware—heads of oil companies and automobile companies—who can't come out as environmentalists or their stockholders' shares would plummet. That's just a fact. But, they themselves are doing everything they can to move things in a better direction. They don't just think about profit in the bottom line. They also think about people, about sustainability of the planet and environmental impact, and so on. And all of this, in my opinion, has to do with our spiritual wellness and our communal well-being. It's very spiritually oriented.

So, I think that this is a very special time for us. We're all more connected in this Information Age and this age of the shrinking world that we live in. This is now almost one global culture. I think that people are waking up to the fact that we have to pull together if we're not going to sink completely under the weight of our own fabrications and delusions.

As I said before, I also think that people are becoming more open to all of this. As people have more experience of technological development, especially in the First World, in America and other places, we've had so much material and technological development, yet people still come up wanting. So, naturally, there's a turning toward looking deeply into timeless values, the perennial philosophy. Spirituality is an "evergreen subject" and it's really coming back in, even beyond the religions and all their isms and schisms.

There's now a greater, more heartfelt interest in a connective spirituality, not just in an inherited belief system that people have to believe in but don't really experience.

So, this is kind of a unique opportunity today, where all of these different timeless wisdom traditions exist side by side in the same place, the same time, the same language. You know, on the same street of every city, we find all of these centers, libraries, bookstores, centers, ashrams, temples, churches. It's all there. And for the first time, we can access these and make a more personal spiritual life and practice that can change our relations and change our community and our world. I feel strongly about this great opportunity.

Of course the down side of it is the overwhelm. We can get overwhelmed by too much information in this Information Age. The up side is that we can make conscious decisions. We do have access. There are no more secrets. You know, the genie is out of the bottle. We have to realize that *we* are the genie! We have the power. It doesn't belong to the priest or to some secret society.

Q - So, I'll make an assumption that when you're interacting with people, they sometimes ask you questions regarding practical issues such as money, sexuality, relationships, things having to do with merging worldly life with spiritual life. How do you approach helping people with those issues?

LSD - Well, I just try to be very honest and answer them the best that I can. I'm not the "Answer Man." I don't know everything. I encourage them to understand that they are their own teacher and that they should cultivate more discernment and discrimination and clear seeing and try to discern the real from the unreal.

Dzogchen has three main practices and the foundational preliminary practice is called "subtle discernment"—discerning the real from the unreal, discerning authenticity from fabrication and so on. I try to encourage people to learn that, to practice that themselves in their daily lives. Then they can make clear decisions. They are not pulled this way and that by what in Buddhism we call "the eight worldly winds"—pleasure and pain, loss and gain, praise and blame, fame and shame. So, rather than be buffeted around by these, we can make emotionally intelligent decisions by knowing what's important. Then we can live by what's congruent with our values, whether or not it's the most comfy or easy way to go. So, I try to be very practical in answering those practical questions. I'd be interested to know what the other teachers you interview find about this.

But, perhaps because I'm called a lama or I'm known as somebody who has lived for twenty years with great sages from India and Tibet, people pose a lot of "not-practical" questions about rebirth, death, visions, out-of-body experiences, communications with the departed, about their spiritual epiphanies and breakthroughs, enlightenment experiences, all kinds of things. So, that's also a certain part of my, let's say, exploration with people who come to me.

Some people ask me about their dreams, about ethical issues like abortion, homosexuality, capital punishment, bringing up their children spiritually, even the ethical dilemma of putting down an aging pet. These are very real ethical dilemmas that people face in life. I try to approach the answering of these ethical questions just as I would the answering of the practical questions. I try to be as straight and as simple as I can on the spot, not just saying, "This is what the Buddha said, so this is what you have to do." You know, I might give my opinion on it, my thought on it. I might also tell them what the Buddha said or what one of my old teachers or someone else did, or something that I observed. But it's definitely not, "This is what you *have* to do!"

I like to take a more exploratory, self-inquiry approach, opening the questions, rather than coming up with the quickest, easiest answer. Sometimes a good question is better than the right answer, if there even is a right answer. Sometimes an "open wondering" approach might help to bring people further than having some answer like a band-aid to patch over the open wound or sensitive area. Sensitivity can be an important and good thing. We shouldn't try to close it over or patch it up too quickly.

And I have a lot of respect for this self-inquiry approach. I think that this is one place where the non-dual traditions of Buddhism and other mystical traditions really come together and have a lot to offer this kind of questioning. It makes sense to be looking into not just the objects and the things in life, but into who we are. If we continue asking and looking into who we are, why we are here, why we're doing what we are doing, how we are doing it, what we are meant to be while here, we will progress spiritually and collectively in the right direction.

Q - For the reader who perhaps senses some form of Awakening, or at least has some degree of interest in the topic, what would you like to say to them?

LSD - I would say this: "American Buddha—awaken! Throw off your chains, your concepts!" But the question is—how? We need to find a way that resonates with our heart and bring it to our lives day after day and year after year and not just imitate somebody else. No more "monk see, monk do!" We each need to find our own true way.

I'm not someone who's going to come and tell you that there's only one true way and it's mine. But, I do think that there's only one true way for each of us. We have to find it. We have to be honest, authentic, sincere and genuine.

And, you know, *lightly*, not so seriously, not grimly. Taking it lightly is very important, with a sense of humor, with a sense of the cosmic absurdity of the entire quest. We need to enjoy the joy of Awakening, the joy of spirit, not think of it as some kind of chore or penance. So, we lighten up as well as "Enlighten up" every step of this Great Way.

As my *dzogchen* master Dilgo Khyense Rinpoche used to say, "With this *dzogchen* practice you can get fully enlightened in three years or seven years or certainly in this lifetime. But, even if you don't, you'll still get off!" [Laughter] Translating from the Tibetan, "You'll still get excited, you'll still get up, you'll still light up." That's the good news.

The good news is that it's actually up to each of us. The bad news is that it's actually up to each of us!

The steering wheel of our destiny is in our own hands. There's no one else to blame. We are not victims. There's a lot of empowerment and blessing and certainty in that. But I think it's also important to look into our motivation, our intention, how selfish we are in life. This is where the rubber meets the road. If we are too self-oriented, if we are just doing for ourselves, caught up in ourselves, spirituality can become like another form of narcissism, self-congratulation, or something. And I feel like we all, including myself, sometimes fall into that in our form of American narcissism. That's okay and understandable, but we should just keep an eye on that and notice that no matter how much people have they can still be unhappy. And a lot of people are unhappy because they think too much about themselves. <u>There is no self!</u> We are doing everything for a self that isn't really there.

On a conventional level, we are here and we do need to take care of ourselves. We need to be a grownup, an autonomous adult, not a dependent child and all of that. But on another level, we are really worshipping at the wrong altar. And that's something to be aware of. Where the rubber meets the road on the spiritual path is whether we are becoming more humble or more peaceful. Are we becoming more happy and fulfilled and content and compassionate?

As we practice self-inquiry and other mindful and contemplative practices we gain more insight toward ourselves, we realize that we are not really who we think we are. And that frees us from a lot of delusions. I truly think that that's the direction that spirituality takes beyond the -isms and schisms. This is the direction of *dharma*. Not just Buddhism, or Hinduism or *vedanta*.

This is the convergence point of the *dharma* today—one *dharma*, a *dharma* that realizes the truth of who we are. It realizes the Buddha-light within one's self, which means with the other, also, within our relations, within everyone and everything.

Biography

Lama Surya Das is one of the foremost Western Buddhist meditation teachers and scholars. Born Jeffrey Miller, he was raised in Valley Stream on New York's Long Island, where he celebrated his bar mitzvah and earned letters in basketball, baseball and soccer at Valley Stream Central High School (class of 1968). While a student at the State University of New York at Buffalo, he attended antiwar protests, marched on Washington, and attended Woodstock. After graduating with honors from college, he traveled throughout Europe and the East, and he has spent nearly thirty years studying Zen, vipassana, yoga, and Tibetan Buddhism with the great old masters of Asia.

Today, Lama Surya Das teaches and lectures around the world, conducting dozens of meditation retreats and workshops in ten different countries each year. Based on his relationship with the Dalai Lama, Surya Das founded the Western Buddhist Teachers Network and has organized three week-long conferences of Western Buddhist Meditation Teachers with the Dalai Lama in Dharamsala, India. He also teaches regularly at Esalen, Open Center, Omega Institute, Interface, at universities in the United States and abroad, and at spiritual centers of all kinds.

Surya Das is the author of *Awakening The Buddha Within: Eight Steps to Enlightenment* (Broadway Books, 1997), which appeared on Publishers Weekly Religion Bestseller list, and on lists at the Boston Globe, San Francisco Chronicle, Denver Post, Rocky Mountain News, and Christian Science Monitor. His new book, *Awakening To The Sacred* (Broadway Books, 1999), combines his extensive background and intense training in Buddhist practices with his remarkable knowledge of other religions, philosophies, and psychology offering a simple guide to creating a spiritual life from scratch and connecting with the sacred in everyday life.

A regular contributor to *Tricycle* magazine, *New Age*, and *Yoga Journal*, he is also the author of *The Snow Lion's Turquoise Mane: 155 Wisdom Tales from Tibet* (1992), and coauthor of *Natural Great Perfection: Vajra Songs and Dzogchen Teachings* (1995).

When he's not meditating, teaching, or attending a retreat, Surya Das enjoys music, dogs, swimming, bicycling, hiking, and haiku poetry. He resides in Concord, Massachusetts, outside of Boston.

You can reach Lama Surya Das through his website at:

www.surya.org

Satyam Nadeen

Interviewed by phone from Atlanta
June 11, 2000

Satyam Nadeen's reputation had preceded him. After reading his two marvelous books From Onions to Pearls *and* From Seekers to Finders, *I knew I wanted him to appear in these pages. His story is, after all, quite remarkable...*

A man—a serious seeker of Truth—makes a fortune in the early days of the marketing of the drug Ecstasy, carefully avoiding the United States market, where it had been made a controlled substance. Some of the drug accidentally slips through into this country and he gets arrested and put into a horrible Federal prison in Florida. In this hellish environment that would cause most of us to curse God and all things holy, he passes his time reading books on religion and spirituality. One day, while reading a book by Ramesh Balsekar, the man spontaneously "falls Awake" when he encounters the phrase, "Consciousness is all there is, and I am That." After a number of years in prison, our now-Awakened man is released and goes on a worldwide many-month-long satsang speaking tour. Finally, he retires to Costa Rica to run a stunningly-beautiful tropical resort he had purchased and turned into a spiritual retreat center. Quite a story, yes?

Now, I'm not exactly sure what I expected when I placed the call to Nadeen in Atlanta on June 11. But whatever it was, it sure wasn't what I got! The man who answered the phone was arguably the most articulate human being I have ever spoken with. Every word flowed from him gracefully, with an incredible sense of ease. Satyam Nadeen refuses to speak from other than personal experience, making what he does say potent with a directness and humor rarely encountered in any walk of life.

Like his mentor Ramesh Balsekar, Nadeen loves to use the term "Source" the way others use words like "God" "Higher Power" and "Presence." I found this to be very appealing, because most terms that we use for the Absolute carry with them some "spin", and this particular word does not.

61

And having a neutral word for the vast, infinite, eternal God-nature of every man, woman and child struck me as a useful thing.

Nadeen has adopted a "no bullshit" approach to questions that have boggled the minds of most of the great thinkers throughout our history, bringing a simplicity and reality to the work.

But most of all, he seems to be such a nice guy! He's funny, without a trace of irony. He knows, but doesn't act like it. He says that his spiritual practice is "to have as much fun as I can every day!" What's not to like about this guy?

After the interview, he invited us to come visit him at Pura Vida, that resort of his. And, I have a confession to make (please don't tell Diana)— I've been spending far more time than I should thinking about how to get us there!

Q - In your experience, is there such a reality as Awakening, Enlightenment, Liberation, or spiritual freedom?

SN - I have a problem with all of those words because as "seekers" we have all been fatally programmed with concepts as to what they might mean. What I do have an actual experience of in myself and in countless other people who I met when I was on a *satsang* tour—more than 92 cities in over three years—was that there is a shift taking place in Awareness. Whether we call that Awakening or just a shift is semantics. And in this new Awareness there is a totally new paradigm happening.

And that paradigm seems to be going away from spiritual tradition for the last umpteen thousand years whereby you needed a Master and spiritual disciplines to arrive at a true knowing of your own essence. This knowing of who you are seems to be happening spontaneously now. And in this knowing, there is total freedom. So that is happening on a larger scale than anyone could imagine.

Q - Some people feel that such a shift may even be necessary for our survival on the planet. Could you comment on this?

SN - I don't think it has anything to do with survival of the species. What we have here is one energy—the Source. And that Source is infinite intelligence and it has a grand design for experiencing Itself in a limited form, in a third dimension. And it's gone along for millions of years without a big shift in awareness and with the tiniest flicker of energy. Anything and everything is possible. So, I don't like to try to second-guess Source as to why this shift is taking place. It's happening! And the result is that, on a very practical level, people are becoming happy for the first time in their lives.

What this has to do with the survival of the whole species who knows, who cares? It's just a mind trip to try to figure it out.

Q - Have you experienced or attained anything distinct from so-called "ordinary" or "normal" human experience?

SN - Well, in "ordinary" experience, everything is experienced through the mind, through the way Source has set up the mind to work. Something in this shift is happening where we're able to transcend the mind.

The mind's function is to analyze and to make better any situation that it judges as not perfect—which is all of life. And, in this shift, we're transcending the normal human predicament whereby we are able to witness the event.

In the "normal" human experience we identify totally with the mind as though its thoughts were actual reality. In this Shift we are moved to identify with the Witness that merely observes the movements of the monkey mind and no longer believe that what the mind tells us is real.

And even though the mind is continuing to judge it in coming up with ways of bettering the situation, this part of us that I call Presence or Witness simply looks at it and says, "So be it. This is what *is*." There's no need to change it. That's not possible in a normal human experience.

And you know what? This has not been talked about that much, because in the past all of the focus of the old paradigm was on bettering yourself or getting to this supposedly exalted state of self-realization. And in that process of trying to accomplish this, the enormous obstacle came up between the doer and the reality of knowing its own essence. Because the only way a doer is possible is through the mind. There is a Higher Force necessary to transcend the mind, and that can't be done by oneself or through the help of another.

Q - Did this shift that you describe seem to happen at a particular moment or event, or did it seem to gradually evolve?

SN - Both. In my own case (and in the experience of virtually everyone I've met who has described this occurring for them) there was a moment of realization that "I am the Consciousness that is all there is." But the ramifications of this realization happen very slowly and gradually and subtly. And it spreads out over years. But, virtually everyone can remember that moment, that insight, we'll call it; an insight where the mind was transcended and all of the old concepts were just dropped for a moment and you experience yourself as just pure Consciousness. And then began the slow, gradual dissolution of all those concepts that are part of the human predicament.

Q - Do you have an experience of growing, maturing, or evolving in this process?

SN - It's a never-ending process that just keeps getting deeper and better. What I call deeper is the understanding of your own essence as Source until the point that the only reality possible is to totally embrace all of existence, just as it is! This runs totally contrary to everything in the human predicament. Human consciousness is designed to try to make everything better. So this process of letting go, allowing, embracing, surrendering is never-ending. Because the subtleties of it can go to the quasi-infinite concepts that have to be dissolved in this process, I could never imagine a point of just tapering off to a plateau.

Q - What is your experience of thought and emotion?

SN - Well, it's still happening the way it always did except that there's a Witness now watching it and not acting on it. It's just allowing the emotions to be. I've become a lot more free in expressing emotions. If anger comes up, or any part of the dark side or the shadow side of existence comes up, I just allow it to be. There's a strange phenomenon happening. If your whole life you've been programmed by the mind to judge anger or rage or envy or any of these emotions as not helpful, then you've repressed it. You've pushed it down.

When this shift takes place, and you allow *what is* to be, it's opening Pandora's Box—they all come screaming out for recognition. So, if you think you're going to peaceful nirvana in this shift—you're not! [Laughter] You're going to go through a period when all of the emotions that you've pushed down—sexual energy, rage energy, any of them—are going to come floating up, jumping up for recognition. And it's time, then, to embrace them and say, "Yes, this is part of my Divine Expression." This is just as real as love, joy and harmony.

Q - Do you have a sense of anything that might be called evil or negative energies within life?

SN - Everything in this human existence as Source is absolutely, totally balanced by freedom and limitation. If we're going to call freedom "good" and limitation "evil" or "bad", then we need to see that there's equal balance in everyone's life. You can never have enough money or power or intelligence to get out of this balance. Everyone is equally subjected to it. It's just part of the Source's experience.

So, what I used to see as evil or negative, I now see as part of the Divine Balance. Source wants to experience all of it. There is nothing excluded. There is no human emotion or experience that has not been experienced by Source. And that's why everyone is such a unique expression of Source because it's not possible with the personality's makeup for just one person to have all of these experiences. You need billions and trillions of people to have all possible experiences. And that's what is happening.

Q - Do you have a Teacher?

SN - No. I hung out with several so-called Enlightened Teachers and what they were saying sounded good in theory but it never rubbed off—it never happened to me. And the actual reality of it was that I never saw any of it actually affect their own personal life either. Again, they are still in that mixture of freedom and limitation. And just because they proclaim themselves Enlightened or their followers proclaim them Enlightened doesn't mean that they got out of the freedom/limitation balance!

And so, you look at someone like Amrit Desai who was judged as lacking in his community and excommunicated and so forth. They were just looking at the one side—they weren't looking at the total picture. So, no I never had a teacher per se that I surrendered to. I tried! Every teacher I had I tried to surrender to but there was just something in me that couldn't quite give away all of my own power to someone else.

At the moment when I did have this shift, I was contemplating a statement that Ramesh Balsekar had made—"Consciousness is all there is, and I am That"—and I had heard that statement for thirty years in various ways, but at that precise moment of my reading it, I was ripe. I was like a mango that has just fallen off the tree. And everything in my entire search, starting with the Catholic priesthood all the way through the Eastern Spiritual route, had prepared me for that moment. None of it was superfluous. It was all part of what happened.

Q - Do you teach?

SN - I share my experience in satsang. However, most satsang teachers that I've known seem to have an agenda that's about what happened with them. In our satsangs I facilitate everyone to share their experience and for everyone else in the room during that sharing to just be in a space of openness to their own inner wisdom. So no matter what that person is saying or what I'm saying, it's irrelevant. The words never have anything to do with the communication of Grace. It's that moment of openness—opening to their own wisdom that constitutes my entire message.

And so, it's sort of a "leaderless satsang" that I'm facilitating. People would like me to speak more, but I'm speaking less. I'm speaking so much less now that I'm doing satsang only at our retreat center in Costa Rica and it's silent satsang. I don't speak at all. I just sit in a circle in the room. It's very, very difficult for me to talk about it anymore.

Q - Do you have a personal spiritual practice?

SN - Yes. I have as much fun as I can every day. That's my personal practice. I never think about God or spirituality any more. It's the most foreign thought to my whole mind. Before this Shift I was a fish that was looking for water. Afterwards I realized that I'm already swimming in the ocean so I just quit thinking about it.

Q - When people ask you questions regarding practical issues such as money, sexuality, relationships, etc. what suggestions do you give?

SN - Well, it depends on the question, but that's maybe why I got off the satsang circuit. I probably talked to more than 10,000 people in those three years and the same old same old questions came up every time. These kinds of questions seem to matter more than just allowing what is to be exactly as it is. Therefore any question like that comes from not yet knowing your own essence. No one who has really experienced this shift would ask a question like that. They just wouldn't.

So, either you're talking to the mind, or you're speaking to pure Awareness. Pure Awareness doesn't ask those questions. To the mind, however, every question you answer raises two more questions. So it's a fruitless thing. The standard answer I give to most questions is, "Don't know, don't care." [Laughter]

Q - Do you meditate?

SN - No...not as a practice, not as a technique. But I love and cherish alone time, time to be quiet, to watch a sunset or listen to the birds. I find myself constantly in beautiful places and I feel nourished and embraced by nature when I can be quiet. So, do you call that meditating? I don't know. I don't care! Please believe me, the search is over. There's nothing to do except enjoy it all. Just enjoy it. What causes enjoyment? Silence causes more enjoyment to me than chaos. So, I love silence.

But I'm also very busy. I'm running two enormous resorts. I have four businesses that are running wide open and that depend on me for daily guidance. And yet in the middle of all of this I don't feel stressed or strung out or tensed up. It's like I know these things have their own life, and all I can do is just be there.

Q - Well, we've somehow already gotten to the final question.

SN - Well, I tell you that there's not much to say. There really isn't. I realized this last October and canceled a whole year of satsangs that were already set up...Australia, Europe, India, Hong Kong, Japan. I just said, "I can't even talk about this, I'm just going to enjoy it."

Q - There will be some readers of this book who may sense some form of this shift taking place in their lives, or at least have a great degree of interest in the topic. What would you like to say to them?

SN - Well, the book found them. The shift found them. The search is over. We're just so conditioned by our past that even when we have found what we were looking for, the mind goes crazy trying to figure out "why and how." You will go through what I call "bobbing in and out" when you experience this shift and you will think you have lost it, but you haven't. It just keeps coming back in waves of understanding and the contrast that is needed for this understanding is for limitation to seem to come back in. And then understanding seems to return. And it feels like, "two steps forward, one step back." That's how this shift goes. Until finally there are no more questions, no more doubt, no more seeking.

Everyone is Source, and they will get it when they get it. The most one can do now is just be and enjoy this Freedom.

Biography

By the second grade Satyam Nadeen, then Michael Clegg, was already "seeking." He wanted to become a Catholic priest and entered the seminary at the age of 12. At 26 he shifted direction and pursued Eastern tradition. For the next 30 years he was an inspired "New Ager", hopping from Maharishi Mahesh Yogi to Guru Maharaji and spending years with Bhagwan Shri Rajneesh. He participated in all of the workshops, diets and disciplines. By the age of 54 he was successful in business and had led a quiet, cultured, luxurious life.

In his search to expand his horizons, he experimented with psychedelics and psychotropics. He embarked on a self-imposed mission to save the world through the manufacture and use of MDMA—Ecstasy. Even though he was manufacturing it within the law (outside of the U.S.) a small quantity slipped through the cracks into the U.S. He was subsequently convicted on a conspiracy charge and sentenced to seven and a half years in federal prison. The DEA took every possession he owned (in four countries), was trying to put his ex-wife away, and place their daughter in an orphanage. In his first book *From Onions to Pearls*, he shares the story of his journey of awakening during incarceration.

While in prison he realized that his lifetime of spiritual searching had brought him no closer to the elusive state he was seeking, so he gave up trying. In this surrender, he found what he was looking for. The next several years were spent in a deepening process he calls the "deliverance" as layers of conditioned ego personality were being peeled away. This story reaches out to those of you who consider yourselves "seekers" of enlightenment and are still waiting to be "finders."

Nadeen's second book is called *From Seekers to Finders*.

You can contact Satyam Nadeen at:

www.satyamnadeen.com

Arjuna Nick Ardagh

Interviewed by phone from Nevada City, California
October 18, 2000

As I mentioned in the Introduction to this work, Arjuna Nick Ardagh had been a friend of mine for a few years when Diana and I moved to Nevada City, California to study in his ministry program at the Living Essence Foundation.

Arjuna is an amazing and complex man. I believe that his first book Relaxing Into Clear Seeing *reveals one of the most revolutionary—yet practical—views of spiritual life that one is likely to encounter anywhere. In it he offers, among many other things, a wonderfully effective process for the acceptance of thoughts, emotions and bodily sensations that often seem to be obscuring spiritual Presence in our lives. This method is being taught in a number of places around the world by a handful of mature practitioners, including myself and Diana.*

Arjuna had been involved in this book project early on so it was natural that he would be selected to appear here as a guest. But we'd have to wait for his interview. In late summer, 2000, I had just completed my training as a minister and Diana and I had moved back to Los Angeles to reinitiate the teaching work that we had put on hold during our period of study.

While we were engaged in the arduous moving process, Arjuna was preparing his third book for publication and continuing to teach week-long Living Essence Training seminars. So, it was actually mid-October before we were able to connect for his interview. This was fine with me because it meant that the questions that he and I had developed together a number of months earlier would now be pretty much forgotten by him, thereby ensuring a fresh, spontaneous interview. I had hoped to conduct this interview in person, but scheduling got difficult, so a phone interview was arranged.

While preparing for the call, I could not help but recall the great gift that Arjuna had given to me during the period following my brother Dave's death just a few months earlier.

69

[Editor's Note: On March 7, 2000 my younger brother Dave—after undergoing an *amazing* spiritual Awakening—was killed while trying to rescue a neighbour who was being brutalized by a man during a two-week murderous hostage-taking spree in Baltimore, MD.]

Diana and I had flown back to Maryland to be with our family for Dave's funeral and immediately after our return to California, she had to leave on a two-week tour for her job. At that same time Arjuna had travelled to Florida to teach. I recall with great fondness and gratitude how he phoned me each day of his trip, sometimes as many as four or five calls a day. He spoke to me with great love and compassion, while all the time urging me to "...sit still...do not avoid facing what is real." His brotherly love and assistance during that time of need will never be forgotten here. In fact, to this day I sometimes affectionately refer to him as my "little brother."

So, with these poignant memories still fresh, I rang Arjuna Nick Ardagh at his home in Northern California on the morning of October 18.

As we spoke on the phone, his image as a tall, thin, elegant yet impish Englishman came to mind. He speaks in a beautifully precise British accent, which lends an air of authority to his words, especially when he warms to the task of describing his unique views on the ordinariness of living an Awakened life in modern times.

Because a number of interviews were already "in the can" by October, I had learned that it was helpful to ask the guest to verbally cue me to indicate that his/her answer was complete, thereby preventing me from "stepping on" their reply. When this was relayed to Arjuna, a hilarious word-dance was interjected into the discussion as he chose to shout "Ho ho ho!" at the end of each answer, no matter how serious or profound the issue being discussed happened to be.

This juxtaposition of the profound with the sweetly eccentric actually describes quite appropriately both this particular interview and the collection as a whole. As you'll find in the next several pages—particularly if you remember to shout "Ho ho ho!" loudly at the end of each statement—Arjuna lives as a constant reminder that Awakened life is a series of paradoxes, often dealt with best through humor. We have had many interactions with this fascinating man and I can honestly say that for all of his wisdom, knowledge, and Awakening ability, he does not take himself seriously. And among the many things that he has taught me, this sense of seeing life (and one's position in it) with love and humor has been among the greatest.

I feel very safe in assuring you that he would advise you to do the same.

Q - In your experience, is there such a reality as Awakening, Enlightenment, Liberation or spiritual freedom?

ANA - These are all words. Enlightenment, Awakening and Liberation are all words. If you are driving down the road and you see a signpost that says Pleasantown, do we know that there such a thing as Pleasantown? You know that there is a signpost but what it points to is another question. These things definitely exist as words and as shared concepts. What they mean is going to be different in the different ways that people use language. It is clear that these terms have no fixed meaning because different people speak about all sorts of things as Enlightenment, liberation or freedom.

Here is what I can tell you honestly from my own experience. Up until about ten years ago, these concepts seemed to be very real to me. There was a strongly-felt sense that there was a person called "me" who was defined as not Enlightened and that if one met the right person or did the right thing that this unenlightened "me" would change into an Enlightened "me." About twenty years were spent trying to liberate this "me", enlighten this "me", trying to free up this "me."

Those twenty years, from ages 14 to 34, were like a dog chasing its own tail. The more effort that was put into trying to free the "me", the more solid the concept of the "me" became and the more solid the concept became of this thing called Enlightenment that "I" had to get to.

About ten years ago I met a man in India whose name was H. W. L. Poonja. He was the first teacher I had ever met who, instead of giving me methods to become free or Enlightened or liberated, asked me, "Who is the one trying to become free? Who are you?" In looking for that one, it became very clear that the whole thing is a concept. There really is no thing that can be found or located called "me" unless I think about it or imagine it. What is actually present is that which is experiencing this moment, and has always been experiencing this moment, which is limitless. It has no limits or boundaries, and is intrinsically free. There is no possibility of anything but freedom for that which has no limits and which is always at peace.

In one sense, Enlightenment, liberation or freedom is that which is actually real and true, has always been real and true, and is real and true right now for everybody. There is also a concept imposed on life that we are right now some small thing called "me" that is not Enlightened, not liberated, not free which needs to become so. That doesn't stand up to examination or investigation. When we try to actually find all of that, it falls apart.

Q - Did this seem to happen at a particular moment or event, or did it seem to gradually evolve?

ANA - Once again, with these questions, in order to be thorough with the answer, it is both and neither, and either one and all sorts of stuff. So, yes, there was definitely a moment in a hotel room in India where for the first and only time, really, there was an absolutely clear, undiluted attempt to find this thing called "me." It happened in a very specific way. There was a conviction that the "me"—this ego—had to be dissolved, gotten rid of or evaporated in order for seeking to end. This had been a very strongly-held idea for many years. At age fourteen, I started to practice meditation and later went on to study and practice with many teachers. For twenty years there was a conviction that it was necessary to free the ego, to get rid of the ego, to dissolve the mind in order for there to be freedom. In other words something big has to happen! In that model, you have to get from point A to point B.

There was a moment, in that hotel room in India one morning, of just innocently looking for this thing, not even realizing what was going to happen. I said to myself, "Okay, we've got to get rid of this ego. Let's find it." It was as if the hand was just stretching out into empty space—but there was nothing that appeared to end the search. So there was a moment—a definite moment—6:30 a.m. on August 29th, 1991. This was when that thing got looked for. But once it was recognized to not be there, you can't really look again in quite the same way. You can return again and again to not finding it, but the recognition—the Realization—happens once. It is as though there is a vague shape in the shadows and you assume it to be, say, an animal. Then you shine a light on it and you see that it is actually not an animal but a tree trunk. Once you have shone the light, even if later it looks like an animal again, now you know what it is. It is a tree trunk. You're not really going to get fooled by that another time. It is finished.

There was a moment of realization. However, it wouldn't really be accurate to say that prior to that point there was a "me" and then there stopped being a "me" or that before that point there was an ego and the ego dissolved or that before that point there was unenlightenment and then Enlightenment struck. It would be more accurate to say that there was a realization that what is really here experiencing this moment has always been free, has always been liberated. And there never has been an ego to get rid of. It's just a concept to describe the way thoughts arise.

There is a moment of realization, but the realization is that there is no significant moment! It is a paradox, you see. Then, in answer to the second part of the question about gradual noticing, my experience has been that the realization is sudden, immediate. But there seems to be something like a constant deepening and integration. All the old ideas and ways of living life from separation and from lack and from there seeming to be a problem arise and get dissolved back into the realization of no-separation, fullness and no problem. So far, it has been my experience that there is no end to that integration.

Some people say that there is an end and that may be true. But my experience has been that every day there is just more freedom. And even though there is already infinite freedom, every day there is more. Every day there is more love, every day more dying of the old. If there is an end to that process, I don't find any hankering to come to that end. Rather than a journey it is like looking into a kaleidoscope. You turn it, and it just keeps changing patterns. There is constant change, constant liberating of every concept, every idea, every everything. There's just deeper and deeper not knowing...deeper and deeper ignorance, actually.

Q - Have you experienced or attained anything distinct from so-called "ordi-nary" or "normal" human experience?

ANA - Absolutely not. No, absolutely not. There is no way to say how much the opposite is true. Ahhhh, what I experience in myself is something so com-pletely and utterly ordinary and basic to life that the very possibility of there being any kind of attainment is ridiculous. What is undeniably true here is that there is this Consciousness or Presence experiencing thoughts and events arising. But it has obviously always been like that because every time any thought was noticed or any feeling was noticed or any event was noticed, who do we suppose was feeling it at any time? There is nothing to be found except Awareness Itself.

And it is also blatantly obvious that this is the case for everybody! Every human being, if you look a little deeper than the gift wrapping (which can be very beautiful), is Consciousness experiencing form—always. Go to the supermarket to get groceries and if you look at the person behind the cash register not as a function, but look at who is really there, it is the same. It is Consciousness experiencing form, maybe with the idea of a separate "me" and maybe not with that idea. But that's just a tiny little concept, that differ-ence. Consciousness experiencing form is everywhere.

Somehow the way my life has unfolded is that I travel around and share this "open secret" with people. That is how my life has unfolded. So many times I find myself sitting up in the front, there are a bunch of people there in the hall and I wonder, "What on earth am I doing here?" I mean, what could possibly qualify one person to speak about what's true for everybody more than another, you know? I know that some people don't agree with this. Some people think that there is a state of realization or Enlightenment and that then a person is in a different state of consciousness. If that is true, then good luck.

But I am really in love with this realization that everybody is the same. It's so delicious to discover that wherever you look there is the same taste everywhere, just with a slightly different disguise. If you see people as who they are, they respond to that being seen. If you see someone as unenlight-ened and burdened and with lots of issues they tend to be obedient to your projections. If you see someone as they truly are, if you see them as Consciousness, they respond that way.

Q - What is your experience of thought and emotion?

ANA - No problem. What is wrong, I mean.....? I remember one time I was sitting with a friend in Seattle. This was a friend who was attending satsang and she was bothered that she was still having thoughts and emotions. She thought it would be better to be in this super-enlightened state where there were no thoughts and emotions.

So we looked out to Lake Washington where there are two floating bridges going right across the lake. When the wind kicks up, the water to the left of the floating bridge is turbulent. Then the bridge itself seems to break the waves, and all the water to the right is still, there is no wave. We looked at these bridges and I said to her, "What do you see on the left of the bridge?" She said that the water was choppy, turbulent. And I asked, "What do you see on the right?" She answered that it was still. Then I asked, "Which side is more wet?" She laughed, because she realized that there is absolutely no reason whatsoever to resist thought and emotion. It is just a concept. Why should there not be thought and emotion? A state of absolutely no thought and emotion is a completely unmanifest state. It is consciousness unmoving. And that is available and has been available for millennia...for eternity.

But now we are playing a game that involves consciousness in form... consciousness incarnate. The thing that makes consciousness incarnate interesting is the play of thought and emotion. If it's resisted it shows up one way. If it's welcomed as the natural display of its own potential then it is wonderful. That is how creativity happens. That is how the deliciousness of love happens. All sorts of things happen through allowing this play to unfold.

Q - You mentioned Poonjaji. What is your current relationship to him?

ANA - I have no relationship to him. First of all, because the person who walked and talked with the body called Poonjaji is now ashes. I do have some of the ashes by my bed but that is not what you usually call a relationship. Then there was what spoke through him or what really touched the heart looking out through his eyes. In the beginning, when I first met him, I fell completely in love with what looked out. And I thought it was something separate that looked out. I thought it was something outside of me that was related to me and leading me home. For a while that seemed to be true and it was a convenient reality to live in, one of devotion and adoration. I went back to see him repeatedly over many years. The last time I saw him was in 1996, a year before he died.

The last time I recall going to see him, it was so clear that what he had always been saying in satsang is just the simple truth—there is no teacher and student. It is all the same Consciousness. There are two different forms. The form of Poonjaji was an elderly Indian man and that is gone. You can't recreate that, it is finished. That is now ashes and it will not return in this creation. But then there was also this magnificent Presence that animated the form of Poonjaji, and that is completely present here, now—everywhere.

One finds it by looking out at creation and one finds it by looking inside to one's own nature. It is everywhere the same—One Taste. That which moved the form of Poonjaji seems to be the same as that which moved the form of Ramana Maharshi and every open window has been a window emanating this same sunlight. If you look out of a window in Madrid, do you see a different sun than if you looked out of a window in London? It is the same sun everywhere.

Now, I hope you don't mind if I go beyond your question a little bit...

Q - Quite all right.

ANA - It feels to me that this is a very sticky and crucial point in where we stand now as human beings. For millennia, Awakening and spiritual life have been viewed in terms of a relationship to a teacher, and therefore hierarchically. So, the teacher is more Awake and I'm less Awake and so on. That, of course, is what contributes to the bliss of devotion and *bhakti*. But holding that idea, that the teacher is separate, also keeps us, in a way, retarded because it means that you get different kinds of groups where everybody is focused on a teacher and everyone is assuming themselves to be somehow separate or different from that.

Now for me, what Papaji pointed to in his lifetime is that this is not necessary. I can only speak from my own experience, but the way he was with me was always really as a friend. He was always willing to reveal his humanness and his simple likes and dislikes and ordinary human reactions to life. That was a great teaching because to recognize the teacher as both Consciousness and as a human being lets one relax. You can also say, "Well, I am also both Consciousness *and* a human being," and the game of duality is then over!

Every teacher I had ever had before was somehow talking down from a podium of some kind. They were talking down and saying, "If you do this, this, this and this, then you will become as great as me." Some teachers even say, "I am the world avatar for this creation," which, of course, creates a huge sense of separation.

To me, every word that Papaji spoke that reached my ears spoke of no difference, no separation, that what is really important is the same in every human being. And for that reason, although I have never loved a human being as much as him, or felt as grateful, I have to now say that there is no relationship. His love and generosity was so great that he destroyed even the relationship. So when he died, really nothing happened—a form dropped. But what was really vibrant still remains to this day.

Q - Do you have a spiritual practice?

ANA - Yes, I do have a personal practice. My practice is called "living human life" and I try to be regular in my practice. [We both laugh loudly]. Sometimes I forget my practice and start doing bizarre and strange things like meditating or holding my breath or something. But the practice that I am really committed to is living ordinary human life.

So my practice involves such *sadhana* as being a parent to two beautiful boys. My *sadhana* involves having to listen when people notice things in me that are a little off and having to return to the humility of not being beyond reproach. My practice includes remembering to do things I said I would do. It includes being willing to be absolutely in the mud of humanity at the same time as being Consciousness. My practice has become to not use spiritual ideas, or fleeting spiritual experiences in any way whatsoever to avoid the curriculum of human life.

These days there are many people whom I also look to as inspiration—people who are willing to live life without censoring what is spiritual or not. One of my favorite friends is Isaac Shapiro, who I think you have also interviewed for this book. What an honest man! He is willing to just climb off any pedestal that he even begins to see being erected, to come back to being a husband and a father. He is someone who is always learning to be human.

And there are many honest people around like that now. I don't think that there is any need for any practice beyond just being here on this planet meeting what life brings you with an open heart.

There is really no goal to reach like this. There is no goal except the living of it in each day. The practice of being human is its own goal in each moment. One doesn't need to be working toward something else. Like having honest relationships—each moment of being honest, of being self-exposed, of being vulnerable is its own reward. You don't have to work toward some higher state. In being a parent with integrity and in really being present for one's children, in the moment of being present there is nothing more. That is its own fulfillment. I cannot imagine any end. Life is so rich and varied that there is no end to the living of it with total willingness—to be Consciousness without any doubt and to be human without any resistance or denial, to embrace the full spectrum of what is available.

My practice is to remember to be willing to be unenlightened and not to retreat into some lofty state of Enlightenment which becomes "holier than" or "separate from." My practice is the willingness to be unenlightened...as unenlightened as Enlightened.

Q - But still, because you do sit in the front of the room at times—when people come with practical questions, maybe about money, sexuality, relationships—how do you address that?

ANA - We have a Foundation here in Nevada City [California] called The Living Essence Foundation. You may notice that we didn't call it the "Get Really Enlightened And Move Beyond The World Foundation!" [We laugh] And we didn't call it the "Go On Retreat And Don't Speak To Anybody Foundation!" And we didn't call it the "Project All Of Your Highest Ideals Onto Somebody At The Front Of The Room Foundation!" We call it the Living Essence Foundation which means that we are interested in living this Presence in the context of an ordinary life without any reservation or censorship at all.

In order to do that, everybody becomes teacher, because one person could not possibly have mastery of living life in Presence in every arena. Someone explores one bit of life and someone else explores another so the *meeting* becomes the teacher rather than a person. We have developed a set of tools to make the thing sort of less confusing. The tools are not to do with Realization. Most of the tools we have are not about realizing the Truth, but living it and reversing the habits that interfere with living this way. I think that you could really sum up what we do as dissolving beliefs or concepts about anything.

Mostly we live our lives with so many layers of beliefs and concepts about how things should be or shouldn't be, what they should look like, and on and on. The tools which we have just dissolve those concepts, back into just being here, where you don't know very much at all.

If people do come with a question about money or relationships, I don't know what is right. I do know that if we can notice where there is some reference like "it should be like this" or "it should be like that,"—this is the problem. We can just realize that we don't know any of this to be absolutely true. If we let go of what we thought was true, we return to an innocence, like a child—not knowing.

I have noticed that any time I am in resistance to life, any time that I am saying "no" to what is in front of me, Presence becomes diluted because Presence is fighting itself in this resistance. Everything is the arising of Presence, so if there is a "no" to what is arising in life it is Presence fighting Itself and creating a dilution of resting as Presence. If we shift from "no" to "yes" to that which is anyway arising, in the "yes to everything" there is absolute Presence, an absolute Resting in yourself. It is that quality of "yes", that quality of unresisting that is more important than the content of what comes.

Q - Do you have a sense of anything that might be called evil or negative energies within life?

ANA - Yes, that's what I mean by resisting. If something is resisted it can appear to become negative. Anger, for example—which is a natural energy, a part of one dimension of life—has a ferociousness. If that is resisted, it can become destructive. It can become ugly. If anger is welcomed, it is just a roar that comes and disappears and maybe doesn't even need to affect anybody else at all.

Sexuality is another good example. Sexuality can be the most divine opportunity to return Home or can equally have a flavor of perversion or violence. And it is all to do with resistance. When sexuality is completely accepted and natural, it becomes beautiful. But if we hold ideas about what should and shouldn't be, that is where all kinds of strange flavors can creep in. It is the same with just about everything, you know? There is the natural movement in life—unresisted—and then there is life with ideas of what should and shouldn't be imposed upon it. It is only when there is resistance that we have the appearance of something being negative.

Q - Some people feel that we as a species are on the brink of a significant shift in consciousness, and that such a shift may even be necessary for our survival on the planet. Could you comment on this?

ANA - Yes, I do feel that is true. I've been traveling and teaching now for nine years, in this way sharing this realization of the indisputably true. The contrast between what happened in 1992 and what is happening now is huge. Just in the beginning of the '90s it was relatively rare and fleeting that people would have the realization of who they really are. And now as I travel to other cities it is pretty much the norm. Almost everybody seems to be sitting in that recognition. Not everybody has necessarily freed up all doubts. But there does seem to be an invisible revolution taking place. It won't be reported in USA TODAY because it's too subtle, too invisible. But, yes, there does seem to be some shift occurring. The whole context of spirituality seems to be shifting.

This is more than just a few people having some realization. It feels to me that the entire context of spiritual life is up for question and reconsideration.

The old model has always been one person being set aside as the teacher, more Awakened, more Enlightened. Because of deep unworthiness, most people who take part in that theater are going to be students or seekers or disciples or something. That has been what spirituality has really been about, hasn't it? Until quite recently, wherever you looked, people had their teacher, and they would call themselves a seeker or a devotee or a student of somebody. Which means that it was always about someone else's realization. Everyone wanted to be a Buddhist, you see.

But now, it seems that there is a possibility for people to be Buddhas [Laughs softly] rather than Buddhists. Rather than being a Christian, there is the possibility to realize that what is behind your own eyes is the Living Christ.

Not only is there a growing wave of realization, but there is also a dying away of old concepts about what spirituality means. As I travel and interact with people, I am seeing the birth of an entirely different kind of spiritual meeting, which I call "co-creative spirituality." It means that there may be a facilitator of the meeting rather like a David Letterman of Consciousness. But it doesn't mean that the one facilitating the meeting is any more realized or Awake. There can now be the realization that the entire room is equally that Consciousness.

Just recently I was in Sweden for an event called the No Mind Festival, about 800 people there altogether. One night we were in a huge tent, 520 people together in the tent and I just found myself saying, "You know, we have spent so much energy looking to someone else, wanting to be somehow guided by or liberated by someone else's Realization. How would it be tonight, even just as an experiment, if we took the someone else's pedestal away and just let this be about you and me?...if we let this be about *everybody* in this tent?" It must have just been the right night or the position of the moon, but that night every person in that tent was willing to accept the invitation. I asked people to just look around the tent and to share their own love rather than look for something from someone else. I asked them to share their own love, to share through their eyes the Presence which is within yourself. Something happened inside that tent that represented, for me, what this is all about. There were 520 people all giving satsang at the same time, with no idea left of something more to attain or someone to turn to and ask questions of. There was an atmosphere of true mutuality, true mutual recognition.

This is what all of this is about, for me. I'm not even remotely interested in being a guru or in having someone else be a guru to me. I'm interested in the possibility that we can be gurus to each other—not in the sense that I've got my thoughts and opinions and you've got yours, but in the possibility that we can meet in a recognition of what is undeniably true, this silent Presence behind the eyes shining forth from every incarnation at the same time. And if that can happen for 520 people in a tent in Sweden, hey, why can't it happen for millions or billions of people? We are all the same, you know? Everybody is that Consciousness. All that prevents it is identification with who I think myself to be. If that shift can happen for that many people in one place, it can happen anywhere and everywhere. Then we have moved beyond the age of the guru, beyond the age of hierarchical spirituality into real Awakening, into a real shift for humankind.

Q - For those readers of this book who may sense some form of Awakening in their lives, or at least have a great degree of interest in the topic, what would you like to say to them?

ANA - The teacher you have always sought, the one who has all the answers, the one who can dissolve all of your doubts and suffering is here on planet earth and available. You just have to know where to look. I would say that we have been looking in the wrong place, in the wrong direction with the old style of spirituality. I would ask anybody that if you are really willing to question deeply, sincerely, without giving up or settling for conceptual answers, if you are really willing to investigate who you are in this moment, this very moment between one thought and another—who hears sound? Who notices movement? Who is that? If you are really willing to look back into that and not give up before the answer (or lack of answer) is absolutely clear, everything you have ever sought for is revealed.

If more and more people are willing to look in the right place, the very foundation of separation, manipulation and greed all comes tumbling down, all becomes resolved. It is the easiest thing in the world to recognize who you are because it is right here. What could be more immediate than your own self? And yet, it is the most challenging thing because it means taking a stand against the ancient habits of false assumption.

This is what I would say to the reader of this book: really, really deeply inquire into who you are. And know that in that inquiry everything that you have ever desired, everything you have ever tried to make happen will be fulfilled.

Biography

Arjuna Nick Ardagh is the founder of the Living Essence Foundation in Nevada City, California, which is dedicated to the awakening of consciousness in the context of ordinary life. Arjuna has maintained a passion for awakening and spiritual inquiry since 1971, when he was in his teens. After completing a Master's Degree at Cambridge University in England, he devoted his life fully to the pursuit of realization of the Truth, and studied with a number of great teachers, both Western and Eastern. After more than twenty years of full time "seeking" Arjuna met his teacher, H.W.L.Poonja, in Lucknow, India, in 1991. Papaji, as he was known affectionately to his students, pointed Arjuna's attention back to the eternal Self present in this very moment. With that meeting the seeking ended. A year later Poonjaji asked Arjuna to return to the West and to pass on the eternal secret of awakening to others.

Since that time Arjuna has traveled extensively both in the United States and Europe, conducting both evening gatherings (*Satsang*) and longer intensives. He has developed a unique approach that is both penetrating in its exploration of the eternal Truth, and also very practical and grounded in addressing ordinary life.

In 1995 Arjuna started the Living Essence Training, which prepares people to facilitate the deepening and stabilization of awakening in others. Arjuna has trained more than 300 people to be certified practitioners of the Living Essence Work, and the Living Essence Foundation has grown to support and make available these tools throughout the world.

Arjuna is the author of *Relaxing into Clear Seeing* (1997), *How About Now* (1999) and is the creator of the *Living Essence Tapes Series*. He speaks regularly at conferences and on the radio and television, and has been featured in magazines in 12 countries. He also teaches a seminar for Business Leaders with David Neenan: Business in Fullness.

Arjuna lives in Nevada City with his two sons, Abhi and Shuba.

For more information about evening events, seminars, the Living Essence Training, books, video and audio tapes of Arjuna's teaching please contact:

Living Essence Foundation
Box 2746
Grass Valley CA 95945 USA
Phone (530) 478 5985
toll free 1-888-VASTNESS
fax (530) 478 0641
e mail: info@livingessence.com
website: www.livingessence.com

Dasarath (David Davidson, Ph.D)

Interviewed by phone from Ithaca, New York
December 19, 2000

During the period when I was engaged in research for this book, I came across a most interesting interview on the Internet. It was a few years old, but the premise was rather extraordinary. The gentleman being interviewed was a Ph.D from New York named David Davidson. He was discussing his theory that the worldwide web offered a metaphorical model for the neurology of a growing global consciousness. In other words, in the same way that the central nervous system could be seen as the body's structural support for consciousness, the Internet could be viewed as the "nervous system" for a wider, more inclusive level of awareness of one another—a place of global identity. I saw that this discussion echoed and very wisely extrapolated positions held by a number of others, including Tim Leary and (in a more theoretical fashion), Teilhard de Chardin.

But the contemporary format of this interview really appealed to me, so I contacted David, who now uses the name Dasarath—which was given to him by his teacher, Poonjaji. We agreed on a time for a phone interview.

Dasarath embodies a most pleasant combination of intellectual depth and the deep ease of being that often accompanies those who live what they teach. This is conveyed very fluidly every time I speak with him. The interview you are about to read is clearly flavored with both of those qualities. But there's a lot more to be found in the next several pages.

As I read and re-read this conversation, I noticed a deeper level of truth each time. Of course, this can be found in the repeated consumption of most legitimate spiritual literature, including each and every interview in this book. But this sense of deepening fell on me rather profoundly in this particular conversation.

During the interview I prepped Dasarath on the basic format, then started to roll tape. We had a good time taping the interview, and then shared a delightful half hour chatting afterward. We also agreed to meet for dinner on his upcoming trip to Los Angeles. A few days later, however, I realized that Dasarath had not mentioned the Internet theory—the very topic which had led me to contact him in the first place! So, I rang him back and taped a ten-minute segment on that topic.

But you will not find a single word about the Internet in this interview.

As I transcribed this fascinating talk, it became very clear to me that the gift that Dasarath had given us was perfect just as it was.

Some weeks later, Dasarath did visit us on his way to a vacation in Hawaii. We shared a lovely dinner and afterward broke out the guitars for a lively jam session.

He's a delightful man and in this interview he offers some of the clearest verbal descriptions of the subtleties of the Awakened condition that I have ever encountered. His choice of words is remarkably lucid and readable— even artful—in that they convey spiritual depth in a very understandable way.

Q - In your experience, is there such a reality as Awakening, Enlightenment, Liberation or spiritual freedom?

D - Well, in one sense you could say it *is* reality, that it's an awakening from what we thought was real to what is actually real—which is free of all thought. That's one way to look at it. In another sense, one could say what my master Papaji used to say—that the whole concept of enlightenment is just a concept that arises out of ignorance. In the silence there isn't any enlightenment, and there isn't any unenlightenment and there isn't any freedom and there isn't any bondage and there isn't anybody to get it!

What a great relief!—freedom from the whole concept of reality. Otherwise, as you know, the words just go around in circles.

Q - This "noticing of reality" in your case...did it seem to happen in a particular moment, or over a period of time?

D - [Pause] Both. There have been many, many moments in my life where there was this recognition. I remember when I was a little boy about 12 years old or so walking to the movies on a Saturday morning. Everything simply disappeared and there was this sense of presence. And in this sense of presence there was a recognition (even for a 12-year-old boy) that, "This is *it*, somehow. *This is what is.*" And then, ordinary consciousness seemed to refocus itself and that was that.

There have been moments like that throughout my life where this that is always here was revealed. I would say, though, that I realized it as more of a continuous background of my own existence when I met Papaji. I can even date it—it was March of 1992. It happened over about a ten-day period of having met the Master and sat with him in a series of one-on-ones, during satsang and in his house at various times. This just crept up and pulled me to it, so to speak, until there was this clear recognition that this is what I am. There was a clear recognition that this is always here, that this presence—the words, as you know, don't do it justice, they never can—call it presence or being-awareness or a sense of stillness or peace, but it's a constant undercurrent.

There's a sense of timelessness. I mean, time really stopped for me then. And I continued to function—I had a watch and all of that. You know it's just numbers going around in a circle. This became very forcefully present in '92.

Even when ordinary consciousness returned, so to speak, when just the day-to-day experience is present, it doesn't obliterate this timelessness. They don't invalidate each other.

It seems like this presence allows for everything, including unconsciousness. It allows for all thought of any kind including body-consciousness. It allows for ordinary existence to take place within it. And yet, what I think is the greatest liberation of all is knowing that ordinary existence and all its ups and downs do not really touch this place. Nor do you ever leave it, although you might think you do.

After the awakening in '92, there were many more times of awakening, some of them in India with Papaji, many others just occurring spontaneously in everyday life. I think it's important for people who are getting all kinds of ideal pictures of what we call realization as an event or an experience to know that after that very momentous transformation in '92, I had a real roller coaster of experiences for a few years. There would be extraordinary times of transcendence and bliss, alternating with all kinds of very intense uncomfortable experiences and mental tendencies arising.

I had moments of fear, worry, doubt, arrogance. They were all coming up in this "space" of consciousness that had been opened up. They were taking place *in the midst of* this realization. This is really very difficult to describe because it's not an either/or thing. It's a real trap to get into "there's only the purity of emptiness." No, it's not! There is this emptiness and in the midst of this emptiness there's a lot of stuff that seems to be going on.

But, what's also interesting is that it didn't matter how many awakenings there were, each time it was the same. Each realization was the same realization. It was the recognition of *being* this awareness, of being this spacious presence. Rather than identifying with all that comes and goes, I was (and am) this awareness. This awareness is the ground of it all. It sees everything playing itself out and it includes everything. It includes emptiness and the realization of being nobody at the same time as it includes being this very specific body-mind process called Dasarath, living out some kind of mysterious destiny. It's all of that.

Q - So would you say, then, that you notice anything that's in any way different or distinct from so-called "ordinary" human experience?

D - Well, you know, anger still feels like anger. There's a pounding in the chest, a tightness of the jaw—the typical physical experiences that are felt. And they are not felt any less than before. In fact, they might be felt even *more* intensely in the sense that there's a greater openness and receptivity. It's like a helplessness in the face of experience. When one realizes that *resistance* to experience is horribly painful, then the allowing of the experience actually frees it up to be what it is.

On the one hand that means it's pretty intense, but—and I think this is the bottom line—on the other hand it's non-existent. It's spacious. This is a very real experience that I have a hard time describing. It's a kind of spaciousness in the body. So that when an experience is arising, it's here. But it's somehow known and felt to be insubstantial or empty. It's just a form within consciousness. That's all that anything is.

And these experiences don't last for very long. They're like little blips on the screen. They come and they go. And that's the blessing of all of this. You know, hell can come and go, lifetimes can come and go in what is a second on the clock!

This frees one up to be truly open and courageous in the face of all experience. One doesn't have to run from any of it.

But, once we get into the description of qualities, it's not really it any more. It's nothing in itself, yet it allows for everything. The Buddhists call it *sunyata* or emptiness, voidness. Sometimes I get it as a spaciousness, as if the space within the atoms—the actual empty, insubstantiality of everything—is vividly felt in my body.

There's a sense of well-being that exists no matter what I'm feeling, even when I have these terrible allergies which I get. Sometimes it's actually hilarious that while I'm sneezing my brains out there's a sense, somehow, of a well-being that's not touched by the allergies or whatever bodily conditions are coming up now as the body ages.

Within that, too, it's laughter, it's happiness, it's joyfulness. But, to give them such tight definition is to somehow...it's somehow lighter than that. A word that I love and that I use a lot—it's a great escape from having to discuss anything—is the word "mystery"—this sense of the mystery of it all, of the impossibility of understanding.

You know, I have a Ph.D. in history; I used to teach. I'm considered an intellectual. Sometimes when people read my stuff they say, "What are you talking about?" It's sometimes very abstruse and abstract. But even in the process of having a mind like that, there is the awareness that *none* of that touches anything; that none of that is a description of this. It's all just the play of consciousness. And there's this mystery that I love. I *love* this mystery! It's incredibly enjoyable, isn't it?

Often, mind or some desire to understand will arise, and go through what I call "walking the dog." You know, when you have to take the dog out to pee for a little while? It gives me a chance to do some thinking. But, it's not as if the mystery is something to be understood. It's something to be *enjoyed*. It's just delightful to me to enjoy it. It's in the enjoyment where it all literally "makes sense."

Q - In this unfolding, is there a sense of evolving, growing, or maturing?

D - Yes, I think that's important to notice, because it's easy to get attached to the eternal unchangingness. It's a great paradox that somehow, on the one hand, the realization itself is always the same, because it's this indescribable mystery that has no qualities. And at the same time, there's clearly an ever-deepening quality to it. That was a bit surprising to me because I had somehow taken an intellectual position that this wasn't so.

Because it has no boundary, it's ever-deepening, ever-expanding, you might say. I remember that Papaji would talk about his experience of it being a deepening love, going deeper and deeper into this ocean of love. So, yeah, I would say that there's some sense of changingness, as long as that's held with it's opposite—unchangingness—being true as well. There's this unchanging quality or reality that has nothing at all going on in it—zero—absolutely nothing at the same time that there does seem to be this dynamic quality of movement.

Q - Perhaps that movement could include thought and emotion.

D - Definitely.

Q - How are thought and emotion experienced by you?

D - Well, they happen! [Laughter] That's the way that I would try to describe my experience of them—they just happen. My relationship to experience shifts from being somebody who is thinking and experiencing something to being the aware space within which thoughts and feelings occur.

And they do come and they go. Some kinds of thoughts have disappeared. They just don't happen much any more. Some kinds of feelings don't seem to happen much any more. But others do, and I think that part of the evolutionary quality is that it's sometimes surprising to see something arise. You know, where did *that* come from? There's something very mysterious about the arising of these tendencies and how they play out.

Thoughts come, feelings come. The whole range of human experience comes. But, they don't stick, you know? It's like the old metaphor of an image in a mirror. Things show up in the mirror but the mirror is never touched or stained by the images which come and go within it.

Q - Is there any sense of anything existing that might be labeled as negative or evil?

D - Well, I don't see anything that you might call an objective entity, like "capital-E Evil" or "capital-D Devil" or that kind of thing. To me, negative and positive, good and evil, God and the devil are all judgments that arise in consciousness. Certain minds have certain tendencies to lock on to them and turn them into absolutes. That happens to be one good description of this whole play of duality or dualism.

I had the good fortune to study for a number of years with a great zen teacher, Joshu Sasaki Roshi. He used to say that we have to hold God and the devil in the same hand. This means that the whole play of duality is held within awareness. And this awareness is not divided. This awareness does not divide into good and evil, although it witnesses the play of consciousness that does so. It sees through that and it sees that everything—all manifestation— is an arising from the same source. And this source, whatever you want to call it—the absolute, or God, or consciousness—is beyond good and evil.

Now, this is a tremendous challenge for people who are attached to good! Because in the play of duality, opposites co-generate. They are mutually-interdependent on one another for their existence. So, the concept of good requires the concept of evil. Once one identifies with goodness, then one needs evil in the world. And one will see evil because, as you know, everything you see is in your own image, so to speak. Everything is a reflection of *your* filter of mind. That's why we can't really have an objective discussion about whether something is good or evil because we're each speaking from a certain place in consciousness and some of these places are like ships in the night.

You know, seeing that the perfection of existence is beyond good and evil doesn't mean that we should remain indifferent to acting upon suffering or be apathetic about constructive action in dealing with abuse, violence, conflict, greed and oppression or whatever else we perceive as unjust in the world. Otherwise, one can get stuck in a kind of fatalism that I think is another big trap in spiritual life. Like, "It's all perfect, so why do anything?"

I think that what matters the most is that people truly follow their deepest heart-instinct. And if that means that you are moved to take constructive action, you do so. In this sense of following the heart, I want to emphasize that we can experience the love that is deeper than our minds, our judgments and our concepts about good and evil. We need to experience the love that is present in the recognition that everything is one.

And, at the same time that one sees the perfection of it all, if one's heart leads one to act on things, then you have to follow your love there. If it's compassion that moves you, so be it. Love or compassion is the true source of appropriate action in the world - deeper than morality. Morality comes as sort of an intellectualization process but prior to that is this love that responds appropriately to what is happening.

In this love we can just acknowledge one another's awareness, and let it be. Am I answering your questions?

Q - Yes, perfectly. Dasarath, did you or do you have a teacher?

D - I've had many teachers in my life. As I mentioned, I studied with Joshu Sasaki Roshi and I had others along the way. But, I had only one guru and that was Papaji, my master Papaji. This is a mystery—the mystery of the guru. I'm writing about it right now. It's so difficult to talk about it. Somehow in the presence of that massive field of silence, this silence could recognize itself. It was, it still is, unbelievable to me in an inexplicable way. He, as my master, was somehow a doorway to infinity.

Q - Do you have a personal spiritual practice?

D - No. But, I sit quietly often, whenever I'm moved to do that. I love to sing from time to time. I can get very devotional sometimes and chant and sing to God in celebration.

But I don't see them as practices in the sense that they're leading some-one somewhere. As you know, there is currently a huge conversation going on about, "Is practice necessary?" and, "Should one practice?" and whether the *advaitin* position is somehow an avoidance of hard work and all of that. Well, my experience of it is that what some might call "practice" is to me just a celebration or an expression of being, rather than some effort, some mov-ing toward a goal.

What Papaji revealed to me more than anything else is that *no one is mov-ing toward a goal.* It's not as if you practice until you get enlightened. Through this grace there's a recognition that there is no one to practice any-thing! And then, in this knowing that no one is practicing, then practice all you want. It's delightful!

It's all part of the creativity of the self that comes up with so many mag-nificently beautiful ways to celebrate itself—to love itself—to communicate itself, which is how I see practice.

Q - Do you teach?

D - Yes, that's pretty much what my life is about in terms of daily activity. It's evolved in a very interesting way. I had somehow expected that I would be teaching in what I thought was some conventional spiritual way of offer-ing satsangs in a traditional advaita form. I have done that and I continue to do that. I have a monthly satsang here in Ithaca and I travel around and do them elsewhere from time to time.

But, I discovered a few years after meeting Papaji that the actual work I do—coaching one-on-one in the workplace and leading retreats in the corporate world—has evolved into a "corporate *satsang*." The clients that I work with come in with certain presenting problems about being effective leaders, or how to work with their boss, or manage their anger on the job, or build teams, or communicate better, the things that coaches ordinarily work with.

And in the process of dealing with that, it becomes evident that a lot more is being offered to them in this coaching work, that freedom or self-realization is actually part of the menu of what's available. And I would say that at least half of my clients are consciously engaged in this, are committed to this, want this.

So, I have been amazed and I remain amazed. That, by the way, is one of the other qualities that I might apply to this indescribable beingness. It's a sense of wonder, or amazement, or awe. Like, "Wow! Look at that!" It's this awe that I sense in my work and again, even though I can say that this is metaphorical, I do sense that this is guru's grace—that it has something to do with Papaji. This work is unfolding for me in such an effortless way. There's this process of awakening to freedom taking place in the ordinary work setting, in the midst of the everyday challenges of work.

So, there's no separation here. There's no mountaintop for me. I'm just immersed in the everyday, dealing in the everyday, witnessing not only the coming and going of my own ordinary experience but also supporting people to be with their ordinary experience and to realize who they are.

And what's interesting is that the more they get in touch with that, the more they see that simply abiding as that is really the ultimate solution to dealing with the ordinary. Somehow, "what to do"—the "right" actions—arise spontaneously and naturally out of the silence, out of this abiding as who you are.

You don't need a million textbooks telling you, "If this happens, do that." You can't write those books fast enough to cover all the situations that come up. It's a lot easier to abide. And I have some clients who, after going to all of those trainings and workshops and so on, are just *thrilled*. "Oh, you mean all I have to do is be quiet?" And somehow consciousness comes up with an appropriate response. And that's amazing to watch.

Q - When people come to you, some of them may come with relatively practical questions about money, sensuality, relationships. How do you approach that with them?

D - It depends on the setting. Typically, in *satsang* I almost always want to refer people back to the silence of the self as the place from which their solution is going to come. You know, I spent twenty years as a trainer and a consultant and I had a private counseling practice for ten years. I don't have the charge, the energy, any more to sit and talk about what to do about money and relationships, and so on.

I recognize that there are legitimate approaches to that, but generally in satsang my approach—for example in a relationship issue—is to have people inquire as to *who* is involved in that relationship. Then from that space of undivided beingness, see what arises in terms of how to treat each other.

Of course, in the corporate setting, I do address the specifics of the situation but I do it within the context of that deeper awareness, so they have an option to fall into that, if they are so inclined.

Q - For the readers of this book who may sense some form of awakening in life, or even just have interest in the topic, what would you like to say to them?

D - I think you just trust your own self. You know, there are a *million* answers. The world is *full* of answers, and they're *beautiful* answers. But, somehow, we ultimately turn to our self because the self is the answer. If you're willing to turn fully to this beingness that's here, to this silence that's here, it reveals everything to you.

So there's nothing you need to know. There's nothing you need to do.

Just be you.

Biography

Dasarath (David Davidson, Ph.D), President of WisdomWork, is a corporate leadership coach and retreat leader. A student of the non-dual traditions for thirty years, he offers satsangs and shares a direct approach to being awake and masterful at work. Dasarath is the author of *Wisdom at Work: The Awakening of Consciousness in the Workplace* (Larson Publications, 1998), and is finishing a new book on *Freedom Dreams*, an exploration of non-dual awareness and his awakening with his Master Sri H.W.L. Poonja (Papaji).

After receiving his Ph.D in History from Yale University and teaching History at Cornell University for five years, Dasarath immersed himself fully in the inner life. He has studied and practiced with masters in *Zen, Vipassana, Yoga* and *Advaita Vedanta*, in contemporary American approaches to enlightenment, as well as investigating his native Judeo-Christian tradition. Most recently, his five-year association with Papaji, who gave him the name Dasarath, radically transformed his sense of identity and teaching work.

While maintaining a private counseling practice for a decade, Dasarath has also given hundreds of seminars on empowerment and high performance, stress and change management, teambuilding, meditation and spiritual development throughout the U.S. His corporate clients have included Corning Incorporated, Cornell University, Carondelet Management Institute, and Harbin Hot Springs Conference & Retreat Center, in addition to a wide range of hospitals, small businesses, and school districts. He has taught at The Omega Institute for Holistic Studies and the Kripalu Center for Yoga and Well-Being. He also founded and moderated the Wisdom-at-Work Internet discussion group for two years with focus on spirituality and awakening consciousness in the workplace. Dasarath currently coaches leaders at Corning Incorporated and presents Wisdom at Work Retreats on the awakening of leadership in the workplace.

Dasarath can be reached at 607-277-0267 tel/fax, e-mail at dasarath@baka.com, and at his website: http://www.letwisdomwork.com.

Alan Cohen

Interviewed by phone from Maui, Hawaii
December 21, 2000

I first met Alan Cohen in late 1996, at a time in my life when change seemed to be in the wind. After studying and practicing seriously with several great spiritual teachers over a twenty-year period, I felt I was at the end of my spiritual rope. I felt almost desperate *to find whatever this Awakening was. I had definitely tasted it but could not understand it, couldn't grasp it, or keep it. It was like being on fire with this incredible burning desire for Truth.*

At that point in time, I was considering traveling to California over Christmas to visit my dear friend Diana, who is now my beautiful wife and Awakened teaching partner. Something in me said that whatever I was seeking was to be found on the West Coast.

Of course, that was totally wrong, since what was being sought was actually found within. And it was completely right, at the same time, but that's a story for another time.

In November of '96 a friend of mine, Shelly Koffler, invited me to go with her to a weekend convention featuring a number of spiritual and motivational speakers where she was scheduled to sing and play. She explained that she would be performing a program of original spirit-based songs at the event.

She'd also been booked to provide musical accompaniment for Alan, who was an old friend of hers. I had read one of Alan's early books The Dragon Doesn't Live Here Anymore *and had loved it, so I was really looking forward to meeting him.*

So, I took the three-hour drive with her. Along the way, I described this feeling of wanting Truth so badly that I'd give anything to find it. As we drove east, the sky darkened and the rain fell. By the time we arrived at the small seaside resort town of Ocean City, Maryland the day had turned bitterly cold and gray. I recall glumly telling Shelly that the weather seemed to me to be a representation of how I was feeling at the time.

91

But once inside the huge hotel meeting room, the brightness and joy of the event was overflowing. I had a really great time and particularly enjoyed Alan's portion of the program. I was totally delighted when Shelly (knowing of my troubled state of mind) told me that she had arranged for me to have a private meeting with him. So he and I ducked into a small side room after his talk, and sat down to chat. He's the kind of man who walks the walk, and this was obvious as we spoke.

Straightaway he asked what he could do for me and I related to him this growing sense of spiritual agitation. I told him that I felt moved to travel west to find my place, but that I was also quite nervous about the prospect.

He looked directly at me and quietly asked two questions:

"Does the thought of moving out west frighten you?" "Yes."

"Does it feel bigger than you can handle?" "Yes," I stammered.

He took a long pause, and then said:

"Then you must go *to California! If it scares you and feels so big, there is* definitely *something waiting for you there!"*

So on this morning—four years later, four days before Christmas in the year 2000—I picked up the phone in my L.A. office. Somehow, I find myself a blissfully happy married man and an ordained minister. And it's now my calling to mentor others in the process of Awakening.

I was smiling as I dialed Alan's number in Maui.

Q - In your experience, is there such a reality that might be called Awakening, Enlightenment or spiritual freedom?

AC - Absolutely. It's the only reason we are here. I've had many moments of enlightenment. They sometimes don't seem to last but they get more frequent and longer. I truly believe that our real nature is enlightenment; we are enlightened beings. We've just been hypnotized to believe we're not. The game is about waking up to remember who we are.

Q - Have you noticed anything that might be distinct or different from "ordinary" human experience?

AC - When I've experienced those moments, I feel deeply at peace, utterly in the moment. The keynote of my being is joy and I remember that all is well—not thinking about the past or the future. I know that there is no death because when I'm in the moment I am utterly alive and it feels great!

Q - Did this recognition happen in a specific moment, or did it take place over a period of time?

AC - It's really both. I've had numerous spikes, you might say, when the windows have opened up and I saw it all as it was. The first one was, I think, when I took LSD in college. Now, some people could rationalize that away, but the truth is that I did have an amazing experience that I cannot deny.

Another time, I was visiting the crypt of Saint Theresa of Lisieux in France and I sat down to meditate for what I had expected would be a minute. Something came over me and I was lifted. I felt like I received a visitation from her energy. I just knew that there was no death and that anything in the material world that I had ever worried about was totally not important.

I felt that recently again when I visited the King's Chamber in the Great Pyramid of Giza in Egypt. We had a one-hour session, half of that with the lights out. I felt a phenomenal life force—this tremendous bliss. I felt a great life force surge through my body.

So, I've had these momentary spikes and sooner or later, you kind of go back to another reality. Yet, at the same time, there's an ever-increasing under-the-surface sense of enlightenment.

There's an undercurrent of growth that's happening all the time, which means that the vibration I'm living in general comes closer and closer to what we call enlightenment. It's an upward curve. It's not so obvious at any given moment but when I look back at who I was three, four, or ten years ago compared to where I am now, there's definitely a growth, a deepening, and an Awakening. So, it's really that surge *and* a gradual awakening.

Q - So you would say that there's a sense of evolving or maturing?

AC - Sure. It's happening all the time whether we know it or not.

Q - How do you experience thought and emotion?

AC - My body feels, my mind thinks, and my emotions go up and down! When I'm in my center—connected to Spirit and clear—I can observe my body, thoughts and emotions with more detachment and they don't seem to have a lot of power over me.

I can also make a choice where I want to go with them. If I get into a thought that's empowering, I can choose to stay with it and grow with it. But if I get into a thought that's debilitating, I can say, "No thank you" and switch my focus in another direction. When I'm at peace, I definitely have more choice about what I indulge in on all of those levels.

Q - Do you have a sense of anything that might be called negative or evil energies in life?

AC - Evil is an interpretation, not a fact. We think that Saddam Hussein is evil and the Iraqis think that we're evil, so who's right? It's really just a momentary judgment. I don't believe in evil. I just think that we can get into thought-spaces or emotion-spaces that block off the flow of life force and we feel unhappy. And we think that something outside did it to us but it's just our own thoughts.

So I prefer to replace the word "evil" with the word "fear." Any time I perceive evil I've gone into a fear space. It's really my own consciousness that I need to correct in that moment, rather than eradicate the world of evil-doers, which is the most counter-productive thing that anyone ever did!

Q - Did you, or do you have a teacher?

AC - I've had many teachers. Bottom line, God is the only real teacher. Spirit is the only real teacher. Inner Being is the only real teacher in the long run.

But it's true that I have had many wonderful people and teachings that have shown up. I studied with Ram Dass and I worked with a mystic in New York named Hilda Charleton for many years. I've worked with *A Course In Miracles*. I love Patricia Sun. Currently, I'm working with a spirit teacher named Abraham.

A lot of very cool people have shown up in my life, and I'm very grateful for them.

Q - Do you yourself teach?

AC - We're all teaching by our being. I have classes and seminars where I am in the role of a teacher, but I'm always teaching more by my energy than by my words. The roles of teacher and student are intermixed. When I teach a class students come forth with the most amazing contributions and shifts and sharings. I learn as much from the students as they learn from the teacher.

So, teaching and learning is always happening; it just depends on which seat you are in at the moment.

Q - Alan, do you have a spiritual practice?

AC - I meditate every day. I pray every day. I've been doing that for many years and it's hard for me to imagine not doing it. I start my day with meditation and prayer. I think it's essential to kick off the day in the right keynote and then everything during the rest of the day follows from that keynote. On the days when for one reason or another I don't meditate, I usually end up wishing that I had!

Q - When you hold a workshop, or speak publicly, I'm sure that people often come with questions regarding practical life issues such as money, sensuality, or relationships. How do you address those issues?

AC - I really like those questions the best because they are very grounded. Some people have a tendency to sort of float off into the ethers. But when somebody's in pain, or just gone through a divorce, or had some financial setback and they're trying to make sense out of it, or they're just falling in love and are seeing new things about themselves in a relationship, those are really good, juicy, tangible handles through which to gain access to spiritual wisdom. So I love those questions and I encourage them.

We can all identify with the human element in those situations in one form or another. So, it gives the other people in the room something that they can tune in with.

Wayne Dyer said that couples sometimes say to him, "We're total soul mates. We're totally one. We both like the same food and the same movies. We even think the same thoughts at the same time."

And he tells them, "Then one of you is unnecessary!"

Q - Some people feel that we as a species are on the brink of a significant shift in consciousness, and that such a shift may even be necessary for our survival on the planet. Could you comment on this?

AC - It's a funny thing. People often ask me, "What trends do you see as you travel around?" I do see trends, but I never dare to say, "This is what's happening," because I know that everyone I meet is basically a reflection of my own consciousness. So, as I grow and open my heart, as I get in touch with my own inner masculine/feminine, these are the people that show up in my workshop!

I'm not quite sure that there's anybody out there at all! [We both laugh] And if there are, I don't know that they're much more than a reflection of where I'm at. And I would imagine that if you would interview twenty different people, you'd get twenty different ideas about what the trends are!

You could interview someone who says that the world has gone to hell in a hand basket. That would be their reality. I wouldn't dare to assume that it was anybody else's reality.

My life is getting better and more joyful. I'm attracting more fun people to play with, but that's just my point of attraction. I think that it's all out there and each of us is seeing with our own eyes.

Q - Well, then, I'll pose the final question this way: in the event that there is someone else out there....

AC - Okay, we can play with that...

Q - ...and you could speak directly to them in the pages of this book, what would you most like to say to them?

AC - I would say "Hello, Self!" I would say that authenticity is the key to enlightenment. As each of us is true to our own passion and our own inner spirit, we begin to attract experiences that empower us to create miracles.

Biography

Alan Cohen is a heart act to follow. One of the most popular inspirational writers and speakers in America, his books, tapes, syndicated column, and transformational seminars have touched the lives of millions of people who have found the courage to believe in themselves and follow their dreams.

Alan's first book, *The Dragon Doesn't Live Here Anymore*, has become a modern metaphysical classic, remaining on best-seller lists for nearly 20 years, used as a college text and foundation for study groups. A survey of Unity ministers cited *Dragon* as "one of the decade's ten most influential books in the Unity movement." A selection from *Dragon* is included in Simon & Schuster's *A Treasury of Light: The Best in New Age Literature*.

A contributing writer for the New York Times #1 best-selling series *Chicken Soup for the Soul* series, one of Alan's pieces has been produced as an episode on the *Chicken Soup* television series. His book of daily inspirational thoughts, *A Deep Breath of Life*, received the *Body Mind Spirit* Magazine Award of Excellence. Alan's books have been translated into ten foreign languages.

Each month Alan's column, *From the Heart*, is syndicated in 60 magazines internationally. His interviews and articles have been celebrated in *Science of Mind, Personal Transformation, New Woman, First for Women, New Realities, Human Potential*, and *Visions* magazines.

A frequent guest on radio and television, Alan has appeared on CNBC's *American's Talking*, as well as many *Good Morning* shows throughout the nation. His presentations are regularly broadcast via satellite on the Wisdom Channel, and he is a faculty member at Omega Institute, America's nation's largest center for holistic education. Alan has addressed personal development organizations throughout the United States, Europe, the former Soviet Union, Indonesia, Greece, and South America, and he guides groups on excursions to sacred sites such as Machu Picchu, Bali, and Egypt.

Alan resides in Maui, Hawaii, where he conducts retreats in visionary living.

Here's how to reach Alan:

Alan Cohen Programs & Publications
455A Kukuna Road, Haiku, Hawaii 96708
Telephone: (800) 568-3079 Fax: (808) 572-1023
E-mail: acpubs@maui.net <mailto:acpubs@maui.net

Antonio Duncan

Interviewed in Los Angeles
January 9, 2001

One day while I was in my office the phone rang. The gentleman who asked for Diana spoke in an accent which I could not immediately recognize. He introduced himself as Antonio. Later, I asked Diana who Antonio was, thinking that he was, perhaps, one of her many friends from her work in the travel industry.

She told me that he was an old friend with whom she used to work in the music business years ago and that he was in town visiting a mutual friend. "He lives in Brazil. In Rio," she commented, when I inquired about his beautiful voice and unusual accent. When I asked her what he does for a living now, she answered with one word.

"Shaman," was what she said.

Well, needless to say, my curiosity was piqued—having never personally met a shaman. So, I was delighted when it was agreed that we would all get together for lunch the very next day.

We joined Antonio Duncan and his pleasant, attractive friend Ann at a restaurant not far from our house and I immediately took a great liking to both of them. Antonio is an intense, dark-skinned man—a smiling, cultured fellow. He gives new meaning to the phrase "talking with one's hands." In fact, his constant gesturing seems to be such an integral part of his delivery that Diana joked to me later that he might go mute if his hands were ever tied down!

As we chatted, he explained how he had mysteriously found his way out of the music business and into crystals, the occult, and shamanism through a rather amazing and humorous episode that is conveyed in this interview. He talked about how his great love for these things led him to become a top lecturer and workshop speaker on the topic of the relationship between crystals and Consciousness in his home land of Brazil. And he told of how he leads tours to a number of sacred places, especially in South America, Mexico and the southwest part of the United States.

He was so engaging (and so "right on" spiritually) that we weren't even halfway through lunch when I found myself inviting him to come back to our house to be interviewed for this book.

While showing them around our place, we took him to the loft-office where I work. When he saw my computer he suggested that we log onto his website, which is primarily about crystals—and is in Portuguese!

As the site downloaded, I noticed that it contained a number of features that I found fascinating, even though I am not all that much into crystals. One section of the site was called "The Crystal Oracle." It involves viewing a page which contains a large number of photographs of various crystals. The viewer selects and clicks on one that vibrationally or esthetically "speaks" most directly to them. A pop-up screen then appears which compares the qualities of that crystal with traits supposedly within the one who made the selection.

Antonio insisted that we try out the Oracle. Diana and I glanced quickly at one another, each with an eyebrow slightly raised. Then we each selected a stone, just to be polite.

I noticed a picture of a stone that I had once held for a few minutes at a friend's house. It had felt good in my hand, so I clicked on that picture. Diana picked hers on the simple basis of an attraction to its color. The shaman activated the cyber-seer and a description of the qualities of each of the chosen crystals appeared on the screen.

Now, I can only report what there is to report. I can only say this as factually and as objectively as I can. The descriptions were so completely accurate for each of us that we were both stopped in our tracks! Bear in mind that the readings were not "correct" in the way that your morning paper's one-size-fits-all horoscope entry catches you in its net of very broad meaning. No, the Oracle scored very direct hits on two people who could not even remotely be called gullible marks.

[His website address is listed in the informational section at the end of this chapter, so try it yourself. We'd be really interested to see what your experience is. Please let us know. And by the way, I also learned that Portuguese is not all that hard to translate into English, especially if one happens to know a bit of Spanish to begin with.]

After that delightful interlude, we retired to the living room, to the tape deck and to four glasses of club soda with lime. I listened carefully—and was amazed at the simplicity, the honesty and the power in this man's words and delivery. Antonio Duncan showed us—once again—that Liberation is universal. I hope you'll agree with me after reading this fascinating discussion with a South American shaman.

Q - In your experience, is there such a reality as Awakening, Enlightenment, Liberation or spiritual freedom?

AD - Yes, there is. And it's just realizing that you are part of the world, that you are part of nature. It's all there. It's realizing about your own power, realizing that the power is not outside of you. It's inside and you create your own reality.

That's what happened to me. Deep down I always knew that was so, and then suddenly, "Hey! I *am* Enlightened!" And that was it. I think it's also learning to consciously create a reality and to have fun by doing it. We were taught when we were children that we had to do things properly like, "If you do what I tell you, you will have an extra allowance or some extra thing." This is not enjoyable...not fun.

My mother's side of the family was totally Catholic and my father's side of the family was a bit into Allan Kardec and spirituality, or spiritism as they call it. Spiritism comes from Catholicism, but they believe in reincarnation and life after death, talking to the spirits, channeling and other things like that. And the Catholics don't believe in these.

So I was born and raised seeing my aunts and grandmother, one side channeling and the others going to Mass. And the Catholic side of the family said that the others had the part of the devil and the others always said, "No, you have to be nice to everybody, everybody has their own interests." I started tending more to my father's side, more to spiritism and when I was about ten years old I started learning in these sessions about the ectoplasm and things like that.

So, spirituality was always part of me. Then I went into the record business and I forgot about a lot of that and got into sex, drugs and rock and roll. But I always had this spark, this relationship with the occult. At the right time, I started to get in touch with shamanism, with the stones (crystals) and all of that. And I came to my own conclusion that Enlightenment is just *being*. And it's perceiving that it's everywhere and everything. God is all that there is! And so, if it's all that is, we are also part of it. And every day is a new learning experience and it's usually just a confirmation, like, "My God, I already knew about that!"

So, Enlightenment is just being free to think and to believe and to be open to receive what the world has to offer you and not be locked into some belief. That is like being in a prison. You don't have to follow all the rules. You just have to be.

Q - Did this seem to happen in a particular moment, or over a period of time?

AD - Well, I would say that unconsciously and subconsciously it was always there. But consciously, that started about fifteen years ago in '86. At that time I started to go into a kind of spiritual search to know who I was. And suddenly, I went into all the right directions and I found really what everything was all about. I started reading about Eastern philosophies and Western philosophies and Native American and Incan and Peruvian and African and Brazilian wisdom and other things. And I found a common point in everything.

It's the very simple teaching of native peoples that's the most direct of all, like, "Honor all living creatures. Honor nature, and the directions of the spirits. Honor everything there is." And to say the same thing, some other people would use, like, dictionaries, and encyclopedias. It could take ten or twenty books of three hundred pages each just to say what a Native American could say in a few words. At the end, it's all the same.

So, that's when I started looking for things and reading about everything. And then some amazing synchronicities started to happen. After you reach a certain point, start meeting the right people, books start falling over your head.

The specific moment was when I was in New York on a trip for the record business. I had read Shirley Maclaine's book *Out On A Limb* and I went to a spiritual bookstore and had an experience exactly like she talks about in that book. A book fell on her head in the shop and that happened to me in East West Books. [Chuckle] Katrina Raphael's book about crystals fell from the top shelf and landed right onto my head! And, at that very moment, I was looking at a flier on the wall announcing that Lazaris would be giving a one-night meeting in New Jersey somewhere. So, I decided to buy the book and to go to the Lazaris seminar.

When I went there, I thought, "My God, everything that I thought I knew is what this man is saying!" He said that you have to have fun while you are creating spirituality. And it hit me that that's it, that's what I needed to do with the crystals. Then I realized that I was already doing this when I was a little boy—four, five, six years old. My grandfather used to make jewelry and he kept his workshop in the garage, so I would go there to watch him working. He would cut stones to use for rings and necklaces and all that and he'd give me the colored stones, the little pieces that didn't serve him. He would give me these. And I was already working with those stones. I remember that I would take those little stones and make circles and patterns with them.

My brother said that I was making mandalas when I was five! So, when I started learning about these things, I knew that I had really been doing this all of my life.

Q - So have you experienced anything that might be called different or distinct from "ordinary" human experience?

AD - Ahhhh, yes, but sometimes people don't perceive what's really happening fully. They don't perceive the synchronicities. Visually, I have had the experience of seeing energies in sacred places or in people. Sometimes, when I'm doing a crystal healing—placing crystals on parts of their body—I see patterns that are like waves of energy. I've never seen a being or something like that, but sometimes I feel presences.

I don't know what it is, but sometimes I start talking during classes. I start saying things as they come and I just let them flow. And I'm not consciously aware of that, it just flows. I don't go into trance. It's not trance channeling. It's just like in the middle of giving a talk or a lecture or when I'm giving a class, I'll be talking about a certain subject and it's like it's for one person to hear. I'm saying something that really happened to them or is presently going on for that person. I'll just look at that person and I'll start talking. [Antonio makes wild and unintelligible talking noises...we all laugh]. And, often it turns out to be great advice for that person.

So, that all started to happen after my first trip to Peru. And I feel like this is part of a past life or something. I don't want to make too much of this. But, I know that there is an energy that is with me that I know is a part of myself. It's a guide and sometimes I feel him as an old Inca, sometimes I feel him as a strong Native American warrior or something. For me, it's all the same. I think it's part of my higher being. Like Lazaris says, "It doesn't matter who I am, what I am, where I come from. What matters is if what I am saying is good for *you*. If it touches your heart, and it's good for you that's what's important."

I often hear some people say, "I was Cleopatra, I was King Tut, I was somebody else." I have personally known more than 150 Cleopatras in my lifetime! Everyone in Brazil says, "I was an Aztec virgin and I was sacrificed in the fire." [Laughter]

Diana - Did you ever notice that no one ever tells you that in their last life-time they were a plumber in Cincinnati?

AD - [Smiling] I know a family, and the woman there lives a very spiritual life. She's at all of my workshops. Her name is Maria Theresa. In her past lifetimes, she says she was the empress Maria Theresa of Austria, her son was Charlemagne, her aunt was Josephine, and her uncle was Napoleon!

So, in this one family there was Napoleon, Charlemagne... [Ticking their names off on his fingers]...Josephine. I mean, what is she doing living in a Sao Paulo suburb?

I've had some other not-so-natural experiences in shamanic rituals. I once drank a sacred beverage as part of an initiation. It was from a cactus called wachuma, also known as San Pedro. It's mixed with water and boiled and you drink that. I was conscious all the time, but I noticed that I could really feel the energy of the plants and the air around me and I could see the vibrational energy around everything. And I could relate to that and feel that everything was all connected. It was like an enhancement of my perception. It was really a great experience.

Now, some people who drink this will tell you amazing stories that they see monsters and they see other beings and extraterrestrials and all that. Sometimes people relate these things as, like, products of their imaginations that come alive. They see things like in a science fiction movie. I think that part of that is their imagination and part of it is their reality. But my experience was very cool, just seeing and feeling energies.

Q - Is there a sense, then, of evolving, growing, or maturing?

AD - Yes. Every day teaches you a new lesson. It's just to keep your eyes open, your ears open and to breathe in what the universe gives you. Everybody has something to contribute to you. It's like everyone who crosses your path is supposed to give you new information, whether very small or very big. It's all growing, growing, and always expanding and never reaches perfection. Perfection is something that's like...inanimate, like it stops. If it's perfect, it doesn't have anywhere to go. So I always say, "Don't try to be perfect. Try always to be better, but don't say that you want to be perfect, because to be perfect is to end."

I have this saying that God is the sum total of everything that exists. And I can't figure how most of the religions represent God as a bearded old man that's usually a father figure. [Quidam sits stroking his big gray beard, smiling]. So, I can see you as that!

My brother always says that he is God and the other day in a workshop a woman sitting near me said, "Ahh, I'm sitting next to God." And I answered, "No, I'm only God's brother!"

Q - How do you experience thought and emotion?

AD - I try to balance them as much as possible. I am more mental than emotional, but I try more and more to release my emotions.

Lately, I am learning a lot about how to express anger, which had been hard for me. Now I learn to say no. That is a very important thing. I'm learning to allow myself to feel more but also to balance that with thought. You have to have that balance to live freely. Sometimes you have to let your feelings go before your thoughts. Sometimes thoughts say, "Hey, don't feel *that* much!"

But I think the thing that's most important for me is to have fun in life. And this is something that has always been with me. If work wasn't fun, I wasn't ready to do it. I had to have fun while I was studying, while I was working. If I have to struggle and to force things, I don't believe in that. While we are here, one of the goals we should set for ourselves is to learn how to have fun. When people are having fun, everybody is fine; everybody is okay. There's no violence, there's no aggression, there's no drama. So, we should always have fun.

And spirituality, too, has to come with fun.

Q - Do you have any sense of something existing that might be labeled as negative or evil?

AD - Yeah, I think that evil and negative energy is manipulation, is denial, is...everything that tells you *not* to have fun! Or everything that tries to take your power by limiting you, by imposing rules and things or by saying that you are bad and that you are not doing things right. Sometimes, I think that parents are doing evil to their children by not, like, letting them go their own way or do their own thing.

I think that evil is related to fear. And at the end, there are two energies. One is love and the other one is fear. They are the opposed energies. And fear comes from ignorance and ignorance leads to judgment.

So, on one side are ignorance, judgment and fear. On the other side of the equation are knowledge, compassion and love. So, whatever is not love, compassion and acceptance is judgment and fear. And that creates violence. That creates all the evil.

Q - Did you or do you have a spiritual teacher?

AD - Well, I would put Lazaris in that category. I see Lazaris more as a consciousness, sort of a group consciousness. I don't see Lazaris as an individual. He's a group consciousness that is very light, very fun to be with. And so I try to read everything that he puts out, and visit his website as much as possible.

There are many people that I would call masters or spiritual teachers. There have been many of them for me. But I think the most constant one, the one I still go back to is Lazaris. He's always telling me something new. Everything he says always causes me to say, "Yes, that's it! That's what I think and feel."

And also there's this guide, this person or energy that is always with me. That's part of my higher self.

Q - Do you yourself teach?

AD - Well, I teach about crystals, which is just another way to teach about Consciousness, about Enlightenment, about living life. I have been having very good response from people who have become my very good friends. It seems that I have made a difference in their lives and that feels really good to me. But, I don't take the position of being a master or a guru. I tell them, "I am like you are. Sometimes I can see a little more, but I give you power to see your own power." I know that people sometimes doubt, but they have to learn about their own power. They need to know that it's their choice, their way of being. Nobody can do their lives for them. I tell them that they have to take responsibility and take care of their own lives. But if I can help them by telling them of one experience or another that I have had or something or another that I might know, like how to place a stone in a particular spot in their house then that's good.

With the stones, the first thing I say is, "Look, the stones, the crystals, they will do *nothing* for you by themselves." If you get stones and just place them around your house, they are just beautiful things, ornamental things in your house. Now, they can be of great help if you empower them with your intention. But, that's the magic phrase: clear intention. Through that crystal you can have the power to do what you need. But, it's not the crystal, it's *you*! You are using the crystal as an instrument to enhance that power which you already have! Because without your power, the crystal cannot do anything; *nothing* can do anything. Be sure that if you empower somebody—like a guru—it's not the guru creating the reality. You are! You are solving the problems, but you think it's the guru that is solving the problems. So, I tell them, "I'm not a guru, and the crystals are not magical beings that will change your life in two minutes!" They need to put their own power into that, and that's the best I can tell them.

Q - Do you have a personal spiritual practice?

AD - Well, I meditate. I have my own rituals with crystals that I do. The biggest part is that I do my mandalas with crystals. I put my attention on the crystals and I place a strong force there to create my own reality the best way possible.

And I like to connect with nature. I always do a kind of ceremony whenever I visit somewhere that I consider a power place in nature. But, it's mostly inside myself where I find the answer to things. It's great now that I'm living in my new house. There's a falcon that lives on the big mountain that's nearby and whenever I start working on something like making a new mandala he comes and he circles around the house a few times and then he flies away. So, it's like he's saying, "Okay..."

You know, the other day we went to Universal Studios. And I realized that we had actually done a ceremony of the four elements while we were there. The first ride was "Jurassic Park" which is all about water. Then we went on the "E.T." ride which is about air. Then "Backdraft" which was about fire. And finally we went on the studio tour where they have the earthquake. So, I realized that I did a sacred ritual even at Universal!

But I don't have any sense that every morning at ten o'clock I have to do this or that. It's whenever I am ready. Sometimes I pass three or four days without doing anything, sometimes I do things three or four days in a row. And I only like to do these things in my house, in my place. When I'm traveling, I just carry one or two stones and I touch them from time to time.

Q - Some people feel that we are on the brink of a significant shift in consciousness, and that such a shift may even be necessary for our survival on the planet. Do you have an opinion about this?

AD - Yes, I really believe that there is a shift going on because two thousand years of indoctrination is now shifting in some ways. The shift is that people are beginning to see that God is inside of each one and that everybody has his own power and that it's a collective thing. It's not one ruler in charge any more. I believe that in the future there will be no more figures like the Pope or the Ayatollah, a major ruler of a major religion. People are becoming more aware now. People are starting to know more about themselves.

Some people say that it's the Age of Aquarius, some people call it other things. But it's really happening. It is a big shift. I dream of a world—and I don't know if I will experience this in this life—but, it's a unified world composed of lots of individuals and there are no two exactly the same.

It's just like what I always say about clusters of crystals. They are made of individual stones and each has it's own uniqueness. One is larger, the other is thinner, the other is shorter. The geometry of the faces are all different from one another. And they can be all together in the same piece, forming a cluster. It's a unity, but it's made of differences.

But we have been living in a civilization that teaches that we have to fit in, be the same, be like the others, don't be yourself, don't be unique. And the big picture is that people are beginning to realize their own power and their own uniqueness. So, people are beginning to realize that we don't have to be the same! We *can* be different and we can accept one another's differences. We can even love those differences.

That's the main point of this shift in Consciousness and spirituality. We are all parts of the larger thing but each is different from the other. Each has something inside that is common to everybody: we are all made of atoms. Instead of saying that God made man in His image and likeness, I say that God created "Atom" (Adam) in His image and likeness!

Q - There will be readers of this book who sense some form of awakening in life, and some who will just have some interest in the topic. Since this is your chance to speak directly to them, what would you like to say?

AD - I'd like to say, "Have fun! If you are having fun, you can be sure that you are growing!" You are expanding in Consciousness. Our biggest enemy is fear. So, we have to expand this Awareness that we are all part of the same big, living cell that we call Mother Earth. And if we f--k up Mother Earth, we f--k up ourselves. So let's get a grip and have fun while we're doing it! Be nice, accept others, live and let live. Be and let be. Have fun while growing.

And you can be sure that all of the power is within. You won't find it outside of yourself. And if you do find it outside, you can be sure that this power has come from inside yourself.

Biography

Antonio Duncan was born in Niteroi, Rio de Janeiro, Brazil. His grandfather was a jeweler, who used to give him little pieces of stones, and Antonio started to collect and play with them, without really knowing he was already working intuitively with their energy. His family was always very interested in spiritual matters, and two of his aunts were trance channelers. Because of this, his curiosity about mysticism awakened very early.

Antonio worked in the international music business for more than 20 years, giving him the opportunity to travel a lot to different parts of the world. In his spare time, he would attend workshops and seminars on shamanic practices, crystals, metaphysics and spiritual growth.

After the Harmonic Convergence, in 1987, he started to study more deeply about crystals and minerals, and after a while he was already giving his own workshops and seminars to share his knowledge of the mineral world. In May 1992 he released his first book, *The ABC of Crystals*, which in a few months became a best seller in Brazil (five printings).

Due to his new activities and the success of the book, Antonio decided to dedicate all his time to teaching and writing, and he abandoned the record business after winning Brazil's greatest prize (The Sharp Prize) as producer for the Best Album of 1993, Zizi Possi's "Valsa Brasileira."

Since then Antonio has been conducting workshops and seminars all over Brazil, and also giving personal readings of his Shamanic Crystal Oracle. In September of 1998 he released his 2nd book, *The Stone Path (O Caminho das Pedras)* which is a dictionary and practical guide to the use of crystals and gemstones. *The Stone Path* is now in its third printing.

Occasionally Antonio takes groups of his students to visit sacred places of the world, mainly in Peru and Brazil, but also in Greece, Egypt, USA and Europe.

Antonio has a site in the Internet, www.crystals.com.br, which is only in the Portuguese language, but it has nice photos of beautiful stones.

Contacts:

> e-mail: duncan@crystals.com.br
> site: www.crystals.com.br
> fax (5521)2709-3347
> phone (5521)2609-2025

Kevin Akash Olver

Interviewed by phone from Sydney, Australia
January 25, 2001

In November of 1999, Diana invited me to travel to Australia with her. I held spiritual gatherings on each of the nine nights I was there. While in Sydney, our dear friend Amelia Allan drove me to a lovely beach home to attend a satsang led by Akash.

We arrived and took seats on the floor among perhaps a dozen other men and women. When Akash first glanced at me there was an immediate sense that I had met him before. In fact, it felt much deeper than that. It was as if he and I had known one another for a long, long time.

I was very impressed with his simple, honest presentation. And at times I found myself thinking the very words that appeared next on his lips. I've had this experience before in certain situations but in this case the sense that "there's only one of us here" was profound.

After the gathering, Akash and I shared a few very warm moments together and promised to stay in touch. A few emails were exchanged in the following months but after a while we fell out of contact with one another.

More than a year later, I wrote to Akash to ask him if he'd like to be part of this book. He immediately replied saying that he'd love to. Naturally, the distance factor pointed toward a phone interview, which we scheduled for after the winter holidays.

I rang Akash and while we exchanged hellos I once again started to get that same feeling that I had had months earlier. He felt familiar to me in the simple sort of way that one might feel a connection with a biological brother or sister. Still, I kept to the plan and explained that the methodology called for me to get right to the interview. He agreed and off we went with the first question. As the interview progressed, he said many things that resonated very deeply with me.

Then we got to his response to the final question and a shiver went up my spine and goose bumps rose visibly on my arms when he said that he'd like

109

to close the interview with a quote from the movie "American Beauty." I sat smiling and saying the words silently along with him as he read the passage.

Out of all possible ways to choose to end his interview, Akash chose a quote that I know and dearly love. In fact, I have it recorded and frequently use it during the three-day Intensive Seminars that Diana and I offer to the public.

Akash and I shared a hearty laugh and agreed that perhaps there really is only one of us here!

Q - Is there such a reality as Awakening, Enlightenment, Liberation or spiritual freedom?

A - Certainly there is liberation from identification with the mind. Up to a certain point, patterns of thought are believed in and taken to be reality. This is false identification, taking a cluster of thoughts to be who we are. On top of this, we then get the idea that there is a right way to be and a wrong way to be. We get stuck in trying to be a certain way and trying not to be another kind of way. This leads to tension and suffering.

The same patterns are carried over into the spiritual search. For example, there may be an attempt to imitate a teacher by trying to be peaceful. And even though it might appear convincing, it is the same mechanism in the mind. It is holding on to a thought—"I should be peaceful"—and trying to be that and trying not to be otherwise. This unnecessary effort keeps us from relaxing into our true nature, which is always at peace.

At a certain point, the games of the mind start to be seen. The energy that has been going into holding on is liberated. And there is a letting go into being, a relaxing into "what is" rather than a clinging to "what should be." This is liberation.

I usually don't use the word "enlightenment" and if I do, it is to refer to a powerful experience of ultimate Truth. Having said that, it is not that there is an experiencer and an experience. There are not two, there is only one. The mind likes to divide into those who are enlightened and those who aren't enlightened. This does not help at all. The mind separates; the heart knows oneness. The true question is whether there is surrender to Being or avoidance and denial of Being.

Q - Did this surrender that you describe seem to take place in a particular moment in time, or was it noticed as a gradual process?

A - There is a moment of absolute absence filled with absolute presence. Deeper than surrender or no surrender....is-ness everywhere, beyond time and space. And subsequently, a process in that the mind engages again, providing the opportunity for increasing alignment with Being. Any parts of the mind that are still hanging on to delusions come up. They need to be recognised, otherwise the same old patterns run and there's a clinging to who one should be. The ego assumes a new identity—"guru." This is one of the traps of spiritual teaching. Great honesty is needed to simply recognise and experience whatever is happening.

Q - Within this recognition that you describe, is there an experience of evolving, maturing or growing?

A - Is-ness is is-ness. Maturing is in the continued surrender to that and in the dissolving of identification with the mind, giving up the ideas of who one thinks one is. This is where the maturing is. Being is Being.

It is not a question of achieving a certain goal or of reaching a certain place. The maturing is in the relaxing into "what is." It is the shift from effort to effortlessness; relaxing from the head to the heart. Even when the mind is moving, it doesn't need to be followed. The mind likes to measure—measuring ourselves against others, where they are, how far ahead they are, how far behind they are. And it measures where we were last week against where we are this week. Putting aside the measuring stick of the mind is one of the surface aspects of maturing.

There is also a deepening that is a mystery, like resting in the support of the whole of existence. Words cannot describe it.

Q - Is there or has there been any sense of anything that might be seen to be different from "ordinary" human awareness?

A - Typical unmatured human awareness is limited and consists of believing in the projection of the mind; belief in whatever movie is running in the mind and appearing to take place in our everyday life. So that movie might consist of "I'm a successful career person" or "I'm powerless in this" or countless others.

Believing in a movie is a form of sleep. In awakening to "what is", the movie is seen for what it is. It is seen to be identification with the ego—the Latin word for "I"—this cluster of thoughts, a play of light and shadow. When this projection, this movie, isn't believed in any more, there is a flowering. The beauty of Being has just been hidden while attention has been on the movie.

In my own experience, there is no extraordinariness in this. Relaxing into the natural simplicity of Being, ordinariness reveals itself as a true flavour of life.

Q - What is your experience of thought and emotion?

A - In the past, the tendency was to go with each thought. A thought would arise and it was as if I'd stick to it and go with it wherever it took me. And when this would happen I would be just moving around on the circumference of consciousness. Now, a thought arises and it is seen. It does not need to be stuck to. It is just what it is, it's just a thought arising or a chain of thoughts arising.

It's a little bit like sitting on a chair and relaxing in the centre of the circus. There can be quite a circus going on all around but there's no following of it, no jumping on the horse and galloping around the outside. And there's no denial or avoidance of it, either. If thoughts are arising, thoughts are arising.

And it's just the same with the emotions. If an emotion arises, it can be experienced. There is a loosening up from clinging to what we want and what we don't want. So for example, if there's a desire to being peaceful, then usually being angry gets judged. It gets thrown into the basement, hidden away and denied. For some people it's the other way around. Being angry seems to be more okay and being softer or calmer is judged. Whatever we favour, we judge the opposite, whether it is in ourselves or in someone else.

When we are willing to see and to experience the opposites, there is freedom. Polarities can still arise, but there is no clinging. Whatever emotion arises can just be experienced. Whatever thought arises can just be seen. There is a resting in what is unaffected by any outer movement or change. That's the shift into acceptance—as in that profound saying, "What is is, and what ain't ain't."

Q - So this leads perfectly to another question; do you have a sense of anything that might be called negative or evil energy in the world?

A - Energy can be expressed creatively or destructively. Evil energy is destructive energy that involves hurting others and ourselves through lack of awareness. And we cannot hurt others without hurting ourselves.

This is a complex question but the answer can be simple. "Evil" and the fear reaction to it are both expressions of darkness. Evil is a power trip fed by fear of powerlessness. It stems from a particular projection, an extreme kind of venomous inner movie. This darkness is the absence of the light of awareness. The light of awareness is the only antidote—to be fully conscious.

Q - Did you or do you have a teacher?

A - Life is my teacher. I have had various teachers and right now you are my teacher. This is the beauty of it, that each moment is a reflection of the wordless. It is right here to be seen and surrendered to in each moment. It is an incredible, delicious being-ness. Each person around us is a mirror to see this, to be this. Each moment is a signpost pointing deeper into this ocean of being. And teachers can offer a wonderful gift of pointing to this. I am tremendously grateful.

Q - Do you have a spiritual practice?

A - No. I have no formal, systematic spiritual practice. However, I have certainly found techniques and maps very helpful for seeing the mechanisms of the mind much more clearly. And consequently my recommendation to others is to use whatever is helpful—not to cling to techniques, not to avoid techniques. If one works, great—use it. Then put it aside when it has done its job.

When we are going somewhere in the outer world, a map helps us find our way. And it is the same in the inner world. We all know how easy it can be to get tangled up in the dense undergrowth of the mind. Experiential maps are very helpful not only for untangling but also, through their use, there is a natural by-product of dropping into Being. Presence is then far more sustainable in everyday life.

I love the old Sufi story about the traveller in the desert who sees a group of men carrying a boat. They're sweating and puffing in the hot sun, many miles from the nearest water. So, the traveller goes up to group of men and asks, "Why are you carrying that boat?" And they say, "Well, quite a while ago we got to this big river and we found this boat. If we hadn't found the boat we wouldn't have gotten across the river. So we're keeping it." They are still carrying the boat even though it is now a useless burden.

Q - I know that you sit with people publicly and that sometimes people come to you with questions of a practical nature such as money, sensuality or relationships. What sort of maps do you try to offer in those situations?

A - I use a variety of experiential maps, particularly in one-on-one sessions. They all clarify the mechanisms of the mind and support letting go into one's true nature. "Spheres of Consciousness" is a specific, practical way of mapping the way that the mind is obscuring Being. People are experiencing amazing results from this as the glue of identification dissolves. "The Polarity Map" is another way of experiencing opposites and defusing projection. I also use the Enneagram.

The first step is to identify what's really going on, not staying with what one thinks is going on, but what is really going on whether this is in the area of sex, money, power or whatever. Then identify what is being clung to and what is being rejected.

You mention money. In our culture, there are some people that are attached to money and have fear of letting go of that attachment. There are others who are clinging to not having money. So there are clingers to each end and both are attached. I'm not talking about letting go of having money or not having money; I am talking about letting go of the attachment. Attachment is based on identification and so the accompanying beliefs need to be seen. In the letting go of attachment, relaxing into Being happens on its own. And it is the same with whatever is arising.

Truth or Presence must be found in the most unlikely place. It can be relatively easy to experience this in a gathering of beautiful people who come together in quiet, in the heart. But that's not enough. It's just not enough. Presence needs to be discovered in the midst of where our deepest identification lies, whether that's in the arena of sex, relationships, money, wherever it might be.

This is the great challenge and the great opportunity. This is the call to live in Truth, as Truth, in the world, in the nitty gritty. I definitely do not say, "Pay no attention to the mind. It is just mind." I've seen a lot of unnecessary suffering that has resulted from that. I would rather say, "See the mind clearly." This clarity is the shining of You and in this shining, it is obvious that you are not what is being seen, you are not the mind. Your true nature is abundantly clear.

The personality has to be seen just as it is and life gives us wonderful opportunities for this. Wherever there seems to be the greatest difficulty in one's everyday life, this is a good place to look. First check what is really happening. What is being clung to? What is being rejected? And then experience it, just as it is. This is relaxing from the head to the heart and it opens up for the shining of who one really is to flood through the layers of personality.

Q - Some people feel that we as a species are on the brink of a shift in consciousness and perhaps that such a shift might be an important shift for the human race. Do you have an opinion on this?

A - There is a call to the human race to awaken. I can't say when this call began. But the call is here and it is here now. So there is no need to wait for a collective wave to carry you. Don't postpone. Answer this call right now, in this very moment. Don't even wait for tomorrow. Respond to the call within yourself.

And then perhaps it can be seen that this call from within is not separate from the call to the whole of humanity. There is only one call and it is up to you whether you answer that call right now or not.

Q - There will be some readers of this book who sense some awakening in their lives. And there will be others who might just have a curious interest in the topic. What would you like to say to those readers in this moment?

A - Don't postpone. Look at whatever you are postponing and see how willing you are to give that up. Postponing is suffering. Life is here now. Being here now is the liberation.

I'd also like to offer a quote from the movie "American Beauty", from the character Lester Burnham:

"I guess I could be pretty pissed off about what happened to me. But it's hard to stay mad when there's so much beauty in the world.

Sometimes I feel like I'm seeing it all at once and that's it's too much. My heart fills up like a balloon that's about to burst.

And then I remember to relax and stop trying to hold onto it. Then it flows through me like rain and I can't feel anything but gratitude for every single moment of my stupid little life.

You have no idea what I'm talking about, I'm sure. But don't worry...you will some day."

Biography

Kevin Akash Olver was born and grew up in England, showing an early interest in altered states of consciousness. After working as a psychologist in the mid-seventies, he established two successful businesses and explored the external world with gusto before going to live and work in India.

Based in Sydney, Australia since 1989, Kevin Akash Olver gives individual sessions, face-to-face and by telephone globally, as well as courses. These are available both for the general public and for corporate leaders, supporting others to discover who they really are and to live to their highest potential, to clarify their values and live according to them. This work has continued to deepen since a powerful realization in 1998 and many people's lives have been touched through his insightful encouragement and finely tuned skills. He is currently writing a book about living and working consciously amid the challenges of everyday life.

Every situation in our lives is an opportunity—a wake-up call—to be true. When we live with genuine integrity, essence qualities such as true intelligence, peace, compassion and joy spread through our experience of life. This is where true happiness resides. Life is a journey of discovering and being who we really are.

This approach is a synthesis of the best of Western psychology and the timeless wisdom of sages. It is about daring to awaken. The Enneagram and other maps are used to identify and clarify the personality type. When habitual patterns are really seen, the glue of identification dissolves in the light of awareness and the qualities of the heart are revealed. Deeper than the psychological level of consciousness lies the energetic level. When held energy patterns are touched by presence, the possibilities are boundless. Concrete, practical methods support stabilisation as living presence in everyday life. The rest happens through grace.

Contact details:

> website: www.akash.com.au
> email: info@akash.com.au
> phone: 61 2 9369 5253
> cell phone: 0413 317 439
> Postal address: PO Box 1506,
> Bondi Junction, NSW 1355, Australia

H. Raphael Cushnir

Interviewed by phone from Tomales, California
February 7, 2001

One of the great learning experiences which Diana and I encountered in making this book was that we should expect the unexpected. At every turn of the road, we found wonderful surprises waiting for us.

This was truly the case in meeting Raphael Cushnir, our next guest. As mentioned earlier, I had developed the basic "wish list" of prospective interviewees very early in the process, even though I left room for others yet to be discovered. By early in the year 2001, I thought that I had pretty much settled who would be in the book but as fate would have it, that plan wonderfully failed to work out and once again the Muse took over and provided an even better back up.

I was at my desk one morning when I got a call from a good friend who lives in Santa Fe. We talked about a variety of topics and eventually this book came up. She told me that she had heard a really amazing interview on a local radio show and that she thought the person speaking would be perfect *for the book. She had felt him to be very genuine in the interview and she was very excited about a new process of spiritual discovery that he had discussed. "Sounds like a candidate to me," I responded. "Who is he?" She chuckled and responded that she had forgotten his name, at which point I sort of filed the whole thing away in the "oh well" file, and forgot about it.*

A few weeks passed. My friend called back with the news that she had contacted the radio station in Santa Fe and gotten the man's name from them. After a bit of quick internet research, I found myself visiting Raphael's website. I really enjoyed what I read there, so I sent him an email and soon he and I were talking on the phone.

There was an immediate sense of connection between us. It turns out that Raphael and I have some mutual friends from my days in the Adi Da work, and we also share a stripped-down, practical version of approaching spiritual life which gave us a lot in common and made for smooth communication

117

from the beginning. Once the interview was completed, I found myself liking Raphael even more. His process of "Living the Questions" seems to me to be a marvelous way of offering the ancient "be here now" teachings to a new generation of modern spiritual seekers, in a fashion which feels original and fresh to me.

It's worth mentioning at this point that during the production of this volume, I had assiduously avoided reading spiritual books. It seemed best to me that wherever possible, I should not allow my writing and editing judgment to be affected by outside influences. This was a little trick I had learned from my time working with musical composers, particularly the Grammy-winning Swiss harpist Andreas Vollenweider. During our time together, he had explained to me that he allowed himself almost no contact with other musicians' work while he was writing or recording an album of his own.

So I had not read Raphael's book Unconditional Bliss *prior to interviewing him. But, since his was among the final interviews conducted for* Wide Awake, *I picked the book up and read it once his interview was finished. I not only thoroughly enjoyed the book but suggested that a number of friends also read it. They, too, reported getting a lot of benefit from the very practical suggestions in it.*

A month or two after the interview, Diana and I had dinner with Raphael in a lovely little Mexican restaurant in Mill Valley, California. We found him to be an engaging and likable man and during our evening together a marvelous time was had by all.

This interview seems to fall into a bit of a unique category in that while most of our guests seem to come from some readily definable spiritual category, i.e. Buddhist, Hindu, Christian-mystic, etc., Raphael offers his wisdom from a place that I might call "secular Awakening." He espouses no exclusive lineage or path. Still, he provides a perspective as spiritually solid and profound as any other presented here.

We hope you'll enjoy this talk and the speaker. And, Alyiah in Santa Fe— thanks for the tip. We owe you one for bringing Raphael to the book and to our readers.

Q - In your experience, is there such a reality as Awakening, Enlightenment, Liberation or spiritual freedom?

RC - Yes.

Q - Would you like to elaborate on that?

[Laughter]

RC - I think that different people can arrive from very different avenues at a place in which they find themselves no longer believing that their freedom or their deepest happiness comes to them from any set of external circumstances. Therefore, they are free to fully participate in each and every moment that they experience. And that full presence, without any conditions, to life as it unfolds moment by moment is, I think, a good way to describe spiritual freedom.

Q - In your own case, did this recognition seem to happen in a particular moment in time, or as a process—over time?

RC - I think the truest answer is both. There was a moment in time when I was so significantly smashed up by life that I became available to a different kind of experience. My previous arrogance and judgmentalness and rigidity could no longer hold any more. And the cracks that became apparent were instrumental in allowing something else to come through.

Then there was a moment when the "something else" did come through. Both of those moments were clear and distinct and remain clear and distinct to me to this day. But I'm also aware that I could never have come to either of them without having lived the life that I had lived up until then.

Q - Is there an experience of anything that might be seen as evolving, maturing or growing?

RC - I think there's a kind of "raw material" to what we are calling spiritual freedom. When it first appears it can be so powerful and transformative that it feels like that's all there is. And yet, most of the work that's required spiritually is about taking that experience and finding out how to live it moment by moment in the most mundane circumstances of everyday life.

Q - Is there any sense that you have lived anything that might be seen as different or distinct from "ordinary" human experience?

RC - Once the door is open by virtue of great practice or great grace or whatever it might be, there are whole hosts of experiences that can come to a person which don't necessarily fit within the confines of what we would ordinarily call "normal" existence. Those kinds of experiences can range from psychic openings to great influxes of physical or non-physical energy. The whole range of paranormal manifestations can be a part of people arriving at greater spiritual freedom.

But, I have an understanding that mirrors some of the wisdom traditions. That is that these circumstances are essentially the fireworks or great display—they indicate that, yes, there is more here than meets the eye. Yet, these things themselves are not really the essence. This essence, at the deepest level, can be given a number of different names—love, emptiness, oneness. And the thing about that essence, from my experience, is that ultimately when we experience it, it feels both totally incredible and absolutely ordinary at the same time.

So, I think that when a person is living in a state of spiritual freedom, there isn't necessarily this feeling of, "Wow, it's a completely different terrain," or "How exciting that all of these different things are happening to me." And certainly not, "Look how special I am because I have been granted the opportunity to experience these things." But instead there is a humility that comes from seeing that truly everything, no matter how ordinary or mundane or how super-fantastic and celestial, is all really infused with the same essence.

Q - What is your experience of thought and emotion?

RC - My experience is that thought and emotion arise sometimes separately, sometimes together, and sometimes created in response to one another. And that they are constantly arising as long as I am living awake in the world. Just being alive creates an ongoing bubbling up to the surface of thought, of emotion, of sensation. And I can choose to link up to any particular thought or emotion and watch the influence between them and watch how it happens in myself—or not.

A better way to say it is that I can witness it or I can become attached to it. Either way, it seems to just be part of the whole and never ending.

Q - Do you have a sense of anything that might be called evil or negative energies within life?

RC - Personally, I do. I hesitate in saying that because I feel that in each moment everything exists and I don't like to label the things that exist in a framework of good/bad or higher/lower. But I believe that in each moment there exists all of the past, all of the present, and all of the future—all of the forces of light and all of the forces of darkness. Together they make up the whole of all that is.

In some circumstances dark forces can become more apparent than usual, either as separate entities or linked up with everything else that is occurring. It is possible for individuals to experience them very deeply, to be influenced by them, in fact even to be placed in great danger as a result of them. And yet, at the same time, that too is ordinary from my perspective. There's nothing about dark forces that is any more spectacular or any more worthy of fixation than any other kind of experience that you might find in that same moment.

I think that dealing with darkness requires a similar but more intense version of the ingredients that all life requires—clarity of intention, humility, radical presence, and fierce love.

Q - Did you or do you have a teacher?

RC - I did not have a teacher in the traditional sense. Some people, myself included, just aren't cut out for gurus and lineages and the whole yoke of devotion and discipline that comes with them. What I did have was mentors—great spiritual friends who were more fully realized than I. They helped point me toward new directions and possibilities.

The other kind of teacher that I have had is more difficult to describe. Swami Muktananda—one of the great authorities in relation to the energy phenomenon known as kundalini—once said, "Ultimately, kundalini becomes the guru." My own spontaneous and unsought-after experience with kundalini reflects this. Embracing the energy and surrendering to it on an ongoing basis creates a kind of non-physical, energetic student-teacher relationship. But this is a huge and delicate topic. Very mysterious.

Q - Do you yourself teach?

RC - This is a problematic term. I usually "share." I share experience. I share with process work. I share with stories. I share with just the day-to-day ordinary parts of my life. The reason I say that the word "teacher" is problematic is because I tend to be wary of people who set themselves up as teachers. I tend to think that each of us knows exactly what we need to know and that we arrive exactly where we need to arrive. And yet, it would be disingenuous to say that there are not people who have come to a deep sense of recognition and therefore really do have something important to pass along.

So, once I get past the problematic part I would say, "Yes, I do teach." But the more I teach and the better I teach results from how much I continue to profess and live my absolute "beginner's mind." Another way to say that is that the more I become convinced that I am a teacher, the less I actually have to offer to others.

Q - Do you have a personal spiritual practice?

RC - I do. I practice something that I call "Living the Questions." This is the basis of what I share with people. Living the Questions is really a kind of meditation in action. I practice it all the time to arrive as fully as possible in each moment, especially the more difficult ones.

But also, Living the Questions over a long period has freed all sorts of energies inside myself. So often, strange as this may sound, I find myself meditating, chanting, or performing asanas in a spontaneous fashion. If I'm open to them in a given moment, sometimes they just happen. They happen and I'm grateful, as opposed to making appointments for them in advance.

Q - I'll assume that sometimes those who you interact with come to you with questions of a practical nature, about, say, money or sensuality or relationships. Can you describe how you work with issues like those?

RC - Well, I don't think that there's a difference between what we call practical issues and what we call spiritual issues. I think there are only the conflicts that people have moment to moment in their lives.

The Living the Questions process that I use with people is the same no matter what the issue. This process entails asking two questions: *"What is happening right now?"* and *"Can I be with it?"* So, if someone arrives saying, "I have a great amount of anxiety around money," or even more specifically, "Should I buy this house?" I'm going to ask them if they'd like to live the questions about it. We'll start with a focus on the body. "Okay, when you think about this issue of buying a home what is your experience? What is happening right now?" And when perhaps the answer arises, "My chest is restricted," or "I'm feeling overwhelmed with guilt"—whatever the response—the companion question is, "Can I be with it? Can I fully accept and open to the experience I have around this question, this conflict?" This process quickly eases a lot of the superficial tension around an issue because the person finds that most distress comes from resistance to the conflict, not from the conflict itself.

Then there's also an opportunity for truths to emerge that are deeper than the original issue. Ultimately, Living the Questions can take people as far as they are willing to go. It can unravel deeper and deeper knots and in the process lead to much greater personal freedom. We can begin with issues about food, relationship, God—really anything at all, no matter how seemingly big or small. The process remains the same and the discovery remains the same.

Q - Some people these days have a sense that we are engaged in a kind of global shift in consciousness, and that if this is true that this shift is important or even essential to us as a race of beings? Do you have an opinion about this?

RC - I know many people who think of themselves as "Light Beings" - people who believe that we are at a transformational moment in our planetary history. They also believe that it's their great privilege and responsibility to help usher in this change of consciousness. And my reaction when I hear this is to say, "Story, story, story, story, story!"

It may be true. I'm not in a position to know. But it's a story no different from a nihilistic story that says that the world is going to hell in a handbasket and that we're the last generation on earth that's going to get to enjoy it. These questions around where we are and what's really happening are part of the great Mystery that we are not able to understand, ever. If we're lucky we can penetrate it from time to time through direct experience but not through mental concepts.

If someone chooses to live the "Light Being" story, bless them. But it's my experience that that story can lead to a great distance from other humans and a great distance from the tremendous amount of suffering and oppression that exists here in this moment. There is a kind of narcissism that can creep into that story, a kind of pride that often is very troubling.

Personally, I'm inspired by people whose transformed consciousness leads them back into the everyday world, into service and activism, working without much of a story at all. These people, and I've been privileged to know many of them, are fighting corporate globalization and exploring new ways of environmental sustainability. They're building new bridges between the prosperous parts of our society and the parts where there is still great disease, great poverty, great suffering. If we could all become passionately committed to healing the earth and its inhabitants, while at the same time losing all sense of attachment to any particular outcome, this, more than anything, could bring about a global shift.

Q - This book will be read partly by people who may have a sense of spiritual freedom in their own lives, and partly by those who may just have a curious interest in the topic. This is your opportunity to speak directly to them. What would you like to say to these readers?

[Long pause]

RC - For most of my life, I was what I would call a great seeker. And I had a really important precept. That was that I would not believe anything that I did not experience directly. I was very lucky to have that precept because it helped me distinguish between what was real for me versus concepts and ideas that came from others which may have been powerful or interesting or intriguing but ultimately not true for me.

On the other hand, sometimes skepticism comes with a certain sort of rigidity, a kind of "prove it to me" attitude that makes it difficult for new experience to arrive in one's life. So I would suggest that it's important to have a healthy skepticism yet at the same time be really open and humble in each moment and to truly understand that we never know what's going to happen next.

Over and over I come into contact with people who are lost in their spiritual searching or lost in their personal pain because they believe that what they have lived until this moment is what they're going to live from now on. They believe that the past they've lived has conditioned their reality to be the same now and forever. And I think that the great miracle of our life here on earth—as well as the great mystery—is that when we stop making assumptions and when we stop pretending to be God, we come to understand that we have absolutely no knowledge about what will happen next. And that lack of any kind of knowing is the very thing which allows us—if we let it seep into every pore of our being—to become available for greater and greater spiritual freedom.

Biography

H. Raphael Cushnir—a writer, teacher and filmmaker—is a proponent of engaged, worldly spirituality. His Showtime Movie, "Sexual Healing," starring Anthony Edwards, Helen Hunt and Jason Alexander, was nominated for two Cable Ace Awards and raised more than thirty thousand dollars for the Minority AIDS Project. Cushnir's book, *Unconditional Bliss: Finding Happiness in the Face of Hardship* was published in 2000 and nominated as Best Psychology Title of the year by the Books for a Better Life Awards.

Cushnir's own access to unconditional bliss came after a period of profound grief. Since then he has traveled the country teaching Living the Questions, his two-step technique for greater presence, in workshops, churches and businesses, as well as on radio and television.

For more information visit Raphael's website:

livingthequestions.org.

Or contact him: hrc@livingthequestions.org

Neelam

Interviewed in Ojai, California
April 10, 2001

Our interview with Neelam was another of the many happy surprises that arose during the preparation of this collection. I had long heard rather glowing accounts of her work from people who had attended her gatherings which, of course, caused me to seek her out almost from the beginning. I have always operated under the presumption that an introduction through a mutual friend is the most direct and effective means to get to meet someone.

Almost a year earlier in Nevada City, California, I had the pleasure of sharing dinner with two gentlemen who were attending a weekend workshop with Arjuna. One was Andy Turner from Las Vegas, who has since become an important member of our team here at Spiritual Freedom Foundation, and is also among my closest friends. Our fellow diner was a tall, friendly surfer-looking dude named Life. I assumed the interesting spelling to be spiritual rearrangement of the more common name "Leif"—which it is. Be that as it may, Andy, Life and I had a grand old time tucking into some salad and pasta and, in my case, a bottle of good local mini-brew.

So when I next heard from Life and he told me that he had not only met Neelam, but was also working for her Fire of Truth sangha, my mind immediately shifted into a slightly smug "soft touch for this interview" pattern. Wrong!

Over the next few months, I tried and tried to arrange the interview without even the tiniest shred of success. Phone calls, e-mails; e-mails, phone calls—I tried everything. I even resorted to my last chance. I called Life and asked him to intercede for me with Neelam. He called back, saying that Neelam rarely did interviews and that he had done what he could to help. Had this all happened early in my stint of collecting interviews, I would have probably just given up. But by now—with more than a year's experience on the project—I had learned that patience was my friend. I also had a deep intuitional sense which told me that this interview was worth the waiting and

125

the effort. So I persisted and sent yet another email to Neelam. Within a day or so she responded, agreeing to meet me for the interview upon her return from her current visit to Israel.

The drive from L.A. to Neelam's home in Ojai was a pleasant hour spent on a lovely sunny day. Arriving early, Diana and I grabbed lunch at a local cafe, then proceeded up the hill to our destination. When we eventually found the house we were warmly greeted on the front lawn by both Neelam and Life. She's a very pretty and tiny woman, and both Diana and I found ourselves needing to bend forward to hug her. But in that greeting I felt a sense of true welcome, like the familiar embrace one gets from an old friend.

We settled in on her back porch to talk in the warmth of the spring sun. As we spoke, that sense of familiarity that I first noticed in the hug intensified until I felt as if I had known her forever. And—as had taken place in several of the earlier interviews—it began to feel to me that her words were appearing on her lips and in my thoughts simultaneously. Our eyes met frequently throughout the conversation in an easy, deep gaze that often lasted well beyond my question or her response. As had happened so often during this literary process, a wonderful sense of true connection—of the Oneness of Being—flavored the interview, so much so that I found myself feeling a bit disappointed when the final question arrived.

But, as we made our way back to the city, it was with both a sense of "mission accomplished" and a feeling of gratitude that Neelam is here and willing to share her understanding of Truth with the world so freely and openly.

Q - In your experience, is there such a reality as Awakening, Enlightenment, Liberation or spiritual freedom?

N - Absolutely. Would you like me to talk a little more about it?

Q - Yes, it might make for a more interesting interview.

[Laughter]

N - You know, when I first knew of something like awakening, it seemed to be something so out of the ordinary and yet it always sounded true to me. And yet, it was like this thing that was sort of out there, so far away from where I was that it just seemed like an almost unreachable goal. Once you wake up, it's just totally amazing because you know the reality of it. You know it's here. It's just like a new relationship, you know? It's really exciting and beautiful and amazing, then you realize that it's just the beginning of something.

So, what I actually thought was that there is this amazing thing called awakening and it seems to be somewhere that you can't reach. Once you reach this place and once you pass the freshness phase, then you realize that this is just a tiny, little step. Before it looked like this great goal that you are going to reach but you see that it's a tiny, tiny little step into reality. You see that you have just made this first acquaintance, that you are just touching something so indescribable, so amazing, so incredible. That's just where it starts, you see?

I say that because what I thought before would be "the thing" turned out to be the very tiniest beginning of something that is totally indescribable.

Q - In your own case, did this recognition seem to happen in a particular moment in time or as a process—over time?

N - There was a process that led to it, a coming in and out of reality. There would be these awakenings, like these amazing things that would happen. And I would just see it and go, "Wow!" And then it would go back to where it was before. And I would have this knowing, this memory of something that had happened in this different reality.

So there would be this back and forth movement of experience. Then there is one particular experience that has shifted into an actual constant change of awareness that just simply knows itself.

From that moment on, there's no coming and going from reality. There's just knowing, right? There's just reality. And then that deepens. We could talk about that—that's actually the interesting part. Because the awakening is just like candy, you just get to taste a little. It's like for kids, you know? [Laughs] You get this little candy, you know? And you say, "Wow, that's amazing!"

So, yes, there was one instant in which it actually shifted into this knowing that there is no such thing as body and person. It all really originates somewhere else. What expresses itself through these forms, these physical, mental, emotional bodies originates somewhere else. So the shift of awareness is into this place of being or truth or whatever. And it happens in one moment and from then on there was and there is just a flowering of it.

Q - Within this flowering, is there an experience of anything that might be seen as evolving, maturing or growing?

N - It's like deepening. Even when I say flowering I have to laugh because at first it is like a flowering. But when it gets difficult, when you really touch in places that are difficult and hard, it's a really deep work—a deep willingness to really, truly take this awakeness, this knowing and touch *everything*, so that there's no place inside where it can't go. Otherwise, we're talking about some kind of awakeness that is held up by an incredible amount of beliefs and tendencies and ideas and stuff that's still within the personality. There's this deepening, which means truly letting go of everything. There's just no way that you can keep anything! It's like you are totally challenged to truly finish every little bit.

And you might choose not to do so, you see? You might choose not to do so. There are a lot of people out there who keep a certain level of awakeness. They exist just to a certain depth. You can see that there's an awakeness, but it doesn't truly reach to everything inside. It's like it doesn't really merge all the way into the Heart, yeah? So, I could talk about deepening or merging, or truly letting everything be touched by that. There is really no place to be or to hide in or to stay in or to know anything.

Especially any kind of knowing. That's always the trick of spiritual teaching. There's a danger of becoming a teacher or of becoming someone who knows something. And any kind of knowing is for nothing, you know? It just doesn't touch reality. It doesn't cut it. There has to be a real willingness to let it go everywhere it wants to. So that's what I call deepening or merging into the Heart. Deepening is the closest that I can come to describing it.

Q - Is there any sense that you have lived anything that might be seen as different or distinct from "ordinary" human experience?

N - I don't know what you mean by "ordinary." This awakening is the most ordinary or most normal way of being that there is. Everything else is not ordinary. This is how we are. It's the most natural way of being. This is who we are. We are not thoughts, beliefs, emotional reactions or patterns, you know. That's not normal or natural. It's just some kind of idea that is being held in consciousness as a way of functioning. But it's not true because it doesn't come from the true being.

Reality is ordinary. It's absolutely, totally, awesomely normal, you know? [Laughs] It's just very simple. It's an absolute and awesome simplicity and normalness. It's the natural way. It's the most ordinary. It doesn't need an intermediary, nothing in between to express itself, to know itself. It's what arises the simplest way. It doesn't need to go through all of the complications that we sometimes go through to express something.

Q - What is your experience of thought and emotion?

N - It depends. It depends on my current relationship with it and what my knowing of it is in the moment. There will be thoughts and emotions that are absolutely irrelevant to my experience and some that will be relevant. These are the places where I would know I still have some identification. But the word "identification" is too much of a word. Perhaps "relationship" is a better term. Things would still matter, there is a mattering to certain thoughts and to certain emotions until they are seen in a real way, a deep way as what they are. And that changes that relationship and when they arise, they just arise as they are. Yes?

Otherwise they arise and there is this habitual tendency to relate to them, to in any way stick with them, you know? Sticky is the best way I can say it. It's like it's time to stick somewhere and you're kind of like, "Well, I don't know!" It starts to get engaged and involved in something. So then it sticks together; there is a relevance. And again, there are places that don't have any relevance whatsoever as they arise. They just arise and they are just what they are. They just pass. They don't even touch on anything.

When this sticking happens, it's my favorite place because that's what shows me what's still there. It's truly my favorite. From my heart, this is my favorite place because this is where I get to be in something that I have not been in before or have refused at some point. In this life, or millions of years ago, I have refused to be someplace and this is where it still sticks.

So when these come up, it's the favorite place to be, because you finally get to be in this which you don't know of. You don't know what it is, you know? It's like it's there and you don't know it, then you get to be there. You get to experience it and you get to totally awesomely know it as yourself. It's a totally amazing thing because here you don't even know yourself as yourself and you get to know it in this place. And it's like, "Wow, my god! It's totally amazing!" Just when you thought it's not there, that it wouldn't be there...there it is! It's awesome! It's just amazing.

And sometimes I hate it. Sometimes there's such a habitual residue of resistance to being how you really are. How you really are is amazing—you can let anything be here. It's just so touching.

Q - Do you have a sense of anything that might be called evil or negative energies within life?

N - No. This is a great idea, you know? I have people come and they talk about evil. I only know this place where something arises which I wouldn't want to face. I still see this arise sometimes in myself. It's the only place where there would be a discrimination of something other than God. It's a place where you don't want to face something—where there's some refusal in being with something. And it's called "negative" and it's called this or that. It's called all of these names. But consciousness can go anywhere. There is no boundary in consciousness. These beliefs just keep you from knowing yourself and they create a very tricky split. Concepts of "good" and "bad" are terrible because it's not true. It doesn't exist like that, you know?

Q - Did you or do you have a teacher?

N - Yes. I have a master. My master is Papaji. When you ask if I have a teacher, I also know that I have always had a teacher. Consciousness is a teacher and that has always been there. I remember having experiences of knowing this when I was six years old—throughout life. So this teacher has always been with me.

But then at some point it manifests in a human form. You see, I would have all of these experiences but there was a part of me that couldn't trust. And it turned out later that I could only really trust through this relationship with a human form. That's why when I met Papaji I could go through this process of discrimination between what is true and what is not true.

So if you find a teacher that is a manifestation of Self taking the form of a person, you have someone to relate to. You start to discriminate within yourself between what is a true impulse that arises in consciousness and what is a habit. You see what is habitual versus what simply arises. Through having a human teacher, you get to such discrimination in places where you yourself don't yet have insight, where you don't trust enough. You probably wouldn't need a teacher if you would trust enough in consciousness itself as it comes. A teacher in human form arises because you yourself have a doubt or need some help in this inner place that just doesn't yet know how to discriminate.

And that's my experience with Papaji. Through this relationship there was a total devotion. At first, it was just a discrimination between what is real and what is not real, between what arises within myself as being true or not true. And then there was this devotion that allowed me to let go of who I thought I was. On this level, it fulfilled the purpose of bringing me to know myself.

Q - Do you yourself teach?

N - Sometimes. Occasionally. [Laughter] I would say that lately it's less and less of a teaching. It actually used to be more of a teaching for a while. You see, Papaji was not a teacher. He was just a being. He made himself available for whatever was going on around him.

But when you say teaching, it seems to relate to some kind of knowing. And that's a difficult place in consciousness. It's a place that acts like it knows, and that's not a true place. So what I do is not so much a teaching as a way of being. It's a way of sharing my experience with other people. Sometimes we just need support to see what is true, what is real. So I have to laugh about this word "teaching" because it implies that I know and you don't know.

Q - Do you have a personal spiritual practice?

N - Being with what is. Just allowing myself to be honest and truthful to what really arises and to be with that. If you mean like a practice of sitting formally for meditation, I don't. If it means spending time with myself deeply, yes. But it's not a formal practice.

Q - I'll assume that sometimes those who you interact with come to you with questions of a practical nature, about, say, money or sensuality or relationships. Can you describe how you work with issues like those?

N - It depends. Sometimes I'll answer these questions if they are relevant to what they are going through. Sometimes these questions do have relevance. But most of the time my job is to just point people to what is really going on. My favorite question these days is to ask, "What is really going on?" Staying with that resolves all of these other issues. That's what really does it.

And yet, sometimes these questions are relevant to the process of discrimination. Sometimes it's important to answer these questions. Who knows how it works?

My general work is to point people toward what is really happening with them because that's where it starts. If you can be with that, then everything else just opens. Then often the questions we usually have about money or diet or whatever are just a result of something else. There's something else going on that we're not dealing with, or not being with. And when we be with it then we suddenly realize, "Ahhh, that's how it is." Everything falls into place. If there's no space for things to fall into, then that's very difficult. And we make that space by being with what is. That's what creates space. Then everything can fall into it, you know?

If we do not create this space, then we start dealing with questions such as money, relationships or diet. But this is all surface. It doesn't address the issue.

Q - Some people these days have a sense that we are engaged in a kind of global shift in consciousness, and that if this is true that this shift is important or even essential to us as a race of beings? Do you have an opinion about this?

N - It seems true that there is a change, but I don't have an opinion about it. I don't know about it. Because when I look all I see is the Self. All I see is consciousness in different forms knowing Itself, not knowing Itself or thinking that It knows Itself.

Q - This book will be read partly by people who may have a sense of Awakening in their own lives and partly by those who may just have a curious interest in the topic. This is your opportunity to speak directly to them. What would you like to say to these readers?

N - I would say be absolutely truthful and honest with yourself. If you think you know something, throw it out. Just be totally honest with your heart. That's what really matters. Reading books, you know, doesn't do it. [Loud laughter] There is such a tendency to pick things up. We often reach out for a book when we are in confusion, when we don't know what's going on. And for us to know what's going on is so much more precious than to know what someone else knows about it. Because then we just adapt everything.

Be honest with what you really know. Be really truthful. In the heart, we all know the truth. It's not something that is just for a few chosen ones. So be honest with yourself about that.

Biography

Neelam was born and raised in Wroclaw, Poland. It was a strong interest and passion for Tai Chi that took her to Germany and then to America to continue her studies. It was in America that she came into contact with the writings of Ramana Maharshi and other spiritual teachers, and her search to reconnect with the truth and reality that she saw in these teachings began.

In this search she had many profound experiences and insights that some wanted to term awakenings, but she knew that there was still more to be known and found. It was in seeing a picture of H.W.L. Poonja, also known as Papaji, in Gangaji's Satsang that she recognized what that more was: her Master. She traveled to meet Papaji in 1994 and it was in early 1995 during a period of deeper surrender to him and the truth that he embodied—that she realized the truth of who she was. In 1996 a new phase in Neelam's life started as she began with Papaji's blessings to give Satsang and to share her realization with those around her. This brought her to travel throughout much of the United States and to different places around the globe and to look deeply at her own self and at the problems and struggles of the modern seeker. In late 1998 Neelam's reflections brought about a period of introspection and change—from extensive travel and bigger and bigger meetings or Satsangs—to a working with people in smaller environments and allowing time for a more complete integration of truth into her self and those who came to her. Over time she saw that it was not only so important for one to know oneself deeply, but also to allow one's deepest knowing and realization to touch all corners of our being and all the different parts of our lives. Her manner of sharing her self addresses this and encourages all that come to meet with her to bring self-honesty, tenderness, and a deep love of truth to oneself and all that surrounds us.

Neelam now lives with her intimate partner just outside of Ojai, California and continues to share of her self and what she knows to be true in a variety of formats ranging from public satsang meetings, to private individual work and group meetings, to weekend intensives and 4 or 5 day long silent retreats.

To contact Neelam, or find out about her schedule, more information is available at:

Fire of Truth
451 Skyhigh Drive
Ventura, CA. 93001
805-649-2272
or with e-mail at
Fireoftruth@compuserve.com
and on the web at
http:// www.neelam.org

Reverend Michael Beckwith, D.D.

Interviewed in his office at
the Agape International Spiritual Center
Culver City, California
July 23, 2001

One of the discoveries I made while compiling this book was that some interviews would be attained easily and some would be more difficult. Over the months, I came to realize that my job was to make the requests, do the follow-up work, and ultimately just relax into the knowledge that those who were meant to appear in these pages would.

I first contacted the Agape International Center of Truth on recommendation from our dear friend Coco. She raved about Reverend Michael, telling me that he is a truly inspired man through whom Truth just pours when he speaks. So, it was with great anticipation that I contacted the Center, which is located just a mile or so from our home here in Los Angeles. Rev. Michael was among the first invited to appear in these pages. But the process of getting him to the interview table was not to be as simple as I had imagined. My call was referred to one of the organization's management people. The initial request was answered with a very cordial but rather disappointing, "We're not sure he can do it. He's very busy and about to leave on his honeymoon trip." I patiently described the scope of the project and asked for the request to be delivered directly to Rev. Michael for a decision.

A few days later I got a phone call from the same lovely woman I had originally spoken with, saying that he would do the interview, but only via e-mail. Now, I had by this point become accustomed to agreeing to phone interviews when it was not possible to meet face-to-face. But I had to ask myself whether I wanted to "break the mold" of the spoken interview and accept Rev. Michael's invitation to allow a pre-prepared written set of responses in the book. To me this was a rather serious issue because I feel a personal sense of responsibility to you, the reader. You and I have a contract within these pages, and I wanted to be certain that I held up my end of the bargain. After all, you didn't pick up this book to read essays, did you?

133

So after some inner wrangling, I made a decision. What came to me was that I would take Rev. Michael up on his generous offer to contribute, but that I would inform you in this preface that the interview was conducted via e-mailed response. This way we could all benefit from the man's wisdom while keeping the integrity of the process intact. So I e-mailed the questions to his assistant. A number of months passed and I got no word back from the Agape office and my deadline was rapidly approaching. After placing a few more calls to the Center, I was delighted to receive an invitation to personally meet with Rev. Michael after all.

As with so many aspects of this book (and life itself, for that matter), I was taught yet another valuable lesson. After all my concerns about whether "to e-mail or not to e-mail," when I finally just relaxed into the reality of "what is" in the situation, the best possible outcome occurred.

I really enjoyed Rev. Michael's company and was thrilled with the gentle power with which he threw himself into the interview. His presence, his clear understanding of Truth and his dynamic descriptions of the spiritual process are just a few of the many reasons why Agape is one of the world's leading transdenominational spiritual centers.

So, to close this Introduction I will say that I found Michael Beckwith to be a most fascinating man who offers us a most profound gift. To quote one statement of his deep vision from the Center's literature:

"We live in a supportive universe governed by universal spiritual principles created to liberate us from the false belief that we are limited by anything outside of ourselves; that freedom is within; that enlightenment is assured; that it is possible to reveal heaven on earth."

I fully agree. I share his vision. And I invite you to do the same.

[Editor's Note: All of the participants in the book were offered the right to approve their final interview and most did edit to some degree. In fairness to the reader, it should be noted that the interview you are about to read was significantly edited by Rev. Michael. I do not see this as a problem, in that it is the overall wisdom being exchanged that should count for the most. But I report this so that you will know that this interview may not read with quite the same tone of conversationality as the others. At the end of the day, however, regardless of format, Truth just Is.]

Q: In your opinion or experience, is there a reality that might be called Awakening, Enlightenment, Liberation or spiritual freedom?

MB: Ha! I like beginning with a question that requires a sense of humor, where you just can't take yourself too seriously in the face of the paradoxically serious! In truth, silence would provide the best answer to this perennial question, because enlightenment begins where the mind stops its insidious demand to conceptualize and categorize that which is in and of itself indefinable and intangible.

You see, generally speaking, individuals live from four levels: self-awareness, awareness of other, environmental and religious. Self-awareness, or self-consciousness, is the realm of attachment to one's own feelings, thinking, personal history and experience. Awareness of other expands consciousness into the beginnings of unselfishness and compassion through interactive roles as mother, father, beloved, child and friend. Beyond the periphery of "me and mine" is relationship to the physical environment, our ecological relationship to Mother Earth. Our innate awareness of "I am more than this" pulls us to unravel the mystery of our existence and to begin thinking about God. But none of these individual or combined awarenesses—is there a plural for awareness?—usher us into that state we call enlightenment, living as a spiritually liberated being while encased in the fleshly garb of an individualized soul on the three-dimensional plane.

And here is where the sense of humor comes in: it is much easier to define what enlightenment is *not*! The tongue cannot speak it, the eyes cannot see it. And yet how natural and appropriate it is for us to aspire not only to define enlightenment, but *to dare to attain it.* So, in my current state of spiritual development, my abridged definition of enlightenment is: that state of consciousness wherein an individual consciously realizes an atonement with an Eternal Presence.

In the human experience there does appear to be a setting-out and a "reaching the goal" of enlightenment. Referring back to the "I am more than this" sense of identity, this stirs up awareness of our immortal nature. Who among us truthfully believes that we are going to die—only other people die! The soul already knows that it is immortal, and, try as it may, the mind cannot out-argue the soul's inherent recognition of its immortality That is our relationship to that within us that was never born and will never die, that "I Am that I Am" of the Christian *Bible* and "Thou Art That" of the Hindu *Vedas.* A step toward enlightenment occurs when this pronouncement rumbles through consciousness and there is an inward response of "yes!" So, to answer this aspect of your question, individuals who align themselves with the reality of existence—whether incrementally or instantaneously—it is they who go beyond living in the limitations of the interactive four levels of relationship to self, other, environment or religion and begin to plumb the eternal, universal verities of authentic spirituality.

Q: In your personal experience, did enlightenment happen at a particular moment, through a particular event? Or did it take place gradually?

MB: Ah, a trick question! You know why? Because until one is enlightened there is no knowing exactly its cause or process! Is it the identity with a personal self—the "Michaelness" of me—who chose to undertake a spiritual quest and *gradually* woke up to the true Self? Or, is it what Shankara's *Advaita* philosophy of nondualism teaches, that separating the Real from the unreal gives instantaneous liberation? Either way, we who consider ourselves as being "on the path to enlightenment" like to think that our commitment to wake up has brought at least some degree of wakefulness, don't we? But, honestly, all I can describe for you is my actual process. You know that old cliché, "It takes one to know one?" There's a great ring of truth to that when it comes to enlightenment because it takes an enlightened being to know an enlightened being. Then, no words are necessary. The Awakened One silently bows to the Awakened One.

I am using words today, with you, and as a spiritual teacher I depend upon words to convey the truth teachings of the New Thought-Ancient Wisdom tradition. Though there are spans of time living in transcendental reality, certainly I am aware that there are yet deeper levels of awakening to attain. Wouldn't it be the height of spiritual arrogance to place a limitation on that which is Limitless? So, now that I have provided a caveat, I'm comfortable revealing something about the staggering grace that continues to guide my pattern of unfoldment.

About twenty-five years ago, when I was a student at USC majoring in psychobiology, there began a series of inner experiences that my text book studies—and self-diagnosis—defined as pathological. I'm relieved to report that since then I've learned that the line between mysticism and madness can be quite thin! But for the year-and-a-half that I was doing astral travel and having telepathic experiences, it was pretty disconcerting! I was simultaneously experiencing an existential dread about life in general and particularly *my* life. There was also this recurring dream of being chased by three men who eventually caught me and drove a dagger into my heart. The dream-pain felt so excruciatingly real. Finally, I screamed and died. When I awoke, nothing in my life was as I had known it. I was drenched in an intoxicating Divine Love accompanied by an unquenchable thirst to understand what just hit me, which led me to a spiritual reader who described in minute detail the life and spiritual practices that are my purpose for being today.

Q: Do you have an experience of growing, maturing or evolving in this process?

MB: No matter what our level of wakefulness, there is always a more expansive Self to be realized. After all, it is really the Infinite realizing its own true, limitless nature in and through individualized incarnation. God's got game! And it is our great privilege to play our part on the game floor of creation. In my acknowledgment that I am awakening, I am simply accessing dimensions of my own true nature, integrating them and expressing them. The difference between my beginner's spirituality of 1975 and today is that I no longer personalize it; I now witness it. Integration has evolved spiritual backbone in my spiritual practices. There are times when I have thought, "Oh, this is *it*!" Almost simultaneously, the rug is pulled out from under my arrogant claim and I accept that growth is limitless!

Q: Is there a sense that you are involved with something that might be seen as different from "ordinary" human experience?

MB: Well, maybe "extra-ordinary" is the best way of describing it. Spiritual awareness is ordinary from the perspective that it is our true nature. But as a collective agreement, humankind has accepted the hypnotic or dream-state of separation from the Source, the illusion of having to go through a "waking up" process to reach enlightenment. There appear to be levels of wakefulness, so you could say that there are states of consciousness that are sub-ordinary, ordinary and extra-ordinary—again it goes on *ad infinitum*. Even as evidence mounts that the collective consciousness is evolving, this does not diminish the ecstasy of what appears to be an awakening process. To me, it is a precious mystery filled with awesome tenderness and fierceness. So when I experience something extra-ordinary—beyond the empirical evidence provided by the five senses—I am grateful that once again the Infinite Absolute has revealed that the invisible is more real than the visible, and that even the visible is this Energetic Stuff condensed into form.

Q: Do you perceive anything that might be described as "evil" or negative energies in the world?

MB: For me there is one word that sums up the whole theme of good versus evil: ignorance. Ignorance of the Infinite Presence that pervades all that there is. It is infinite and does not contradict its own nature. There cannot be any person, place or thing outside of the infinite. Not realizing our own true nature, we cut ourselves off from this Infinite Intelligence, Infinite Divine Love, this causes a variety of forms of suffering. When an individual perceives that they are cut off from the Source of Life, these thoughts are forms of energy. Eventually, energy condenses into form—thoughts become things, self-created circumstances and so on. From this comes a conviction that evil or negativity has a separate life of its own and a whole industry builds up around it! This is not to deny the appearance of negative phenomena that occur in our world—this is real enough to persons who suffer. Nor does it permit us to be callous about relieving the causes of suffering in this world. But the greatest gift we can give to another is to offer practices that bring about spiritual wakefulness, because it is through meditation and prayer that an individual wakes up to their own true nature. Then it is understood that there is nothing more powerful than the Eternal Presence in which we live, move and have our being.

Q: What is your experience of thought, sensation and emotion?

MB: Many people are convinced that emotions and sensations precede thoughts, and because of this they rely heavily on their influence in forming conclusions about themselves, others and life in general. My own practices have revealed that thought precedes sensations and emotions. Emotion is a reaction to perception and sensations are reactions to input of the five senses. Awareness is a "place" continuously bombarded by every form of input, including that of the collective consciousness of our entire universe with its prejudices, preconceived notions, definitions of reality, truth, and so on. Those perceptions that stick to us—that we grasp onto—become the contents of our awareness and describe the quality of our consciousness. To me, the reality is that through meditation and prayer the cultivation of an awareness of universal spiritual laws underpinning the universe becomes the touchstone of choice—responses to outer and inner stimuli. In other words, there comes an alignment with an intuitive knowing that causes emotions and sensations to express a passionate compassion, loving-kindness, wisdom—all the higher faculties of our soul-nature.

The existence of the Godhead is proclaimed in and through every particle of creation. This is reality. Of course then there is thought *about* reality. Most people don't experience reality; they experience their opinion about reality. And then they get mad at a God they don't even believe in! The whole point of spiritual practice is to develop a direct communion with the One Reality that ultimately frees us from all false belief in an existence separate from our own God-self.

Q: Did you or do you have a teacher?

MB: There have been many great souls who have influenced and continue to grace my spiritual path. At a young age I was inwardly guided to understand that I was to learn from the inner teacher, and yet to remain open and receptive to all true teachers, whether they were in a physical body or not. But it wasn't my destiny to surrender my life to one teacher or guru in particular. In my twenties, for about seven years I immersed myself in the teachings of East and West. I was blessed to experience s*atsanga*—spiritual fellowship—with many great ones. I used to travel to Ojai in the '70's and listen to Krishnamurti. I developed great love and respect for Paramahansa Yogananda and his path of Self-Realization Fellowship. The Sufi master Inyat Hazrat Khan deeply affected me. The spiritual brilliance of Sri Aurobindo I found to be a very expanding experience, including his influence on Dr. Ernest Holmes, through whose Consciousness Studies School of Ministry I eventually became an ordained minister. Dr. Daniel Morgan, founder of the Guidance Church of Religious Science, gave me a strong foundation in Western metaphysics. George Washington Carver, Walter Russell, Joel Goldsmith, Jesus the Christ, Emerson, philosophers and the Kemetic teachings have all contributed and enriched my spiritual life and practices.

A New Thought minister named Homer Johnson—he made his transition in 1983—taught me the meaning of humility, love and compassion. For hours I would sit with him, drenched in the power of his prayer to a most available and responsive Infinite Presence. While at Morehouse College, I was privileged to be introduced to Dr. Howard Thurman, a great theologian and teacher.

Each person's life has its own unique pattern of spiritual unfoldment. Mine has included Sufi, Christian, Hindu, Buddhist, African Shamanism, Ancient Wisdom and New Thought traditions, as well as philosophy, science and social activism. You know, $2 + 2 = 4$ whether you are in China, Africa or the United States. So whether you hear truth from a Sufi master, a Hindu guru, a Buddhist master or a Christian mystic, if they have gone beyond the three-dimensional experience and realized the Eternal Presence, it's going to contain the same universal experience of one who has touched the hem of the garment of Truth.

Q: Do you have a personal spiritual practice?

MB: Every morning and evening I meditate and pray, and throughout the day I am conscious of being enveloped in a Presence that causes me to remain in a continual state of communion with love, joy and peace—the qualities of this Presence in my very soul. I work out each morning to keep the body temple fit and follow a predominantly vegetarian diet—without being a fanatic—because of the vibrational differences within foods. Service is my work, both in my spiritual community and the larger global community. About twice a year, I go on a silent retreat which assists in clearing out the dust and grit of the journey that we don't always notice is present in consciousness. But my mainstay is meditation; it's just something I do all the time. You know what they say, "Don't leave home without it."

Q: It is said by some people that we as a species are in the midst of a shift in consciousness. Some even say that such a shift is very significant in the evolution of mankind. What is your opinion about this?

MB: I'm glad you asked, because this is something I'm really passionate about! I am often privileged to sit among visionaries whose inward sight sees beyond the world of external appearances, and they are shouting from the rooftops that a new world is emerging! The mass media camouflage this evolutionary breakthrough because their radar picks up only the chaos, the static within this process, not the music of it! I strongly sense strands of an emerging world culture united on an ethical basis of humankind's highest development spiritually, philosophically, educationally, scientifically and socially.

Earlier radical visionaries have predicted such a world. In fact, some have told us of times in the earth's history where such cultures have already existed. We also have examples of communes and co-ops that are forming based on the idealism of cooperation. I see this as a trend that recognizes and appreciates what indigenous cultures have practiced for a long time. You might call it an "all for one and one for all" type of mentality, or in modern philosopohical parlance, the "the highest good of the whole" that becomes the foundation for ethics, standards, values and principles that determine decision making, law-making, social structure and so on. In this kind of society every individual is honored and encouraged to contribute their unique gifts to the community. With what some call our progressive technological advances, this shift is not coming a moment too soon because our high tech/low touch society has created tremendous pollution, a buildup of nuclear armaments beyond what we will ever use, and an insatiable culture of materialism.

Just earlier this month I was privileged to facilitate the Synthesis Dialogues with His Holiness the Dalai Lama and individuals who are spiritually motivated social activists. Granted, each of us has our roles to play—you're writing this important book and I'm being interviewed for it—we get to make a contribution in stirring up the consciousness of its readers, who ideally light a fire in others to awaken and contribute their gifts to the planet. But these individuals are placing their existence in conditions where they could lose their lives for the sake of saving others, the planet and so on. What gives them the courage? A genuine love of humankind, plain and simple. This fuels their vision of world peace and causes us to see through their radical actions that we must never give up living our true natures of goodness, peace, love, joy and bliss. We can bring "heaven on earth" by experiencing it within our own beings right where we are, *now!*

So I am optimistic. I actually see emerging what Dr. Martin Luther King Jr. called the "beloved community" in the midst of the seeming chaos.

Q: For those readers of this book who may sense some form of awakening or spiritual progression in their lives or at least have interest in the topic, what would you like to say to them?

MB: For the neophyte or experienced traveler on the spiritual path what is to be understood is that That which is fueling the hunger for Truth is the Eternal Truth itself residing in every soul. Open the heart in complete trust so that Divine Guidance may illuminate your walk to spiritual awakening. Dimensions of yourself will be revealed that you cannot now imagine exist. Familiarize yourself with the experiences of those who have traveled the path to enlightenment, including the many dark nights of the soul they faced with great spiritual courage and backbone. Let them be a light unto your own unique pattern of unfoldment. Each soul has a unique romance with the Infinite, so trust where your inner spirit is leading you because it will always be closer and closer to your authentic being.

Biography

Visionary Founder and Spiritual Director of one of the world's largest and most rapidly expanding transdenominational communities in the New Thought-Ancient Wisdom tradition, Rev. Dr. Beckwith is more than a spiritual teacher to 8,000 local members, affiliate members and thousands of friends worldwide—he is a transformational phenomenon! His is a spiritually passionate voice, announcing to all beings that they are beloved and essential emanations of the Universe.

In the 1970's Dr. Beckwith began a contemplative journey that, along with extended periods of meditation, included seven years of study embracing the major religions of East and West. In 1986, Dr. Beckwith's inner vision revealed a world united on an ethical basis of humankind's highest development spiritually, philosophically, educationally, scientifically and socially. Today, Dr. Beckwith oversees a network of twenty ministries and outreach programs. His renown as a harbinger of the world's quest for peace has drawn into his visionary orbit individuals whose names are synonymous with this goal. Arun Gandhi, grandson of Mohandas K. Gandhi, shares with Dr. Beckwith the national co-directorship of "A Season for Nonviolence," an organization that promotes and teaches the principles of nonviolence embodied by the great Mahatma Gandhi and Dr. Martin Luther King, Jr. A recipient of many humanitarian awards, in January 2000 he and his party received a dignitarial welcome from India's government with a luncheon held in honor of his contribution to revitalizing the Gandhian principles in the West. Along with other of the nation's stewards, he shares the distinction of being a founding member of the Association for Global New Thought, convening organization of the Synthesis Dialogues with His Holiness the Dalai Lama in Dharamsala, India, and this year in Trent, Italy.

In addition to being a father of two magnificent adults, Dr. Beckwith is a grandfather of two treasured grandsons. His creative achievements include authorship of *40 Day Mind Fast Soul Feast*, available at Agape's Quiet Mind Bookstore located in Culver City, California. In December, 2000, Dr. Michael Beckwith married Dr. Rickie Byars-Beckwith, Music Director of the Agape International Choir, and co-author with him of the songs sung by the Choir.

If you would like to contact Rev. Michael Beckwith, you can reach him at:

Agape International Center of Truth
5700 Buckingham Parkway
Culver City, CA 90230
Phone: (310) 348-1250
Fax: (310) 348-1255

Matthew Fox

Interviewed by phone from Oakland, California
July 24, 2001

The discussion you are about to read was the very last interview I con-ducted before handing this book over to the publishers. It—along with this preface—was completed just a few days before my deadline.

Matthew Fox had been on my "A List" of possible guests from the begin-ning of the project, which started with the Saniel Bonder interview some fif-teen months earlier. It was just difficult to get Matthew to sit still long enough to talk to him.

This in no way surprised me. After all, I knew that I was seeking to talk with a man who is among the most significant and important "spiritual out-laws" of our time. And he's also an incredibly busy fellow!

In a single lifetime he's managed to be dismissed by the Pope from his position as a Dominican monk and be silenced by the Vatican for his won-derfully progressive views on spiritual issues. He's authored more than 24 books on an amazingly wide variety of spiritually-significant topics and is the founder and president of the world-renowned University of Creation Spirituality in Oakland, California. He's been the recipient of numerous awards for his contributions to the spiritual well-being of the world, includ-ing the Courage of Conscience Award which had previously been given to the Dalai Lama, Mother Theresa, Rosa Parks and others.

So, I persisted diligently in working through the process of getting Matthew's staff to agree to this conversation, right down to the last minute before the book was due to go to press. And I am so happy that I did!

When I finally found myself ringing his number he was still busy! The first words that he said to me were, "Can you hold on for just a minute? I have my publisher on the other line discussing the deadline for my next book." I had to laugh.

I found myself liking this man immensely from the very beginning of the conversation. He is relaxed and humorous, even while discussing issues of

143

very serious impact, as you will see. It wasn't very long into the conversation before I began to realize that Matthew's contribution to this book would make the wait well worth it. His leadership role in reviving the awareness of the Western mystic tradition represents an essential "rounding out" of the collection of interviews presented here. And his respect for (and propagation of) the wisdom of indigenous peoples adds another crucial flavor.

I also greatly appreciated a critical point which Matthew raises in this discussion. He wisely suggests that the deeply negative occurrences of life— as well as the bliss, the happiness and the positive events—can be profoundly transformative. I find this to be a critical perspective, especially for those of us who come primarily from the Eastern tradition. All too often we tend to concentrate on the Light, forgetting that our shadow-self can play an equally-important role in revealing Truth to us.

In this book I have been very careful not to "play favorites" or suggest that one guest's contribution is more important than another's. Each brings a unique view of wisdom and each is as powerful as the next. But I offer this advice before you begin reading: take this man's words very *seriously! There is a lot to absorb in the next several pages especially if you are at all interested in the serious impact that Western mysticism has had on our lives and on our culture.*

But be forewarned. Matthew Fox also shares with us a note of most sober alarm. He reminds us that the ecological clock is ticking; that mankind as a species is nearing the end of our ability to continue to survive as a race unless we make some serious personal/spiritual/political changes—now! This call to personal responsibility is not one of the cheery aspects of Awakening. But it comes with the territory and Matthew makes it very clear that we need to accept this duty earnestly and proactively. And I love him for that important admonition.

One last word about my own behavior in this interview. Perhaps it was the ebullience of knowing that this book was headed to press within days; maybe it was just that I shared so many "Ah, yes!" moments with the guest. I don't know. But I allowed myself to get more verbally involved with this interview than in any other. You'll notice that I bantered more with Dr. Fox than in any of the other conversations. It felt natural and spontaneous, so I did it and allowed it to survive the editing process. I trust that you'll grant me this indulgence in the final interview of a long project. But mostly, I hope that you enjoy the interview. So, off we go...

Q - In your experience, is there such a reality as Awakening, Enlightenment, Liberation or spiritual freedom?

MF - Well, of course. I think we have many awakenings. In the Christian tradition I think the most common word would be *metanoia*, or transformation. It's also sometimes called conversion, but that's been sucked in by proselytizing compulsions. Although the whole idea of being "born again" has been distorted by fundamentalism, the idea is that birth happens many times in a lifetime. The word that I like the best is from my friend Meister Eckhart, the great 14th century mystic and heretic, who used the word "breakthrough." In fact, he invented the word breakthrough in German. This word is a good parallel to the word *satori* in the Buddhist tradition.

And I think we have many breakthroughs. Eckhart says that "for the person who is awake, breakthrough does not happen once a year, once a month, once a week, once a day, but many times a day." And I think that is very beautiful and very real. It can happen with birds singing, it can happen in a conversation, it can happen with the news of the death of someone we love, or the news of the birth of someone we love. It can happen in a lecture or while reading a book. It can happen running, it can happen meditating. So I very much subscribe to the word *breakthrough* to name all of that. It's a common reality, of course, and possible for all of us.

Q - This breakthrough as you describe it...did it seem to happen in a particular moment, or as a sort of a process over a period of time?

MF - I would say it happened both as a process and with breakthrough moments. I definitely am in the school of process. I saw a tee shirt once that said. "I've been born again...and again...and again...and again..." That's me. So, I can think about walking in the woods when I was a child or reading Tolstoy's *War and Peace* when I was in junior high school. I told a friend that it blew my soul wide open.

That's the reason I went to the Dominican order—to explore what happened in my soul, if you will. I think that our breakthroughs often follow a break*down*. Alcoholics Anonymous is a good example of that. Many people would say that their first spiritual experience was when they broke down through alcoholism or divorce or some other negative experience. I think that having polio when I was twelve was a breakthrough in the form of a breakdown. For me, losing my legs was a breakthrough. It turned out to be temporary, but no one could tell that at the time. I met a very contemplative monk who would visit me in the hospital and he showed me another path to life which I did not know about at that time.

And then there's study. Study has always been a breakthrough experience for me. I believe that study is one of the yogas, one of the spiritual disciplines. I know that is true in the Jewish tradition. Studying *torah* is a prayer. And it can happen in worship, art, music and in teaching and in writing books. Oh my goodness, I get very high writing books. There are many breakthroughs. So, the answer is yes to all of the above!

Q - So I get the sense that you feel that there is a deepening or evolving of this over time.

MF - Oh, absolutely. If we weren't evolving and deepening, we wouldn't be part of the universe, which is constantly evolving and deepening. I think that there's a scary thing about fundamentalism in all of its forms—it freezes people. And not just the religious forms do this, but the whole state of fear and control that tempts us at times. Facism freezes our souls. It's scary because it really aborts the evolution of our souls, and therefore the evolution that we can make to the community and, indeed, the evolution of the universe. I think that the new creation story from science really awakens our consciousness about how every being—*every* being—is involved in evolving.

This fits very well with, again, Meister Eckhart's theology that God, too, is evolving. Eckhart says, "God becomes as creatures become." So that as we evolve, you might say that the faces of divinity become more diverse and grow. And as the universe grows—and it is growing—it's like divinity's "belly" is growing since the universe is God's womb. So there's evolution going on everywhere! Why wouldn't it go on in our souls? Eckhart has a great line about this. He says, "God is delighted to watch the soul enlarge." And that says it all. We are here to enlarge our souls, to grow our souls. And of course, that's evolutionary.

Q - So would you say, then, that you notice anything that's in any way different or distinct from so-called "ordinary" human experience?

MF - Well, of course. First of all, I really want to stress something that I alluded to earlier. And that is that breakdowns are part of the process. It's what the mystics call the *via negativa*. So, in grief work, for example, Joanna Macy says that when the heart breaks the universe can pour through. I also alluded to AA, as another example of the fact that we have to bring in the dark night of the soul, the *via negativa*, and realize that this too is part of the breakthrough process although it doesn't always feel like it or look like it. The darkness we enter, the despair, the shadow are all a deep part of the process. We don't want to confuse people and say that it's just a straight path of light because it by no means is. And I just want to put that on the table.

Q - Thank you.

MF - But getting back to your question, even our grief work goes to extraordinary levels. For example, Mechtild of Magdeburg, a 13th century mystic says, "There are times when the lantern goes out. And the memory of the lantern goes out, and even the memory of the beauty of the lantern goes out." I mean, it can really get dark. But this is part of the journey. And it can be amazing and extraordinary to people—the experience of nothingness, for example. But those are very real experiences, they are part of the journey. Any healthy tradition will help us to name it and to find practices to allow us to stay there.

I happen to think that a big reason why our culture at its ordinary level is so set up for addiction—whether it's drugs, alcohol, shopping, or anything else—is that we've not been told exactly what you're asking. We haven't been told that ordinary people have extraordinary experiences. And in the *via negativa*, there are extraordinary experiences of bottoming out.

The same is true with joy and ecstasy! We're not prepared for joy in our culture! [Laughter]. We're lucky if we can buy some momentary happiness. So, at both ends of the spectrum—the *via positiva* (the joy) and the *via negativa* (the suffering, the emptiness and darkness)—there are extraordinary experiences which are available to ordinary people, to everybody. And we must let them know that and give them tools by which to endure both the joy and the suffering. Otherwise, we settle for a really mediocre life, where religion takes over instead of true spirituality.

Q - I'm so thrilled to hear this from you, Matthew. It is true that "I am That" is a great realization. But, then the baby starts crying or the boss is yelling at you. In that moment it can feel like, "I realize that I am That...so what?" We need to learn how to live an honorable life as That in the middle of a world where there are murders and rapes.

MF - And bills to pay! [Laughter]

Q - Yes! Thank you. So, how are things like thought and emotion experienced by you?

MF - Well, I welcome them as the influx of the creative spirit and the angels who ride on the highways of intuition. Especially at night when dreaming, I often wake up with interesting thoughts, and I don't take credit for them. I think they come from the powers of the universe including angels, literally—spirit powers. And they make life interesting. I couldn't get along without them! They strengthen us and they challenge us and they heal us. So I think it's about having an open heart and mind to listen for revelation, if you will, or for the communication that comes our way.

It's not unlike the breakthrough we were talking about earlier, it can happen day or night. It can happen in our sleep or when we wake up. It can happen when we encounter someone during the day. It can happen when we are at work ourselves. We can see all of this as the creative process, and for me the creative process is God trying to rush through us. Eckhart has a beautiful sermon on the Holy Spirit as a "rushing river" and it's all about creativity, about how this river brings rejoicing to the soul and to the community. He bases it on a Psalm which says that spirit is a river that runs through the soul or something like that.

I find this to be a very real experience and I think that our culture is very reticent to honor the power of creativity that is everywhere. Take, for example, this so-called debate going on in this country about education. All the politicians are talking about is how many exams the schools should give to the kids. I *never* hear the word creativity! I think that if we would set our sights on reinventing education by teaching creativity and learning the discipline that goes with it, that would be the way to do it. Creativity is what makes our species so unique, so powerful and so dangerous! Why wouldn't we zero in on that?

So our honoring of the power which is creativity is grossly underdone. I think all these forces you mention—thought, emotion, etc.—are the power of creativity trying to wake us up. There is a time for thought and (as in meditation) a time for no-thought. And this dance is very important. But it doesn't mean putting down thought.

Q - Did you have a teacher?

MF - Yes. I've been trying to recover this lineage called "Creation Spirituality" which is a mystical tradition of the West. It comes through the wisdom literature of the Hebrew Bible, for example, the prophets and also of Jesus who is now acknowledged by the greatest scholars as coming from the wisdom tradition. It also comes through in the works of Hildegard of Bingen, Thomas Aquinas, Francis of Assisi, Teilhard de Chardin and others in our century, for sure. But I was alerted to this tradition by Pere Chenu, a wonderful French Dominican theologian who I studied with in Paris in the late '60's. He was the one who named the Creation Tradition for me, so he was my mentor. He was forbidden to publish by Pope Pius XII for twelve years, but he was a wonderful being and a great soul.

This is the lineage of the historical Jesus, but also of the cosmic Christ, and it's a very ecumenical tradition. Meister Eckhart has been more roundly approved of by Hindu and Buddhist scholars than by Christian ones. Even Aquinas has passages that are very *zen*, about letting go of mind and so forth. There are amazing correspondences and bridges. Once you get into the deep mystics of any tradition you find them talking a common language.

Q - Including physicists!

MF - Absolutely. I work a lot with scientists of many types, not just physicists. For example, Rupert Sheldrake the British biologist and I wrote a book together on angels and another called *Natural Grace*. My latest book *One River, Many Wells* is about the idea that when you go down into your well—whether it be a Buddhist well, a Jewish well, a Christian well—if you go deep enough you come to one river which is the river of Divine Wisdom. The river is not different, the wells are different. And we've often confused the well with the river and that is the beginning of religious wars and all sorts of nonsense.

Q - Do you teach?

MF - Oh yes. I started a university of spirituality, The University of Creation Spirituality here in downtown Oakland five years ago, and I teach both here and on the road. I teach at Hollyhock, an island off Canada and I'm going there in a few days to teach a course with Andrew Harvey. So, I teach on the road and I teach at our school.

Q - What do you teach?

MF - Well, Creation Spirituality is the oldest tradition in the bible and as I said, it's the tradition of both the historical Jesus and of the cosmic Christ and of the Celtic people who never lost the Cosmic Christ awareness in nature. It's the tradition of the greatest mystics of the West *and* of prophets struggling for social and eco-justice. It's the tradition within which our dialogues with science have always taken place. That's why Aquinas was condemned three times by the Church before he was canonized as a saint—because he was making use of Aristotle's work. In the 13th century Aristotle was the hot scientist of the time, his work coming in through Islam.

It's ecumenical. It's feminist, which is why it's been ignored and condemned so often by the Church because it honors the wisdom of Sophia (the feminine) and it honors the wisdom of women's experience. So, it's been a minority tradition in the West, often neglected or condemned, which is why I was beaten up by the Vatican. But because it's about cosmology it's about "original blessing" instead of "original sin" and it starts as the universe's blessing. It's not anthropocentric and so it very much feeds into a time like ours when ecology is the number one moral issue of our time. The survival of our species and so many others depends on the deepening of our spiritual practice and awareness in realizing that all beings are sacred and all of our relationships are sacred.

It also draws heavily on the indigenous wisdom. We're starting a program at our university that we're calling "Recovering the Indigenous Mind." It'll be run by an Oneida woman. It's very important that we honor and learn from the indigenous traditions which have been so beaten up over the last centuries both by modern philosophies and religious bigotry.

Q - Yes, and as a result we've lost the family, we've lost the tribe. To me, this is a core loss.

MF - Exactly. That's right. We've also lost our kinship to the earth and to the cosmos, which is "the big family."

Q - Many people report that there seems to be something like a "shift" taking place in Consciousness and that this shift may be of real importance to us as a race. Would you care to comment on this, Matthew?

MF - Oh definitely. I've been on the road for thirty years, but even ten years ago there was still a lot of resistance to all of this. I heard a lot of, "Yes, but...yes, but." But around ten years ago it seemed like the dam broke and there was a shift—a noticeable shift. People started to say, "Yes, and...yes, and!" They started to ask, "Where can this take us?"

And I've seen this, "Yes, and..." build in the last ten years. There's no question about it. Look at the bestsellers on the New York Times list and books about spirituality and spiritual practice are well-represented there. The very word "spirituality" used to be a word that Protestants could not deal with at all! I know when my first book came out there was a lot of static around that, but spirituality itself has kind of entered the mainstream.

But, there's a danger in that, too, in that there are plenty of whacko, superficial and oddball things floating around in the name of spirituality. So, it's a mixed blessing for spirituality to be entering the mainstream and we have to be very alert. But overall, it's not only a good thing, but a *necessary* thing. I don't think our species can survive at the rate we're going. We are not a sustainable species on our present path of behavior—period. There is no question about that. We are destroying the very nest in which we live. Therefore, we have to change. And how do humans change? Well, I don't think we can depend on governments to do the changing. I think we have to change spiritually and then take that *into* government, take it into our professions and our work world.

Our Doctorate of Ministry program here is just phenomenal. It's grown to four hundred students in just three years. It's the only program like it in the world and it's all about bringing spirituality into the work world. So we have engineers and business people, therapists, social workers, journalists, artists, clergy all getting their Doctor of Ministry degree because they feel this shift that you are asking about. They *know*!

They feel that in academia—their preparation to become attorneys, businesspeople, therapists or scientists—they had *no* training about spirituality in their profession. I hate to say it, but it's even true about most clergy as well.

So, they're making up for lost ground, if you will. And then they do what I call infiltration. They take their spirituality and the new cosmology into their professions and shake things up. And that's how we're going to change things!

Q - I think it may go the other way, as well. I know a number of therapists who report that once many of their clients get past the issues of immediate pain they are facing, they see that they are really seeking something deeper than what therapy can provide. So, I believe that the "calling" is actually coming from both directions.

MF - You bet. Spiritual direction is what a lot of people are really looking for. I know a therapist who tells me that whenever she first meets a client she gives them my book *Original Blessing* and that 90% of them don't come back! [Laughter] I'm not sure if I should take that as a compliment or not. But, it's her experience that what I call "toxic religion"—things like the issue of original sin—is eating away at people's self esteem. But once you can undo that, everything begins to flow again.

Q - How about you personally? Do you have a spiritual practice?

MF - Sure. I mean, I try to be alert as to what's working and what isn't. I'm a very busy guy but I usually do a five or ten-minute meditation in the morning when I get up. I do some yoga and then I try to find time during the day to walk, preferably by water if possible, to empty my mind that way. And during the day, with the work that I do—whether it's writing, lecturing or administering the university—I find it important to connect with the spiritual practice which is inherent in the work world because that's where we put so much of our energy.

So, I don't have a "packaged practice," you might say. But earlier we used that word "evolution" and I think that our methods evolve—*should* evolve—as our situation evolves. When I get out of being the president of a university, I'll be a much calmer person. So I'm sure that my spiritual practice will take on a much calmer hue.

We also do a lot of art as meditation in both the Masters and the Doctorate program and I practice what I preach. I love working with artists. It's a very important way for me to center.

Reading the mystics is also a very important part of my spiritual practice. It's one of the joys of my work that I get to read them and re-read them because I teach them and because I'm writing books and trying to put them into practice.

So I read Meister Eckhart, Thich Nat Hahn, Aquinas. I'm currently working on a book on John of the Cross—by the way, I recommend his poetry, not his commentaries! I think he did the commentaries just to keep the Inquisition off his back. So, stick with the poems! [Laughter] I've also done two or three books on Hildegard of Bingen. And the historical Jesus is worthy of our attention—the whole wisdom tradition. Today we're so blessed because we can draw on so many sources. I love reading the *Upanishads* and the *Vedas*, but we can draw on so many spiritual traditions, as long as we don't just stay on a superficial level. That's why it really helps to have a tradition like Creation Spirituality which allows us to go deeper into whatever you are reading. It's a methodology for reading deeply.

Q - I assume that in your position people often come to you with questions of a practical nature, perhaps regarding money, sensuality, relationships, etc. How do you approach serving them?

MF - Well, of course there's no one approach. It depends on the person. But I have to look at these things in my own life, too. The Lakota people talk about "all our relations." They say that all prayer is about becoming aware of and healing *all* of our relations, whether it's the relationship to our body, our food, who's making the food, who's selling the food, what's in the food. About two years ago, I found that I have diabetes and this has really awakened me because I read every package and bottle that I pick up to see the sugar content and it's shocking. For example, you order iced tea on an airplane thinking you're ordering something healthy for you, but it's got like fifty-nine grams of sugar in it, for God's sake!

The whole system of industrial capitalism is just pouring stuff into our bodies and into our minds through television and other ways. It's truly toxic and scary. So we have to be more and more alert on a daily basis and we have to love our bodies. Again, organized religion has not made that a priority! Our bodies are fourteen million years old. There's something sacred to cherish here.

And relationships—if I had a one-sentence formula for solving that one I'd be running the world [Laughter]. It's a great mystery. Obviously we are always dealing with divine powers and shadow powers whether we're dealing with our own souls or others. We have to be alert and, again, it's a creative process.

When I married Jerry Garcia and his wife I told them that marriage is not a noun, it's verb. Every day is an act of creativity between people. That's how we have to see it. And like any act of creativity, there's no insurance policy, no guarantee. But it's full of surprises, and that's the joy of it. I always encourage people to stay at it as long as they can.

Q - Well, Matthew, the final question is actually an opportunity for you to speak directly to the readers of the book. Some may have gotten the book because they are having breakthrough experiences in their own lives, others may just be curious about the topic. What would you say to them?

MF - Well, I'd ask them to listen to their hearts. And if the heart has been blessed with either a small opening or a big breakthrough, I'd ask them to realize that this is important work of the spirit that's coming upon them. And they want to pay attention to that and let the spirit through. That can mean, of course, developing meditation practices but it can also mean study and learning about traditions, especially their own tradition. A lot of Westerners think that they have to go East and that's because Western religion has often ignored spirituality. But I think as my work has demonstrated, we have great mystics from the West such as Hildegard of Bingen, Meister Eckhart, Nicholas of Cusa and others who come out of our own tradition but have the same impact, really, as many of the creative teachers of the East. I think that the East has kept to its practices better and so there are a lot of practices that we can invoke such as yoga, for example, and meditation and others.

Also, of course we can look to the indigenous wisdom. You know, Carl Jung once said that he never dealt with a North American at the level of spirituality when he didn't find an Indian inside. So, we're not just European-Americans, Asian-Americans, African-Americans. We're all native Americans in the sense that we're on their land and this is where their spirits were honored for centuries. So we can be open to that. Many people are very moved when they hear Native American drumming or experience dancing or enter a sweat lodge for the first time. So, we should not ignore the beautiful, powerful contribution of the indigenous wisdom.

Certainly, my writing and the writing of many others has been to recover the treasures of the Western mystical tradition and (especially in my most recent book) to put them into the same pool with the treasures of the Eastern traditions. I think that's where we have to be as a species today.

We can't be hiding behind our denominational boxes. It's too late for that. We need all the wisdom we can get. So, whenever there's an opening in our hearts and in our souls, that's wisdom trying to pour through, so let's give it some attention.

Biography

Matthew Fox, a postmodern theologian, has been an ordained priest since 1967. He holds Masters degrees in philosophy and theology from Aquinas Institute and a Doctorate in spirituality, *summa cum laude*, from the Institut Catholique de Paris.

Fox is president of the new University of Creation Spirituality and Co-director of the Naropa Oakland MLA in Oakland, California. Fox is author of 24 books, including the best-selling *Original Blessing, A Spirituality Named Compassion, Passion for Creation: The Earth-Honoring Spirituality of Meister Eckhart, The Reinvention of Work, Sins of the Spirit, Blessings of the Flesh* and *Natural Grace* (with Rupert Sheldrake).

In addition to his work as a writer and teacher in the San Francisco Bay Area, Fox is a lecturer whose travels throughout North America, Europe and Australia have brought his message of ecological and social justice, mysticism and blessing to eager and ever-growing audiences.

Fox received the 1994 New York Open Center Tenth Anniversary Award for Achievement in Creative Spirituality. In 1995 he was presented the Courage of Conscience Award by the Peace Abbey of Sherborn, Mass. Other recipients of this award include the Dalai Lama, Mother Theresa, Ernesto Cardenal, and Rosa Parks. In 1996 he received the Tikkun National Ethics Award in recognition of contributions made to the spiritual life of our society. Fox has twice received the Body Mind Spirit Award of Excellence for outstanding books in print: in 1996 for *The Reinvention of Work* and in 1997 for *Confessions: The Making of a Post-Denominational Priest*. In May 2000 he was awarded an Honorary Doctor of Letters degree from The University College of Cape Breton, Sidney, Nova Scotia, Canada.

In a review of his autobiography *Confessions: The Making of a Post-Denominational Priest* in the March 11, 1996, Publishers Weekly says, "This highly charged autobiography of a priestly life will stand as a lasting memorial to the difficulty of maintaining certain articles of faith and dogma at a time of shifting cultural paradigms. Fox's portrait of himself...is likely to become a classic."

Matthew Fox's latest book is *One River, Many Wells,* published by Jeremy Tarcher, Inc.

You can reach Matthew Fox in the following ways:

The University of Creation Spirituality & Naropa Oakland
2141 Broadway, Oakland, CA 94612
website: www.creationspirituality.com
email: ucs-naropa@csnet.org
Ph: 510-835-4827   Fax: 510-835-0564

Epilogue

As I mentioned in the very beginning of this book, we were halfway through the completed interviews before it dawned on me that the methodology would turn out to be so important. I understood from the beginning that the strategy of asking identical questions in each conversation would carry with it some uniqueness. But I could not know how profoundly meaningful this was to be. It took a comparison of the first several completed chapters for me to begin to sense the fullness of what was being revealed in this process.

Clearly, each guest expresses his or her version of Awakening (or Enlightenment, nirvana, satori, spiritual freedom, etc.) in a way unique to them. While we find general agreement among them, what seems equally striking to me are the differences that appear. It dawned on me that if we had elected to arrange this book by question, a different and rather startling view might have emerged. The variations in the way different body-mind organisms view this topic stands out more clearly. Appendix I demonstrates how my version of such a "cut and paste" might look. I encourage you to use this as a guide to do your own rearrangements, making use of the book as one might with a Seminar booklet.

For example, the very first question on the basic reality of Awakening was one that I thought would be rather uniform in response. But even this inquiry revealed a significantly wide range of responses.

So, what are we to make of this? We might tend to question whether these people are even talking about the same thing! Is there, in fact, *anything* that might be called a unified experience of Awakening or living as Awareness? As we ponder this, we get tantalizing tastes of a delicious subtlety that I could not have known would arise. We edge toward a mysterious Place which revealed itself during the creation of this book.

The answer to this dilemma of diversion came to me in the following statement:

Whatever is true about Awakening
must be true in this very moment,
and must be true universally.

In a nutshell, whatever the Divine may be, it *must* be infinite and eternal. In my first days in Catholic school I was taught that the catechism clearly describes God as infinite, eternal, almighty, all-knowing, all-seeing, all-present. Most religions from around the world and throughout the ages have put a strong emphasis on the fact that God exists as an infinite and eternal entity and is in some way knowable by man. I find this to be entirely significant.

If this is correct—if God is infinite and eternal—then God-nature *must* be present here and now! Simply by definition, the word "infinite" *must* include the very place where I sit. And it must include me—and you! We must, by our very nature, be absolutely *drenched in* and *dripping with* the Divine Being, or else God <u>cannot</u> be infinite!

The same is true if we consider the word "eternal." There can be no time, no generation, no moment, *no instant* that is somehow mysteriously removed from total God-ness! How could it be otherwise?

What audacity of thought or lunacy of intention could make us seem to exist *outside of* that which is infinite and eternal? Where within endless time and limitless space could God be hiding in order to somehow manage to avoid being present in us as we sit together in this blessed moment? Clearly, whatever God is, he/she/it exists everywhere and in every moment.

I'm reminded of a story from the life of H.W.L. Poonjaji (known affectionately as Papaji) who is mentioned in a number of interviews in this book. He had been the final living disciple of the great advaitin master Ramana Maharshi. Papaji had a period early in his life when he was "visited" with visions of Krishna. These appearances were apparently quite revelatory and, of course, emotionally stunning to the young Poonja. This was so much the case that when he eventually met Ramana, he was quick to regale the great Indian saint with prideful stories of his encounters with the Blue God.

Papaji later recounted that Ramana quizzed him deeply on these Divine meetings, and then finally asked, "So, tell me, is it true that Krishna would arrive, meet with you, and then go away?" When the younger man answered yes, Ramana softly replied, "Of what use is a God who comes and goes? Find out what remains."

So, as I was reading these interviews and pondering their shared meanings and the differences among them, a simple view of the Divine fell over me again. And in such a moment of relaxed acceptance, doubt is shredded like a kite in a hurricane.

These men and women are, indeed, unique. Each one sees with their own eyes, and speaks from their own place. Each, like a kettle, whistles the Awakened Song at his or her unique pitch. But each exists as a part of the whole, like a facet cut into a precious gem. Each is a unique expression of the vast, still Presence that we call God, the Divine, the Almighty and the thousand other names we sing as we contemplate the awe-some and paradoxical Divine Mystery that we call life.

This gracefully accounts for what appears to be the variable points of view among our guests in these pages. In allowing for (no, luxuriating in!) the truth that each and all are unique manifestations of a unified Divine Personality, we can *enjoy* the singular and collective beauty of the many flowers which make up the garden.

And, as we simply relax our tendency to separate and categorize, a fundamental and profound vision is made available to us. We see that there is a tremendous gift offered to us by our guests and their varied points of view. As we begin to enjoy (rather than be confused or bothered by) the wide spectrum of ideas offered, we may see that *our own* unique understanding of spiritual freedom is also welcome here! After all, if as mentioned earlier God is infinite and eternal, then at some root level of identity, *you too* are fully Divine.

At many points along the way in my spiritual development, I have been surprised (or even disillusioned) when I learned that one or another of my spiritual heroes was actually human, just like me! I suppose I really wanted to believe that there would come a time when I would be fundamentally different. I now realize that what I *really* wanted was to be somehow magically relieved of the pains and fears which are a necessary part of embodied existence. I wanted to believe that I could somehow avoid touching all the bases on my way to home plate. But now I realize—thank God—that human beings remain human beings, imperfections and all.

Now, it's true that the recognition of spiritual freedom within my own being did, in fact, bring about some measure of radical growth, as is commonplace among those who fully allow such a shift to take place. But these areas of extraordinary change seem to arise *within* our basic nature as men and women. The fundamental shift has been within the process of *Witnessing* all that arises, not within the content of what is arising moment to moment. The flowering seems to be ongoing yet seems profoundly ordinary. This is my humble understanding of the process, borne out by deep personal observation, and echoed by the words of our friends in these pages.

But many of us have held some form of longstanding belief that this transition was superhuman in nature—that spiritually-liberated men and women were somehow perfect or in some way advanced far beyond us. Their condition often seemed to be far, far from our own "where are my car keys?" kinds of lives. I suggest that the answer is in the word "editing." Think about it. In the books you may have read about saints, sages, gurus, teachers and holy people did *any of them* appear as normal, so-called ordinary men or women? I can honestly say that I have read *hundreds* of such books and in almost every case, Master Mumpety-Ump or the Reverend Sri Swami So-and-So is depicted as beyond human frailty, certainly not shown to be like you and me. I find this unfortunate and disturbing.

By far, most spiritual teachers whom I and my collection of friends have met are, in fact, quite human. This would include a number of so-called big names in the field.

But imagine yourself to be a disciple of a profoundly charismatic, deeply spiritual man or woman. You are a follower of Truth who was lucky enough in this lifetime to meet a massively-Awakened teacher or mentor. Even if you *know* that your teacher still exhibits some of our shared, less-than-beatific traits, would you write about those "feet of clay" in a book? Of course not. A good writer or editor would paint the best possible picture of the man or woman they have entrusted to guide their spiritual evolution.

I think that human nature practically *requires* us to creatively edit what we tell others (especially in writing) about such beings. And this is correct and good. I have no problem with the "best foot forward" syndrome even when it applies to spiritual leaders.

But in reading these often highly-sanitized accounts of Awakened beings, we may have accidentally been poisoned with the unconscious belief that these men and women were *fundamentally* different from us. The books written seem to imply that they never drove too fast, never snuck into a movie theatre, never overspent the budget, never got drunk at the Christmas party, and never had wild sex or said the f-word—even if they did! So, it follows that since I might still do some or all those things, *I cannot possibly be Awakened!* How sadly misdirected! And how utterly damaging!

But we are adult men and women. Can we not accept and allow our spiritual guides to be as human as we are? Is it necessary —or even beneficial— for us to see them as hovering a few inches from the earth? And further, isn't it unfair to *them* for us to demand such exaggerated, seemingly perfected lives from them? So I implore you to relax these conditioned beliefs. Stop imagining that your spiritual icons are superhuman. Read beyond the edited accounts of their lives and begin to simply love and honor them for being the flesh-and-blood spiritual visionaries which they are.

Yes, we *should* endeavor to live the best, most wholesome lives possible. Yes, it *is* true that one is better off to avoid as many of the vices of human life that one possibly can. But please—let's not throw the enlightened baby out with the bath water. In accepting yourself *as* your Self, a new and more beautiful—yet still completely human—life awaits you.

After all, if your spiritual role-models exist as ordinary men and women and still live lives of spiritual freedom—*so can you*! Once you outgrow the outrageous self-demand that you must be perfect before you can claim your birthright of spiritual freedom, you will see that what you have sought has always been the case.

Then you will encounter what I believe is the most significant discussion on this topic. One of the general themes surfacing in these interviews is that spiritual Awakening is no longer a rare event, something to be found behind the cloistered walls of the monastery, convent or ashram. Rather, it is being recognized as a condition available to ordinary men and women everywhere. Falling into direct recognition of Truth has become a form of human evolution which is simply available as a much more widely present reality in these times. What does this mean for you in a purely practical sense? If you *are* in fact Awakened—or engaging the process in some form—what then? Why is it important? What is the significance of your soul's liberation?

We need only look at the world with honest and courageous eyes to see the need for the cultivation of spiritual freedom. Despite our many efforts and great advances, mankind is walking a perilous path toward an uncertain future. I tend to agree with Matthew Fox's comment in the final interview of this book: "...we are not a sustainable species on our present path of behavior—period."

As we relax into this condition of Awareness, we may discover that it's really not about "me" anyway. The so-called separate one who had so ardently sought Enlightenment ultimately surrenders into a powerful and ecstatic Understanding that "I" is not—and has never been—separate at all! Whoever and whatever "I" is, it is felt to be mysteriously connected to all else that exists. We who speak from these pages have observed that in our teaching and sharing workshops the attendees report the very same qualities which we have noticed in our own Awakening. They describe an ecstatic reality in which "I" is seen to be vast, infinite, eternal and still. Identification with the apparently separate one relaxes and we see our true Nature to be the ecstatic "field" within which "I" arises. "I" begins to live as *Consciousness Itself.*

So, as our habits of separative thought softly yield to a more universal Vision of Truth, we begin to sense that whatever happens to "me" impacts the entirety of existence. When all that exists in life is seen to be arising as a mysterious aspect of my own Being-ness, my behaviors begin to reflect a brilliant and more universally-inclusive Divine Love. From this radically-shifted perspective there arises a sense of true stewardship. After all, if I am intrinsically and ecstatically at one with all that exists, will I not care for our Mother—the earth—with a loving Heart and a responsible hand? If all beings are seen to be appearing as part of my own true Self, who will I batter or steal from or hate? You see, the true significance of Awakening is not personal. It is universal. The Awakened Heart becomes the very means through which the entirety of manifest existence becomes purified and made Bright.

And it begins in the smallest and simplest of ways. Not all of us are called to sit at the front of the room and teach, nor would it be a good thing if we all did. Living spiritual freedom within an ordinary human life seems to be the highest calling in this age. As more of us begin to take our Awakening sensibilities into our families, schools, workplaces and social lives we become "stealth Blessers." Our presence becomes a source of Radiance for all whom we meet.

As we relax into the naturalness of simply *being*, it will be noticed by those around us, The Blessing is shared and our friends' tendencies toward the clinging to the habits of separative thought are eased. After all, if *you* as an ordinary non-guru type can live from freedom, so can every man and woman who encounters you. This is my hope for and vision of the New World.

Remember, if God *is* infinite and eternal, then you are in this moment (and have always been, and will always be) Divine. I don't care what you eat or drink, you are at heart the vast Being spoken about in all scriptures. Even if you sometimes fall down and skin your knees spiritually, your *nature* is Already-Free, totally and eternally adrift in the infinite ocean of Divine Oneness. No sin has ever touched (or can ever touch) the One who you truly are!

In this very moment, at the very core of your being—without need of change or improvement—you are the unbearably beautiful Light of the World.

Would you like to see what life looks like to the Awakened being? Just open your eyes—now—wherever you are as you read these words. Look around. What you see is the vision of truth.

Listen—just now. What you hear in this very moment is the soft whispering of your own freedom.

Touch your own face—your fingers rest on the consecrated body of God.

Linger here and rest. Never leave.

This moment is your destiny.

Appendix I

In the preparation of this book, I tried very hard to maintain a reasonable journalistic stance. I did my very best to *not* allow my own taste as a Lover of Truth to "flavor" any of the thousands of tiny decisions which go into a project of this type. My goal, essentially, was to get out of the way and give the speakers the podium. I worked very hard to bring the collected interviews to you in the purest form available—as close to the exact words of the guest as originally conveyed to me.

In preparing this Appendix, however, I realized that I must abandon that journalistic posture. This is because *someone* had to choose and edit the responses you are about to read. This task was formidable, but also revealing and enjoyable. As you read through the dissected text ahead, just remember that you are consuming *my* choices. I also elected to present this Appendix to you in alphabetical order by last name for your convenience of reference.

If you are that rare creature who is on fire for Truth, I offer a suggestion: dissect the book again on your own. Choose your own edited sections. Look at it from as many different, self-generated angles as you can imagine. There are a lot of gems hidden in these fifteen conversations.

So feel free to use this book playfully. And if anyone in this book (including me) has said something that hit you in the heart, make contact with them—now!

Q - In your experience, is there such a reality as Awakening, Enlightenment, Liberation, or spiritual freedom?

Arjuna - "...in a way, Enlightenment or liberation or freedom is what is actually real and true and has always been real and true, and is real and true for everybody."

Michael - "In truth, silence would provide the best answer to this perennial question, because enlightenment begins where the mind stops its insidious demand to conceptualize and categorize that which is in and of itself indefinable and intangible."

Saniel - "Ahhhh.....yes! That's my answer! We could call it by any of those names, any other name. We could call it by no name at all. Something has occurred that has amounted to a radical shift in my whole existence, and I use terms like those to describe it."

Alan - "Absolutely. It's the only reason we are here...I truly believe that our real nature is enlightenment; we are enlightened beings. We've just been hypnotized to believe we're not. The game is about waking up to remember who we are."

Raphael - "I think that different people can arrive from very different avenues at a place in which they find themselves no longer believing that their freedom or their deepest happiness comes to them from any set of external circumstances. Therefore, they are free to fully participate in

161

each and every moment that they experience. And that full presence, without any conditions, to life as it unfolds moment by moment is, I think, a good way to describe spiritual freedom."

Surya - "Yes, absolutely. In fact, some wisdom masters say that it's the only reality, but that's a little too idealistic, I think. Enlightenment is definitely possible. Wisdom is within us. We only have to realize the truth of who and what we are—reality."

Dasarath -"Well, in one sense you could say it *is* reality, that it's an awakening from what we thought was real to what is actually real—which is free of all thought. In one sense, that's a way to look at it. In another sense, one could say...that the whole concept of Enlightenment is just a concept that arises out of ignorance. In the true Silence there isn't any Enlightenment, and there isn't any unEnlightenment and there isn't any freedom and there isn't any bondage and there isn't anybody to get it!"

Antonio - "Yes, there is. And it's just realizing that you are part of the world, that you are part of nature. It's all there. It's realizing about your own power, realizing that the power is not outside of you. It's inside and you create your own reality."

Matthew - "...I think we have many breakthroughs....And I think that is very beautiful and very real. It can happen with birds singing, it can happen in a conversation, it can happen with the news of the death of someone we love, or the news of the birth of someone we love. It can happen in a lecture or while reading a book. It can happen running, it can happen meditating. So I very much subscribe to the word *breakthrough* to name all of that. It's a common reality, of course, and possible for all of us."

Catherine - "My experience...what I most deeply sense has no words, has no description. It's so utterly implicit that everything is so completely *drenched* in it that *any* word is reductionistic."

Wayne - "There is an event that happens through an organism, a body-mind mechanism that is called Awakening, or Enlightenment or whatever. And what constitutes this Enlightenment or Awakening is that a false notion—a belief in a sense of personal doership, a sense that 'I am the center of the universe...I am the one who is doing'—that false notion falls away."

Satyam - "I have a problem with all of those words. What I do have an actual experience of...[is] that there is a shift taking place in Awareness...This knowing of who you are seems to be happening spontaneously now."

Neelam - "What I actually thought was that there is this amazing thing called awakening and it seems to be somewhere that you can't reach. Once you reach this place and once you pass the freshness phase, then you realize that this is just a tiny, little step. Before it looked like this great goal that you are going to reach but you see that it's a tiny, tiny little step into reality. You see that you have just made this first acquaintance, that you are just touching something so indescribable, so amazing, so incredible. That's just where it starts, you see? I say that because what I thought before would be 'the thing' turned out to be the very tiniest beginning of something that is totally indescribable."

Akash - "Certainly there is liberation from identification with the mind... This is a false identification, taking a cluster of thoughts to be who we are. On top of this we get the idea that there is a right way to be and a wrong way to be. We get stuck in trying to be a certain way and trying not to be another kind of way... There is just being."

Isaac - "There's just a seeing that what is Awake has always been Awake and until you know that, there's just a sense of life that was asleep, although you didn't know it was asleep."

Q - Did this seem to happen at a particular moment or event, or did it seem to take place gradually?

Arjuna - "...there was a moment of realization. However, it wouldn't really be accurate to say that prior to that point there was a 'me' and then there stopped being a 'me', or that before that point there was an ego and the ego dissolved, or that before that point there was unenlightenment and then Enlightenment struck. It would be more accurate to say that there was a realization that what is *really* here experiencing this moment has always been free, has always been liberated. And there never has been an ego to get rid of. It's just a concept to describe the way thoughts arise."

Michael - "Until one is enlightened there is no knowing exactly its cause or process!"

Saniel - "In doing my work, I've noticed that for some people it's more during a period of time whereas others can point to an instant. I'm kind of a curious combination of the two."

Alan - "It's really both. I've had numerous spikes, you might say, when the windows have opened up and I saw it all as it was. Yet, at the same time, there's an ever-increasing under-the-surface sense of enlightenment. There's definitely a growth, a deepening, and an Awakening. So, it's really that surge *and* a gradual awakening."

Raphael - "I think the truest answer is both."

Surya - "Buddhists have been debating this for a couple of centuries, 'Is enlightenment sudden or gradual?' One of my masters said that it's about suddenly awakening and then gradually cultivating, maturing and developing it and ironing out what we've realized or glimpsed."

Dasarath - "Both. There have been many, many moments in my life where there was this recognition."

Antonio - "Well, I would say that unconsciously and subconsciously it was always there."

Matthew - "I would say it happened both as a process and with break-through moments."

Catherine - "It was very much triggered by meeting Poonjaji, of course, in that the recognition came upon me as something that felt very famil-iar...In his presence I just felt how simple the whole thing was and, in a way, it was reverberating in my being... All that's happening is that there's a greater and greater consistency in this noticing, or in this ongoing recognition."

Wayne - "*Every* event happens at a particular moment by its very nature! And it can be notionally linked to preceding events. But—which events do you connect it to? I mean, it's an arbitrary process. Do you connect it to being dropped out of your crib at age two, or do you connect it to med-itating for twelve years? Both are events that preceded that one, but which one is causative? This notion of process has to do with causation—what causes the subsequent event? And the understanding is that *everything* causes the subsequent event! Nothing is independent."

Satyam - "Both. In my own case (and in the experience of virtually every-one I've met who has described this occurring for them) there was a moment of realization that 'I am the Consciousness that is all there is'. But the ramifications of this realization happen very slowly and gradual-ly and subtly. And it spreads out over years.

"But virtually everyone can remember that moment, that insight, we'll call it; an insight where the mind was transcended and all of the old con-cepts were just dropped for a moment and you experience yourself as just pure Consciousness."

Neelam - "There was a process that led to it, a coming in and out of real-ity. There would be these awakenings, like these amazing things that would happen. And I would just see it and go, 'Wow!' And then it would go back to where it was before. And I would have this knowing, this memory of something that had happened in this different reality.

"So there would be this back and forth movement of experience. Then there is one particular experience that has shifted into an actual constant change of awareness that just simply knows itself. From that moment on, there's no coming and going from reality. There's just knowing, right? There's just reality. And then that deepens."

Akash - "There is a moment of absolute absence filled with absolute pres-ence. Deeper than surrender or no surrender .... is-ness everywhere, beyond time and space. And subsequently, a process, in that the mind engages again, providing the opportunity for increasing alignment with Being."

Isaac - "The Truth is that it only happens now, and the whole idea of grad-ually or suddenly just is now. They're both just ideas that don't have any validity. So, if you want to speak in terms of time, it's an ongoing deep-ening of the recognition of That."

Q - Have you experienced or attained anything distinct from so-called "ordinary" or "normal" human experience?

Arjuna - "No, absolutely not. Absolutely not. There's no way to say how much the opposite is true. Ahhhh, what I experience in myself is something so completely and utterly ordinary and basic to life that the very possibility of there being some kind of attainment is ridiculous. What is undeniably so here is that there is this Consciousness or Presence experiencing thoughts and events arising... there's nothing to be found except Awareness Itself.

Michael - "Well, maybe 'extra-ordinary' is the best way of describing it. Spiritual awareness is ordinary from the perspective that it is our true nature. But as a collective agreement, humankind has accepted the hypnotic or dream-state of separation from the Source, the illusion of having to go through a 'waking up' process to reach enlightenment."

Saniel - "Yes. This Awakening or Realization that has taken place—the prepositions get awkward—'for me', 'in me', 'to me', 'as me'—I don't know...it's not an objective event which happened that I experienced per se, it's a shift in the subject Itself that I am. And, yes, it has so dramatically distinguished the life post that event from what was previous to it that it's kind of a great divide in my history as a human being. So, yes."

Alan - "When I've experienced those moments, I feel deeply at peace, utterly in the moment. The keynote of my being is joy and I remember that all is well—not thinking about the past or the future."

Raphael - "Once the door is open by virtue of great practice or great grace or whatever it might be, there are whole hosts of experiences that can come to a person which don't necessarily fit within the confines of what we would ordinarily call 'normal' existence. Those kinds of experiences can range from psychic openings to great influxes of physical or non-physical energy. The whole range of paranormal manifestations can be a part of people arriving at greater spiritual freedom."

Surya - "I think that human experience includes the Divine. So, no, I wouldn't make any special claims for myself. I could say that I'm the same as you and everyone else, and that I know that. Not everyone does."

Antonio - "Ahhhh, yes, but sometimes people don't perceive what's really happening fully. They don't perceive the synchronicities...For me, it's all the same. I think it's part of my higher being. What matters is if what I am saying is good for *you*. If it touches your heart and it's good for you, that's what's important."

Catherine - "Well, you see, what is often called 'normal' human experience is really an obsession with illusion. What I would call the experience of direct presence is the *lack* of obsession with the illusory thoughts and the mental formations that arise mostly in imagination. So from my point of view, "normal" consciousness, as we might understand it on a planetary level, is very <u>*abnormal.*</u>

"So, this is a kind of a collective hallucination in madness. The so-called 'awakened condition' is no big deal...It's just your natural relaxation. It's when you are no longer obsessed with what is untrue."

Wayne - "The experience that happens through this organism is a product of its nature. It's capacity for experience is determined by its senses—its ability to experience touch, smell, taste, sight, hearing. In the absence of any one of those senses, experience is different.

"...What is absent in the sage is this false sense of an authoring of the 'me'."

Nadeen - "Well, in 'ordinary' experience, everything is experienced through the mind, through the way Source has set up the mind to work. Something in this shift is happening where we're able to transcend the mind.

"The mind's function is to analyze and to make better any situation that it judges as not perfect—which is all of life. And, in this shift, we're transcending the normal human predicament whereby we are able to witness the event."

Neelam - "I don't know what you mean by 'ordinary'. This awakening is the most ordinary or most normal way of being that there is. Everything else is not ordinary. This is how we are. It's the most natural way of being. This is who we are. We are not thoughts, beliefs, emotional reactions or patterns, you know. That's not normal or natural. It's just some kind of idea that is being held in consciousness as a way of functioning. But it's not true because it doesn't come from the true being.

"Reality is ordinary. It's absolutely, totally, awesomely normal, you know? [Laughs] It's just very simple. It's an absolute and awesome simplicity and normalness. It's the natural way. It's the most ordinary. It doesn't need an intermediary, nothing in between to express itself, to know itself. It's what arises the simplest way. It doesn't need to go through all of the complications that we sometimes go through to express something."

Akash - "Typical unmatured human awareness is limited and consists of believing in the projection of the mind; belief in whatever movie is running in the mind and appearing to take place in our everyday life. So that movie might consist of 'I'm a successful career person' or, 'I'm powerless in this' or countless others.

"Believing in a movie is a form of sleep. In awakening to 'what is', the movie is seen for what it is. It is seen to be identification with the ego—the Latin word for 'I'—this cluster of thoughts, a play of light and shadow. When this projection, this movie, isn't believed in any more, there is a flowering. The beauty of Being has just been hidden while attention has been on the movie.

"In my own experience, there is no extraordinariness in this. Relaxing into the natural simplicity of Being, ordinariness reveals itself as a true flavour of life."

Isaac - "Yes. What's considered normal is a sense of separation. It's funny because you can't really call it an experience but it's a recognition in which all experience is seen to be just the filter that gets looked through. Yet there's no one looking and there's no filter.

"But, in the sense of being somebody that knows something or that is something...it doesn't seem so any more."

Q - Do you have an experience of growing, maturing, or evolving in this process?

Arjuna - "There is constant change, constant liberating of every concept, every idea, every everything. There's just deeper and deeper not knowing...deeper and deeper ignorance, actually."

Michael - "No matter what our level of wakefulness, there is always a more expansive Self to be realized. After all, it is really the Infinite realizing its own true, limitless nature in and through individualized incarnation."

Saniel - "The basic radical shift simply is so. And, I have come to refer to it as a 'second birth.' There's a biological as well as a spiritual logic to this that is closely linked into the circumstances that produce our birth into human form to begin with. So, calling it a second birth is not just a metaphor.

"...If we look at an infant, and then at what happens afterward, there are tremendous changes. But, the condition of being a born human being stays the same. Likewise, in this shift that has occurred there is something about the essential nature of it that's just a given now.

"And the changes are happening on every level of my existence. It's as if at the moment of Awakening booster rockets were fired and it took my transformation process into an ongoing warp speed. And it's more or less continued that way."

Alan - "Sure. It's happening whether we know it or not all the time."

Raphael - "I think there's a kind of 'raw material' to what we are calling spiritual freedom. When it first appears it can be so powerful and transformative that it feels like that's all there is. And yet, most of the work that's required spiritually is about taking that experience and finding out how to live it moment by moment in the most mundane circumstances of everyday life."

Surya - "Yes, I think so. I don't think there's any static state. If it's just a state then it's not the real thing, it's not the natural state or how things actually are, which is a little more mysterious or a little more flowing than fixed. But our experience of it, our realization of it does seem to deepen."

Dasarath - "I would say that there's some sense of changingness, as long as that's held with it's opposite—unchangingness—being true as well.

There's this unchanging quality or reality that has nothing at all going on in it—*zero*—absolutely nothing at the same time that there does seem to be this dynamic quality of movement."

Antonio - "Yes. Every day teaches you a new lesson. It's just to keep your eyes open, your ears open and to breathe in what the universe gives you. Everybody has something to contribute to you."

Matthew - "Oh, absolutely. If we weren't evolving and deepening, we wouldn't be part of the universe, which is constantly evolving and deepening."

Catherine - "Definitely. Definitely, this blaze of...consciousness...it's ongoing. It's always new, fresh. So, yes, there's always a deepening, always yet another moment to embrace. And, it has nothing to do with goal. It's a 'journey without a goal', as Trungpa Rinpoche called it. I once asked Poonjaji, 'Is this ongoing for you?' And he said, 'All the time. Every moment, even this moment'."

Wayne - "I liken that to the experience of walking around without a stone in your shoe. What is that like—to walk around all day without a stone in your shoe? Isn't it *wonderful* that you don't have a stone in your shoe? Aren't you astounded at every moment...that you're walking around without the stone in your shoe?

"There is no experience of *not* having a stone in your shoe except when you *do* have a stone in your shoe and the stone is removed! Then there's the experience of the absence of the stone in your shoe. This is the experience of Enlightenment—the experience in the moment of the *absence* of something. So, is there a deepening of the experience of not having a stone in your shoe?"

Nadeen - "It's a never-ending process that just keeps getting deeper and better. What I call deeper is the understanding of your own essence as Source; understanding that the only reality possible once you realize who you are is to totally embrace all of existence as it is! This runs totally contrary to everything in human consciousness. Human consciousness is designed to make everything better. So this process of letting go, allowing, embracing, surrendering is never-ending. Because the subtleties of it can go to the quasi-infinite concepts that have to be dissolved in this process, I could never imagine a point of just tapering off to a plateau."

Neelam - "It's like deepening. Even when I say flowering I have to laugh because at first it is like a flowering. But when it gets difficult, when you really touch in places that are difficult and hard, it's a really deep work—a deep willingness to really, truly take this awakeness, this knowing and touch *everything*, so that there's no place inside where it can't go...There has to be a real willingness to let it go everywhere it wants to. So that's what I call deepening or merging into the Heart. Deepening is the closest that I can come to describing it."

Akash - "Is-ness is is-ness. Maturing is in the continued surrender to that and in the dissolving of identification with the mind, giving up the ideas of who one thinks one is. This is where the maturing is."

Isaac - "Ahh, yes, you know...there's the absolute level where nothing is happening, or what you could call Shiva, and then there's the play of energy, called Shakti or consciousness and in this play of energy, somehow Consciousness is revealing Itself to Itself. There are patterns seen which are not personal in any way. Somehow there's a sense of deepening, but there's no one that's deepening. Consciousness is having a play with itself."

Q - What is your experience of thought and emotion?

Arjuna - "It's just a concept, you know? Why should there not be thought and emotion? A state of absolutely no thought and emotion is a completely unmanifest state. It's consciousness unmoving. And that is available and has been available for millennia...for eternity.

"But now we're playing the game that involves consciousness in form, consciousness incarnate. And the thing that makes consciousness incarnate interesting is the play of thought and emotion. If it's resisted it shows up one way. If it's welcomed as the natural display of its own potential then it's wonderful. And that's how creativity happens. That's how the deliciousness of love happens. All sorts of things happen through allowing this play to unfold."

Saniel - "Thought and emotion are natural functions of this living organism that I am. So, they are me. I have thoughts, I have emotions...I give myself permission to experience them all. And they always have things to show me.

"There are patterns of thought and emotion that are very characteristic to Saniel Bonder, some of which can get *real* aggravating to me, as well as to others, at times. And I work with them. My motivation to change patterns of thought and emotion, where there is that motivation, often springs from a desire to live more harmoniously with people, to make changes in my life that feel important to me."

Alan - "My body feels, my mind thinks, and my emotions go up and down! When I'm in my center—connected to Spirit and clear—I can observe my body, thoughts and emotions with more detachment and they don't seem to have a lot of power over me."

Raphael - "My experience is that thought and emotion arise sometimes separately, sometimes together, and sometimes created in response to one another. And that they are constantly arising as long as I am living awake in the world. Just being alive creates an ongoing bubbling up to the surface of thought, of emotion, of sensation. And I can choose to link up to any particular thought or emotion and watch the influence between them and watch how it happens in myself—or not. A better way to say it is that

I can witness it or I can become attached to it. Either way, it seems to just be part of the whole, and never ending."

Surya - "You know, in Buddhist philosophy the three poisons or afflictions—greed, hatred and delusion—sort of include thoughts and emotions. In other words, delusion is an emotion as much as greed or anger or hatred or lust or avarice...Thoughts and intentions create our world and they create our emotional experience and our feeling world, too. This is not just an intellectual intention."

Dasarath - "Thoughts come, feelings come. The whole range of human experience comes. But, they don't stick, you know? It's like the old metaphor of an image in a mirror. Things show up in the mirror, but the mirror is never touched or stained by the images which come and go within it."

Antonio - "I try to balance them as much as possible. I am more mental than emotional, but I try more and more to release my emotions. But I think the thing that's most important for me is to have fun in life... While we are here, one of the goals we should set for ourselves is to learn how to have fun. When people are having fun, everybody is fine; everybody is okay. There's no violence, there's no aggression, there's no drama. So, we should always have fun. And spirituality, too, has to come with fun."

Matthew - "...Our honoring of the power which is creativity is grossly underdone. I think all these forces you mention—thought, emotion, etc.- are the power of creativity trying to wake us up. There is a time for thought and (as in meditation) a time for no-thought. And this dance is very important. But it doesn't mean putting down thought."

Catherine - "Well, in my own perspective of this...everything is absolutely welcome and has it's own play. It has it's own place, you could say...So, the arising of thought comes and it has its own place, its own usefulness or lack thereof. And a discriminating awareness will know the difference.

"And the arising of emotion, same thing. Emotions are generally born of thought. Thought precedes emotions generally, so some emotions have their usefulness and some don't.

"And in this resting in clear presence, discernment deepens. There are many aspects of this [process] that are maturing on their own without any effort. And in that quiet presence, there is greater and greater love, greater and greater kindness."

Wayne - "Thought and emotion arise. The full range of thought and emotion arise, and are expressed in accordance with the nature of the organism, and they pass. And then new ones arise. But the experience of it is only by an identified individual. In the absence of an identified individual, there is no subsequent experience of what is happening. *There is simply what is happening!*

Nadeen - "There's a strange phenomenon happening. If your whole life you've been programmed by the mind to judge anger or rage or envy or any of these emotions as not helpful, then you've repressed it. You've pushed it down. [But] when this shift takes place, and you allow *what is* to be...you're going to go through a period when all of the emotions that you've pushed down—sexual energy, rage energy, any of them—are going to come floating up, jumping up for recognition. And it's time, then, to embrace them and say, 'Yes, this is part of my Divine Expression.' This is just as real as love and joy and harmony."

Neelam - "It depends. It depends on my current relationship with it and what my knowing of it is in the moment. There will be thoughts and emotions that are absolutely irrelevant to my experience and some that will be relevant. These are the places where I would know I still have some identification...And again, there are places that don't have any relevance whatsoever as they arise. They just arise and they are just what they are. They just pass. They don't even touch on anything...How you really are is amazing—you can let anything be here. It's just so touching."

Akash - "In the past, the tendency was to go with each thought. A thought would arise and it was as if I'd stick to it and go with it wherever it took me. And when this would happen I would be just moving around on the circumference of consciousness. Now, a thought arises and it is seen. It does not need to be stuck to. It is just what it is, it's just a thought arising or a chain of thoughts arising."

Isaac - "Thoughts and emotions come up. They're impersonal. There's nobody that's thinking them, they are happening by themselves. If anyone thinks that they're in control of thinking, all they need to do to prove that it's *not* them doing the thinking is to try to *stop* thinking... They will see really clearly that there's no thinker, or anybody that's doing it. It's just that the *activity* of thinking produces the sense of a thinker.

"...And so, thoughts and feelings come and at moments they can look personal; at moments they can look serious; at moments they can seem solid. But, there's the recognition that they're really nothing."

Q - Do you have a sense of anything that might be called evil or negative energies within life?

Arjuna - "Yes...If something is resisted it can appear to become negative. So anger, for example, which is a natural energy, a part of one dimension of life which has a sort of ferociousness, if that's resisted it can become destructive. It can become ugly. But if anger is welcomed, it's just a roar that comes and disappears and maybe doesn't even need to affect anybody else at all.

"...But if we hold ideas about what should and shouldn't be, that's where all kinds of strange flavors can creep in. It's the same with just about everything, you know? There is the natural movement in life—unresisted—and then there is life with ideas of what should and shouldn't be imposed upon it. And, I would say that it's only when there is resistance that we have the appearance of something being negative."

Michael - "For me there is one word that sums up the whole theme of good versus evil: ignorance—ignorance of the Infinite Presence that pervades all that there is. It is infinite and does not contradict its own nature. There cannot be any person, place or thing outside of the infinite. Not realizing our own true nature, we cut ourselves off from this Infinite Intelligence, Infinite Divine Love. This causes a variety of forms of suffering. When an individual perceives that they are cut off from the Source of Life, these thoughts are forms of energy. Eventually, energy condenses into form—thoughts become things, self-created circumstances and so on. From this comes a conviction that evil or negativity has a separate life of its own and a whole industry builds up around it!"

Saniel - "Yes...I don't feel that evil is intrinsic to Being such that it's untransformable, but I do feel that evil is a force in the world, one of the forces in the world that we would do well to take very seriously.

"...I'm hopeful that as more men and women do relax into a non-separate, Awakened participation into reality, we will more and more be able to counter human evil (in all of its forms) without reducing it or minimizing it as just some form of pathology within the psyche of the individual."

Alan - "Evil is an interpretation, not a fact...It's really just a momentary judgment. I don't believe in evil. I just think that we can get into thought-spaces or emotion-spaces that block off the flow of life force, and we feel unhappy. And we think that something outside did it to us, but it's just our own thoughts. So I prefer to replace the word 'evil' with the word 'fear.' Any time I perceive evil I've gone into a fear space. It's really my own consciousness that I need to correct in that moment, rather than eradicate the world of evil-doers, which is the most counter-productive thing that anyone ever did!"

Raphael - "Personally, I do. I hesitate in saying that because I feel that in each moment everything exists and I don't like to label the things that exist in a framework of good/bad or higher/lower. But I believe that in each moment there exists all of the past, all of the present, and all of the future—all of the forces of light, and all of the forces of darkness. Together they make up the whole of all that is."

Surya - "I don't think there's a devil or really any absolute good or bad. I think that these are relative notions. Of course, there is negativity, and harmfulness, and unwholesomeness in the world, and corruption, and so on. That's for sure. There's plenty of oppression, injustice and greed and cruelty and meanness. But, the shadows are also nothing but light. There's no such thing as absolute darkness. I also don't think there's any perfectly unmitigated good.

"So, in the realm of duality, long live wide discrimination and discernment between good and evil, helping and harming, wholesome and unwholesome, skillful and unskillful, virtue and vice. We need to make those discernments for ourselves for the benefit of one and all."

Dasarath - "Well, I don't see anything that you might call an objective entity, like 'capital-E Evil', or 'capital-D Devil' or that kind of thing. To me, negative and positive, good and evil, God and the devil are all judgments that arise in consciousness. Certain minds have certain tendencies to lock on to them and turn them into absolutes. That happens to be one good description of this whole play of duality or dualism."

Antonio - "I think that evil and negative energy is manipulation, is denial, is... everything that tells you *not* to have fun! Or everything that tries to take your power by limiting you, by imposing rules and things, or by saying that you are bad and that you are not doing things right...I think that evil is related to fear. And at the end, there are two energies. One is love, and the other one is fear. They are the opposed energies. And fear comes from ignorance and ignorance leads to judgment.

"So, on one side are ignorance, judgment, and fear. On the other side of the equation are knowledge, compassion, and love. So, whatever is not love, compassion, and acceptance is judgment and fear. And that creates violence. That creates all the evil."

Catherine - "No, I call it ignorance. I don't have any sense of what is called evil whatsoever. I just see that there are different types of densities and that when one is very, very asleep to their own nature of their clear, clear pristine presence...then pain ensues and that pain can instigate very, very painful acts, acts of suffering."

Nadeen - "Everything in this human existence as Source is absolutely, totally balanced by freedom and limitation. If we're going to call freedom 'good' and limitation 'evil' or 'bad', then we need to see that there's equal balance in everyone's life. You can never have enough money or power or intelligence to get out of this balance. Everyone is equally subjected to it. It's just part of the Source's experience.

"So, what I used to see as evil or negative, I now see as part of the Divine Balance. Source wants to experience all of it. There is nothing excluded. There is no human emotion or experience that has not been experienced by Source.

"And that's why everyone is such a unique expression of Source because it's not possible with the personality's makeup for just one person to have all of these experiences. You need billions and trillions of people to have all possible experiences. And that's what is happening."

Neelam - "No. This is a great idea, you know?...I only know this place where something arises which I wouldn't want to face. I still see this arise sometimes in myself. It's the only place where there would be a discrimination of something other than God. It's a place where you don't want to face something—where there's some refusal in being with something. And it's called 'negative' and it's called this or that. It's called all of these names. But consciousness can go anywhere. There is no boundary in consciousness. These beliefs just keep you from knowing yourself and they create a very tricky split. Concepts of 'good' and 'bad' are terrible because it's not true. It doesn't exist like that, you know?"

Akash - "Energy can be expressed creatively or destructively. Evil energy is destructive energy that involves hurting others and ourselves through lack of awareness. And we cannot hurt others without hurting ourselves.

"This is a complex question but the answer can be simple. 'Evil' and the fear reaction to it are both expressions of darkness. Evil is a power trip fed by fear of powerlessness. It stems from a particular projection, an extreme kind of venomous inner movie. This darkness is the absence of the light of awareness. The light of awareness is the only antidote—to be fully conscious."

Isaac - "That can happen in a moment, but it's clearly just a projection of thought. There's no such thing. It's just a pattern, you could say, in consciousness, of thinking something should be different and really believing it for a moment. But ultimately, there's no such thing."

Q - Did you or do you have a teacher?

Arjuna - "I can only speak from my own experience, but the way [Papaji]...was with me was always really as a friend. And he was always willing to reveal his humanness and his simple likes and dislikes and ordinary human reactions to life. And that was a great teaching, you see, because to recognize the teacher as both Consciousness *and* as a human being lets one kind of relax. You can say, 'Well, I am also both Consciousness and a human being', and the game of duality is then over!

"To me, every word he spoke that reached my ears spoke of no difference, no separation, that what is really important is the same in every human being."

Michael - "There have been many great souls who have influenced and continue to grace my spiritual path. At a young age I was inwardly guided to understand that I was to learn from the inner teacher, and yet to remain open and receptive to all true teachers, whether they were in a physical body or not. But it wasn't my destiny to surrender my life to one teacher or guru in particular...You know, 2 + 2 = 4 whether you are in China, Africa or the United States. So whether you hear truth from a Sufi master, a Hindu guru, a Buddhist master or a Christian mystic, if they have gone beyond the three-dimensional experience and realized the Eternal Presence, it's going to contain the same universal experience of one who has touched the hem of the garment of Truth."

Saniel - "...I have many teachers. I had two great Master Initiators—Ramana Maharshi and Adi Da. There were other great enlightened or awakened beings who influenced particularly my early...spiritual quest. One of them, Neem Karoli Baba came back around later as very helpful to me...and, I learn from other humans all the time.

"So, I have to give a more complete answer to that question because to just say that I don't have a teacher is kind of misleading. I don't have a single, primary Teacher. My wife Linda is a constant teacher to me. Our cat is a constant teacher to me."

Alan - "I've had many teachers. Bottom line, God is the only real teacher. Spirit is the only real teacher. Inner Being is the only real teacher, in the long run."

Raphael - "I did not have a teacher in the traditional sense...What I did have was mentors—great spiritual friends who were more fully realized than I. They helped point me toward new directions and possibilities.

"The other kind of teacher that I have had is more difficult to describe. Swami Muktananda...once said, 'Ultimately, kundalini becomes the guru.' My own spontaneous and unsought-after experience with kundalini reflects this. Embracing the energy and surrendering to it on an ongoing basis creates a kind of non-physical, energetic student-teacher relationship."

Surya - "Yes, I've had many teachers. I had a guru, a root guru, the late Tibetan master Karmapa and others like His Holiness Dilgo Khyense Rinpoche and Kalu Rinpoche. These are my root gurus.

"My first guru was Neem Karoli Baba who gave me my name Surya Das. He is always with me. They are all always with me."

Dasarath - "I've had many teachers in my life...But, I had only one guru, and that was...my master Papaji. This is a mystery—the mystery of the guru... Somehow in the presence of that massive field of silence, this silence could recognize itself. It was, it still is, unbelievable to me in an inexplicable way. He, as my master, was somehow a doorway to infinity."

Antonio - "There are many people that I would call masters or spiritual teachers. There have been many of them for me. But I think the most constant one, the one I still go back to is Lazaris. He's always telling me something new. Everything he says always causes me to say, 'Yes, that's it! That's what I think and feel'."

Matthew - "Yes. I've been trying to recover this lineage called 'Creation Spirituality' which is a mystical tradition of the West. It comes through the wisdom literature of the Hebrew Bible, for example, the prophets and also of Jesus who is now acknowledged by the greatest scholars as coming from the wisdom tradition. It also comes through in the works of Hildegard of Bingen, Thomas Aquinas, Francis of Assisi, Teilhard de Chardin and others in our century, for sure. But I was alerted to this tradition by Pere Chenu, a wonderful French Dominican theologian who I studied with in Paris in the late '60's...This is the lineage of the historical Jesus, but also of the cosmic Christ, and it's a very ecumenical tradition...Once you get into the deep mystics of *any* tradition you find them talking a common language."

Catherine - "Oh yes, I do, and probably will continue to. I studied Buddhism for seventeen years prior to meeting Poonjaji, and...I had a lot of one-on-one time with some of the real greats—Krishnamurti, Trungpa Rinpoche and many others who weren't my personal teachers, but were great influences.

"And I feel that the way I approach life is that everyone and every circumstance kind of ends up being one's teacher. People who call me teacher are wonderful teachers to me, and I feel so honored and privileged to know them.

"So, I feel a sense of sitting there kind of awestruck by this universal intelligence speaking through so many people over time, crossing so many ages and cultures."

Wayne - "I do have a guru—Ramesh Balsekar in Bombay...I love him more than life itself."

Nadeen - "No. I hung out with several so-called Enlightened Teachers, and what they were saying sounded good in theory, but it never rubbed off —it never happened to me.

"So no, I never had a teacher per se that I surrendered to. I tried! Every teacher I had I tried to surrender to, but there was just something in me that couldn't quite give away all of my own power to someone else.

"At the moment when I did have this shift, I was contemplating a statement that Ramesh Balsekar had made—'Consciousness is all there is, and I am That'—and I had heard that statement for thirty years in various ways, but at that precise moment of my reading it, I was ripe. I was like a mango that has just fallen off the tree. And everything in my entire search, starting with the Catholic priesthood all the way through the Eastern spiritual route, had prepared me for that moment. None of it was superfluous. It was all part of what happened."

Neelam - "Yes. I have a master. My master is Papaji. When you ask if I have a teacher, I also know that I have always had a teacher. Consciousness is a teacher and that has always been there. I remember having experiences of knowing this when I was six years old—throughout life. So this teacher has always been with me."

Akash - "Life is my teacher. I have had various teachers and right now you are my teacher. This is the beauty of it, that each moment is a reflection of the wordless. It is right here to be seen and surrendered to in each moment. It is an incredible, delicious being-ness. Each person around us is a mirror to see this, to be this. Each moment is a signpost pointing deeper into this ocean of being. And teachers can offer a wonderful gift of pointing to this. I am tremendously grateful."

Isaac -"I'd say all of life, ultimately! Yes, all of life—every moment ....You know what's funny about this is that I met Papaji and, yes, he pointed me at myself and I could say that he was the manifestation of myself. And at the same time, you know, what limits does Consciousness have? It's just everything. It's like, I've really been playing with this one, because it almost feels too narrow to say that I have something like a lineage. This will be fun for some of the people stuck on lineage."

Q - Do you teach?

Saniel - "I'm going to resist labeling it, and see if I can actually describe it. I teach the most direct approach that I can take responsibility for at any given time that will help others duplicate this, we could say 'condition of awakeness', or quality of integration and wholeness; non-difference between the human and transcendental Divine dimensions of being. And I also teach my best sense of the most integrated, balanced, sane and natural way to live beyond that transition, not only for the individual, but also for us cooperatively. So I make a big emphasis on mutuality.

"I've defined this as being as true as you possibly can to your own self or being, in all of the testing moments of life while cooperating with others who are really doing the same, consciously so at whatever stage of awakeness or integration they might be. That's a pretty good summary."

Alan - "We're all teaching by our being. I have classes and seminars where I am in the role of a teacher, but I'm always teaching more by my energy than by my words. The roles of teacher and student are intermixed. When I teach a class students come forth with the most amazing contributions and shifts and sharings. I learn as much from the students as they learn from the teacher.

"So, teaching and learning is always happening; it just depends on which seat you are in at the moment."

Raphael - "This is a problematic term. I usually 'share.' I share experience. I share with process work. I share with stories. I share with just the day-to-day ordinary parts of my life...

"So, once I get past the problematic part I would say, 'Yes, I do teach.' But the more I teach and the better I teach results from how much I continue to profess and live my absolute 'beginner's mind.' Another way to say that is that the more I become convinced that I am a teacher, the less I actually have to offer to others."

Surya - "Yes, I teach. I teach the *dharma*. I teach American Buddhism. I teach *dzogchen*. I teach meditation, chanting, Tibetan energy yoga, self-inquiry, ethical and compassionate action, seva (service). That's what I teach, all based in the Mahayana Buddhist tradition, and the *dzogchen* lineage."

Dasarath - "Yes, that's pretty much what my life is about in terms of daily activity. It's evolved in a very interesting way...I have a monthly satsang here in Ithaca, and I travel around and do them elsewhere from time to time. But, the actual work I do—coaching one-on-one in the workplace, and leading retreats in the corporate world—has evolved into a 'corporate satsang'."

Antonio - "Well, I teach about crystals, which is just another way to teach about Consciousness, about Enlightenment, about living life...But, I don't take the position of being a master or a guru. I tell them, 'I am like you are. Sometimes I can see a little more, but I give you power to see your own power.' I know that people sometimes doubt, but they have to learn about their own power. They need to know that it's their choice, their way of being. Nobody can do their lives for them. I tell them that they have to take responsibility and take care of their own lives."

Matthew - "Oh yes. I started a university of spirituality, The University of Creation Spirituality here in downtown Oakland five years ago, and I teach both there and on the road."

Catherine - "Well, I have held regular sessions called *Dharma Dialogues* over the last eight years in the U.S. and Europe. I could describe it as a sharing. I could say that this instrument called Catherine is being played by some mysterious musician... You know it's such a flow of phenomena happening all the time. So let's say that in one moment I have on a hat that represents sharing (as in *Dharma Dialogues*) and in another moment I'm schmoozing with my friend on the phone or I'm being a sister—dealing with my brother who has AIDS. A number of my friends are going through cancer treatments, and I try to comfort them in that.

"You know, I don't feel a particular role, but I feel that this expression, this manifestation basically gives itself away. That's all it seems to be doing, in different ways and in different roles: teacher, friend, sister, daughter, whatever."

Wayne - "I teach *nothing*! In a most profound sense, what I teach is nothing. And...the nothing that I teach is that which is also everything. I have no doctrine or dogma or techniques associated with teaching, so calling it a 'teaching' might be begging the question.

"...So what I do is I come and I sit down and see what happens. Each time it's a little different. Sometimes people love it, become completely enthralled, mesmerized—it's the most astounding thing they've ever heard. And most people leave at the break! *There's just nothing to do, you know?* They're like, 'Man, this is the most *worthless* of teachings!' It's an absolutely worthless teaching—there's nothing there! So, it takes a particularly foolish kind of disciple to be interested in this *nothing*! But those are the ones that I delight in being with and talking to. Because in the absence of wanting to get something, the world shakes."

Nadeen - "Well, I share my experience in satsang...I encourage, I facilitate everyone to share their experience and everyone else in the room to just be in that space of openness to their own inner wisdom. And no matter what that person is saying, or what I'm saying, it's irrelevant. The words never have anything to do with the communication of Grace. It's that moment of openness—opening to their own wisdom that constitutes my entire message.

"And so, it's sort of a 'leaderless satsang' that I'm facilitating. People would like me to speak more, but I'm speaking less. I'm speaking so much less now that I'm doing satsang only at our retreat center in Costa Rica and it's silent satsang. I don't speak at all. I just sit in the room in a circle. It's very, very difficult for me to talk about it anymore."

Neelam - "I would say that lately it's less and less of a teaching...You see, Papaji was not a teacher. He was just a being. He made himself available for whatever was going on around him.

"But when you say teaching, it seems to relate to some kind of knowing. And that's a difficult place in consciousness. It's a place that acts like it knows, and that's not a true place. So what I do is not so much a teaching as a way of being. It's a way of sharing my experience with other people. Sometimes we just need support to see what is true, what is real."

Isaac - "I can say that there's a Resting as the Essence that we all are. And, there are a few ways that this plays out, but mostly what happens is that a person will ask a question and as I'm simply being That in them Which they are already, suddenly they see it from that perspective. And they see the question from the other way around, or they see it from There. And usually there's laughter or whatever happens.

"And, of course there are times when someone is asking something from another level, and I can just respond from experience at the time. But mostly, it's this play of recognizing what's true in someone—in everyone, actually—in every moment. And just enjoying that together."

Q - Do you have a personal spiritual practice?

Arjuna - "Yes, I do have a personal practice. My practice is called 'living human life' and I try to be regular in my practice. Sometimes I forget my practice and start doing bizarre and strange things like meditating or holding my breath or something. But the practice that I am really committed to is living ordinary human life.

"So my practice involves such *sadhana* as being a parent to two beautiful boys. My *sadhana* involves having to listen when people notice things in me that are a little off and having to return to the humility of not being beyond reproach. My practice includes remembering to do things I said I would do. It includes being willing to be absolutely in the mud of humanity at the same time as being Consciousness. So my practice has become not using spiritual ideas or fleeting spiritual experiences in any way whatsoever to avoid the curriculum of human life.

"...My practice is to remember to be willing to be unenlightened and not to retreat into some lofty state of enlightenment which becomes 'holier than' or 'separate from'. My practice is the willingness to be unenlightened...as unenlightened as Enlightened."

Michael - "Every morning and evening I meditate and pray, and throughout the day I am conscious of being enveloped in a Presence that causes me to remain in a continual state of communion with love, joy and peace—the qualities of this Presence in my very soul. I work out each morning to keep the body temple fit and follow a predominantly vegetarian diet—without being a fanatic—because of the vibrational differences within foods. Service is my work, both in my spiritual community and the larger global community. About twice a year, I go on a silent retreat which assists in clearing out the dust and grit of the journey that we don't always notice is present in consciousness. But my mainstay is meditation; it's just something I do all the time. You know what they say, 'Don't leave home without it'."

Saniel - "Not in the sense of an identifiable routine that I do every day. My practice is to identify the leading edge impulses that are coming up for me in my life; to question and test them and then to see how everything stacks up; then to determine the priorities of what are the most auspicious and the most necessary things to do—auspicious and necessary for me, yes, but also for everybody, for the totality. We need to do those things and to keep on seeing, investigating, looking into, expressing more, daring more often. Daring, recognizing and persevering is one of the triads that I've come up with—ways to characterize the daily ongoing practice that I feel is important."

Alan - "I meditate every day. I pray every day. I've been doing that for many years, and it's hard for me to imagine not doing it. I start my day with meditation and prayer. I think it's essential to kick off the day in the right keynote, and then everything during the rest of the day follows from that keynote. On the days when for one reason or another I don't meditate, I usually end up wishing that I had!"

Raphael - "I do. I practice something that I call 'Living the Questions.' This is the basis of what I share with people. Living the Questions is really a kind of meditation in action. I practice it all the time to arrive as fully as possible in each moment, especially the more difficult ones.

"But also, Living the Questions over a long period has freed all sorts of energies inside myself. So often, strange as this may sound, I find myself meditating, chanting, or performing asanas in a spontaneous fashion. If I'm open to them in a given moment, sometimes they just happen. They happen and I'm grateful, as opposed to making appointments for them in advance."

Surya - "Yes, I practice daily meditation, chanting and some yoga, prayer and some of the Tibetan rites and rituals. Also, I consider service an important practice. I consider my teaching or pastoral work, spreading and preserving the *dharma*, bringing teachers from the East to the West, building monasteries and meditation centers here, the interfaith work, all as spiritual activism. They are kind of my *bodhisattva* mission, my spiritual practice, my own growth in the work."

Dasarath - "No. But, I sit quietly often, whenever I'm moved to do that. I love to sing from time to time. I can get very devotional sometimes and chant and sing to God in celebration...But I don't see them as practices in the sense that they're leading someone somewhere...My experience of it is that what some might call 'practice' is to me just a celebration or an expression of being, rather than some effort, some moving toward a goal."

Antonio - "Well, I meditate. I have my own rituals with crystals that I do. The biggest part is that I do my mandalas with crystals. I put my attention on the crystals and I place a strong force there to create my own reality the best way possible...And I like to connect with nature. I always do a kind of ceremony whenever I visit somewhere that I consider a power place in nature. But, it's mostly inside myself where I find the answer to things."

Matthew - "Sure. I mean, I try to be alert as to what's working and what isn't. I'm a very busy guy but I usually do a five or ten-minute meditation in the morning when I get up. I do some yoga and then I try to find time during the day to walk, preferably by water if possible, to empty my mind that way. And during the day, with the work that I do—whether it's writing, lecturing or administering the university—I find it important to connect with the spiritual practice which is inherent in the work world, because that's where we put so much of our energy.

"So, I don't have a 'packaged practice', you might say. But earlier we used that word 'evolution', and I think that our methods evolve—*should* evolve—as our situation evolves."

Catherine - "No. I did at one point. I used to go from retreat to retreat but I never liked the idea of a practice, and I never liked practicing. I was not one of those people who enjoyed having a daily meditation practice. I would do it as a form of discipline—kind of a drudgery.

"But, I notice now that I love the sitting, the quiet, because I'm not doing anything! You know, it's just total relaxation. I don't in any formal way do that in my own life, because for the most part I live a very quiet life. My life itself is very meditative, it has that quality of relaxed, present Awareness very effortlessly."

Wayne - [Long pause...then Wayne shakes his head].

Q - For the transcriber...that's a "no".

Nadeen - "Yes. I have as much fun as I can every day. That's my personal practice. I never think about God or spirituality any more. It's the most foreign thought to my whole mind. Before this shift, I was a fish that was looking for water. Afterwards I realized that I'm already swimming in the ocean so I just quit thinking about it.

"...I love and cherish alone time, time to be quiet, to watch a sunset or listen to the birds. I find myself constantly in beautiful places and I feel nourished and embraced by nature when I can be quiet. Silence causes more enjoyment for me than chaos. So, I love silence."

Neelam - "Being with what is. Just allowing myself to be honest and truthful to what really arises and to be with that. If you mean like a practice of sitting formally for meditation, I don't. If it means spending time with myself deeply, yes. But it's not a formal practice."

Akash - "No. I have no formal, systematic spiritual practice. However, I have certainly found techniques and maps very helpful for seeing the mechanisms of the mind much more clearly. And consequently my recommendation to others is to use whatever is helpful—not to cling to techniques, not to avoid techniques. If one works, great—use it. Then put it aside when it has done its job."

Isaac - "I've recently come out of a three-week period where I've tried to practice...but it's kind of fallen in on itself again. I think that mostly it's just the enjoyment of being...and there's such an interest in it. And because of my life being what it is, being available to satsang, people seem to keep wanting to talk to me about it. If anything is my practice, it's just being available to that interest and serving that interest. So that's probably the strongest practice."

Q - When people ask you questions regarding practical issues such as money, sexuality, relationships, etc. what suggestions do you give?

Arjuna - "We have a Foundation here in Nevada City. It's called *The Living Essence Foundation*...which means that what we are interested in is *living* this Presence in the context of an ordinary life without any reservation or censorship at all.

"Now, in order to do that, *everybody* becomes teacher, because one person could not possibly have mastery of living life in Presence in every arena. Someone explores one bit of life and someone else explores another and so the meeting becomes the teacher rather than a person. So, we have developed a set of tools to make the thing sort of less confusing. The tools are not to do with Realization; most of the tools we have are not about realizing the Truth, but about living it and reversing the habits that interfere with living this way. I think that you could really sum up what we do as dissolving beliefs or concepts about anything."

Alan - "I really like those questions the best because they are very grounded. Some people have a tendency to sort of float off into the ethers. But when somebody's in pain, or just gone through a divorce, or had some financial setback and they're trying to make sense out of it, or they're just falling in love and are seeing new things about themselves in a relationship, those are really good, juicy, tangible handles through which to gain access to spiritual wisdom. So I love those questions and I encourage them.

"We can all identify with the human element in those situations in one form or another. So, it gives the other people in the room something that they can tune in with."

Raphael - "Well, I don't think that there's a difference between what we call practical issues and what we call spiritual issues. I think there are only the conflicts that people have moment to moment in their lives ...Then there's also an opportunity for truths to emerge that are deeper than the original issue. Ultimately, Living the Questions can take people as far as they are willing to go. It can unravel deeper and deeper knots, and in the process lead to much greater personal freedom. We can begin with issues about food, relationship, God—really anything at all, no matter how seemingly big or small. The process remains the same and the discovery remains the same."

Surya - "Well, I just try to be very honest and answer them the best that I can. I'm not the 'Answer Man'. I don't know everything. I encourage them to understand that they are their own teacher and that they should cultivate more discernment and discrimination and clear seeing and try to discern the real from the unreal.

"...And I have a lot of respect for this self-inquiry approach. I think that this is one place where the non-dual traditions of Buddhism and other mystical traditions really come together and have a lot to offer this kind of questioning. It makes sense to be looking into not just the objects and the things in life, but into who we are. If we continue asking and looking into who we are, why we are here, why we are doing what we are doing, how we are doing it, what we are meant to be while here, we will progress spiritually and collectively in the right direction."

Dasarath - "It depends on the setting. Typically, in satsang I almost always want to refer people back to the silence of the self as the place from which their solution is going to come.

"Of course, in the corporate setting, I do address the specifics of the situation, but I do it within the context of that deeper awareness, so they have an option to fall into that, if they are so inclined."

Matthew - "Well, of course there's no one approach. It depends on the person. But I have to look at these things in my own life, too. The Lakota people talk about 'all our relations.' They say that all prayer is about becoming aware of and healing *all* of our relations...And relationships— if I had a one-sentence formula for solving that one I'd be running the world...It's a great mystery. Obviously we are always dealing with divine powers and shadow powers whether we're dealing with our own souls or others. We have to be alert and, again, it's a creative process.

"When I married Jerry Garcia and his wife I told them that marriage is not a noun, it's verb. Every day is an act of creativity between people. That's how we have to see it. And like any act of creativity, there's no insurance policy, no guarantee. But it's full of surprises, and that's the joy of it. I always encourage people to stay at it as long as they can."

Catherine - "Well, again, I suggest to people that they be natural—be very natural. So, if what is naturally arising feels good and wholesome and celebratory is to be in partnership, hallelujah!...If two people are celebrating in trust, in deep love (including a deep friendship-love) in partnership, then that's great, that's really a blessing.

"And, if partnership is not arising in life, I see no problem with that whatsoever. There's a great intimacy available for anyone resting in presence.

"The Buddha taught what is called *sila* or ethics as a way to deepen concentration, because he understood that if your behavior is not appropriate, is not skillful, you cannot have a quiet mind...and as we get more and more soft and quiet, a very heightened sensitivity comes—greater than any moral or ethical system that I know of."

Wayne - "Make as much many as you possibly can. F--k as many people as you possibly can. Eat as much as you can. Live as long as you possibly can. And enjoy life! What's so difficult about that?"

Nadeen - "Well, it depends on the question, but, that's maybe why I got off the satsang circuit. I probably talked to more than 10,000 people in those three years and the same old same old questions came up every time. And any question like that comes from not yet knowing your own essence. No one who has really experienced this shift would ask a question like that. They just wouldn't.

"So, either you're talking to the mind, or you're speaking to pure Awareness. Pure Awareness doesn't ask those questions. To the mind, however, every question you answer raises two more questions. So, it's a fruitless thing. The standard answer I give to most questions is, 'Don't know, don't care'."

Neelam - "It depends. Sometimes I'll answer these questions if they are relevant to what they are going through. Sometimes these questions do have relevance. But most of the time my job is to just point people to what is really going on. My favorite question these days is to ask, 'What is really going on?' Staying with that resolves all of these other issues. That's what really does it."

Akash - "I use a variety of experiential maps, particularly in one-on-one sessions. They all clarify the mechanisms of the mind and support letting go into one's true nature. 'Spheres of Consciousness' is a specific, practical way of mapping the way that the mind is obscuring Being. People are experiencing amazing results from this as the glue of identification dissolves. 'The Polarity Map' is another way of experiencing opposites and defusing projection. I also use the Enneagram.

"The first step is to identify what's really going on, not staying with what one thinks is going on, but what is really going on, whether this is in the area of sex, money, power or whatever. Then identify what is being clung to and what is being rejected."

Isaac - "I guess it depends on what book I've just read or how things seem at that particular moment....But it's so funny because a week later I might hear what I say and cringe. I guess, you know, there's the willingness to be naked and honest, as honest as I know how, anyway. And, usually when people see that what they are speaking about isn't as personal as they thought, that takes a huge bite out of it right there. There's a recognition that it's universal—whatever they're dealing with, I'm dealing with, too. I think that's more important than what I actually ever say."

Q - It's said by some people that we as a species are in the midst of a shift in Consciousness. Some even say that such a shift is very significant in the evolution of mankind. What's your sense of that?

Arjuna - "Yes, I do feel that is true...the contrast between what happened in 1992 and what is happening now is huge...Just in the beginning of the '90's it was relatively rare and fleeting that people would have the realization of who they really are. And now as I travel to other cities it's pretty much the norm. Almost everybody seems to be sitting in that recognition. Not everybody has necessarily freed up all doubts. But there does seem to be an invisible revolution taking place. It won't be reported in USA TODAY because it's too subtle, too invisible. But, yes, there does seem to be some shift occurring. The whole context of spirituality seems to be shifting.

"...We're all the same, you know? Everybody is that Consciousness. All that prevents it is identification with who I think myself to be."

Michael - "I'm glad you asked, because this is something I'm really passionate about! I am often privileged to sit among visionaries whose inward sight sees beyond the world of external appearances, and they are shouting from the rooftops that a new world *is* emerging! The mass media camouflage this evolutionary breakthrough because their radar picks up only the chaos, the static within this process, not the music of it! I strongly sense strands of an emerging world culture united on an ethical basis of humankind's highest development spiritually, philosophically, educationally, scientifically and socially."

Saniel - "I see human history as a continually quickening evolutionary process. That's one of the reasons why I have tremendous respect for many traditions. I'm not partial to the view that there is <u>an</u> absolute truth, at least in words, that always was so and always will be so. There are qualities of existence that appear to be very fundamental to our nature and to the nature of reality. The human species is itself an evolving *science*, not just *scientists*.

"We are part of an event that is unfolding. And from that sort of large-view perspective, I do see that we appear to be in a time when a quickening is intensifying. The acceleration is accelerating. And, as you said, many people have a similar view. So, yes, I feel that it's critical for survival.

"...all the issues facing us are just *screaming* for us to get Awake and grounded and be able to look each other in the eye and say, 'Yes, I know my Godness, but *don't bow to me!*' Let's bow to one another, and let's bow to all of the other creatures on the earth."

Alan - "People often ask me, 'What trends do you see as you travel around?' I do see trends, but I never dare to say, 'This is what's happening' because I know that everyone I meet is basically a reflection of my own consciousness...

"I would imagine that if you would interview twenty different people, you'd get twenty different ideas about what the trends are! You could interview someone who says that the world has gone to hell in a hand basket. That would be *their* reality. I wouldn't dare to assume that it was anybody else's reality.

"My life is getting better and more joyful. I'm attracting more fun people to play with, but that's just my point of attraction. I think that it's all out there, and each of us is seeing with our own eyes."

Raphael - "I know many people who think of themselves as 'Light Beings'—people who believe that we are at a transformational moment in our planetary history. They also believe that it's their great privilege and responsibility to help usher in this change of consciousness. And my reaction when I hear this is to say, 'Story, story, story, story, story!'...

"If someone chooses to live the 'Light Being' story, bless them. But it's my experience that that story can lead to a great distance from other humans, and a great distance from the tremendous amount of suffering and oppression that exists here in this moment. There is a kind of narcissism that can creep into that story, a kind of pride that often is very troubling.

"Personally, I'm inspired by people whose transformed consciousness leads them back into the everyday world, into service and activism, working without much of a story at all. These people, and I've been privileged to know many of them, are fighting corporate globalization and exploring new ways of environmental sustainability. They're building new bridges between the prosperous parts of our society and the parts where there is still great disease, great poverty, great suffering. If we could all become passionately committed to healing the earth and its inhabitants, while at the same time losing all sense of attachment to any particular outcome, this, more than anything, could bring about a global shift."

Surya - "Yes, I think that there is a shift happening. And I think that even political leaders and people from the most diverse walks of life from many countries are really calling for a spiritual revolution. We're realizing that we do have enough resources, but they are inequitably distributed. There's enough knowledge to live together harmoniously, but we are not meeting on a common ground, and we need to do so.

"...I think that this is a very special time for us. We're all more connected in this Information Age and this age of the shrinking world that we live in. This is now almost one global culture. I think that people are waking up to the fact that we have to pull together if we're not going to sink completely under the weight of our own fabrications and delusions.

"...There's now a greater, more heartfelt interest in a connective spirituality, not just in an inherited belief system that people have to believe in but don't really experience.

"...So, this is kind of a unique opportunity today, where all of these different timeless wisdom traditions exist side by side in the same place, the same time, the same language....It's all there. And for the first time, we can access these and make a more personal spiritual life and practice that can change our relations and change our community and our world. I feel strongly about this great opportunity."

Antonio - "Yes, I really believe that there is a shift going on because two thousand years of indoctrination is now shifting in some ways. The shift is that people are beginning to see that God is inside of each one and that everybody has his own power and that it's a collective thing ...But we have been living in a civilization that teaches that we have to fit in, be the same, be like the others, don't be yourself, don't be unique. And the big picture is that people are beginning to realize their own power and their own uniqueness. So, people are beginning to realize that we don't have to be the same! We *can* be different and we can accept one another's differences. We can even love those differences.

"That's the main point of this shift in Consciousness and spirituality. We are all parts of the larger thing, but each is different from the other. Each has something inside that is common to everybody: we are all made of atoms. Instead of saying that God made man in His image and likeness, I say that God created 'Atom' (Adam) in His image and likeness!"

Matthew - "Oh definitely. I've been on the road for thirty years, but even ten years ago there was still a lot of resistance to all of this. I heard a lot of, 'Yes, but...yes, but.' But around ten years ago it seemed like the dam broke and there was a shift—a noticeable shift. People started to say, 'Yes, and...yes, and!' They started to ask, 'Where can this take us?'

"And I've seen this, 'Yes, and...' build in the last ten years. There's no question about it. Look at the bestsellers on the New York Times list and books about spirituality and spiritual practice are well-represented there... spirituality itself has kind of entered the mainstream."

Catherine - "Well I have no idea whether or not we are in a shift. From one perspective it might look that way...But then, you look at the world, you look at the huge populations in China and the Middle East and Africa and you might not get the sense that there's really so much shifting there. But, of course, it can happen fast. Who knows?

"...I find that I just don't have much interest in future speculation. Given that we simply cannot know, so much of what I used to think was going to happen didn't happen and things I thought wouldn't happen did. Just watching the unfolding is enough. It takes up the whole screen, and prevents putting in any future picture".

Wayne - [Belly laugh] "I think that it's a delightful notion. And, it'll certainly draw people in! I mean, *everyone* wants to be part of the <u>*Big Shift*</u>! You'd hate to be left out of this big *cosmic occurrence*. I mean if you don't catch the wave it's like not getting into the rising stock market!"

Nadeen - "What we have here is one energy—the Source. And that Source is infinite intelligence and it has a grand design for experiencing Itself in a limited form, in a third dimension. And it's gone along for millions of years without a big shift in awareness and with the tiniest flicker of energy. Anything and everything is possible. So, I don't like to try to second-guess Source as to why this shift is taking place. It's happening! And the result is that, on a very practical level, people are becoming happy for the first time in their lives.

"What this has to do with the survival of the whole species who knows, who cares? It's just a mind trip to try to figure it out."

Neelam - "It seems true that there is a change, but I don't have an opinion about it. I don't know about it. Because when I look all I see is the Self. All I see is consciousness in different forms knowing Itself, not knowing Itself or thinking that It knows Itself."

Akash - "There is a call to the human race to awaken. I can't say when this call began. But the call is here and it is here now. So there is no need to wait for a collective wave to carry you. Don't postpone. Answer this call right now, in this very moment. Don't even wait for tomorrow. Respond to the call within yourself.

"And then perhaps it can be seen that this call from within is not separate from the call to the whole of humanity. There is only one call and it is up to you whether you answer that call right now or not."

Isaac - "It seems that way to me at times, but at other times it doesn't seem like *anything* is happening. It's a funny play, you know? It's like when you really look at it, you can't describe this instant *at all*. And so, if you can't describe it, all you can do is live it. You can't really say if it's evolving or whatever the hell is happening.

"So, it's like—in anybody's experience—all we can really describe is what we put a frame around. We can't ever describe the moment, it's just this funny play of thinking that we know what's going on which gives us time and space and all the rest of the funny stuff."

Q - For those readers of this book who may sense some form of Awakening in their lives, or at least have a great degree of interest in the topic, what would you like to say to them?

Arjuna - "The teacher you have always sought, the one who has all the answers, the one who can dissolve all of your doubts and suffering is here on planet earth and available. You just have to know where to look. And, I would say that we've been looking in the wrong place, in the wrong direction with the old style of spirituality. I would ask anybody that if you're really willing to question deeply, sincerely, without giving up or settling for conceptual answers, if you're really willing to investigate who you are in this moment, this very moment between one thought and another—who hears sound? Who notices movement? Who is that? If you are really willing to look back into that and not give up before the answer (or lack of answer) is absolutely clear, everything you have ever sought is revealed.

"If more and more people are willing to look in the right place, the very foundation of separation, manipulation and greed all comes tumbling down, all becomes resolved. It's the easiest thing in the world to recognize who you are, because it's right here. What could be more immediate than your own self? And yet, it's the most challenging thing because it means taking a stand against the ancient habits of false assumption. This is what I would say to the reader of this book: really, really deeply inquire into who you are. And know that in that inquiry everything that you've ever desired, everything you've ever tried to make happen will be fulfilled."

Michael - "For the neophyte or experienced traveler on the spiritual path what is to be understood is that That which is fueling the hunger for Truth is the Eternal Truth itself residing in every soul. Open the heart in complete trust so that Divine Guidance may illuminate your walk to spiritual awakening. Dimensions of yourself will be revealed that you cannot now imagine exist. Familiarize yourself with the experiences of those who have traveled the path to enlightenment, including the many dark nights of the soul they faced with great spiritual courage and backbone. Let them be a light unto your own unique pattern of unfoldment. Each soul has a unique romance with the Infinite, so trust where your inner spirit is leading you because it will always be closer and closer to your authentic being."

Saniel - "Oh...have courage. Persevere. So many of my brothers and sisters are struggling so hard. There are so many of our generation who have lost hope, and despaired to the point of giving up. So that's my first recommendation—have hope. And even when you don't have hope, persist and endure. Persevere. Try not to shut down on the possibility that you, too, can awaken. If you do shut down, try to be as easy on yourself as possible.

"If awakening is something that you feel desperate for in this lifetime, and you haven't been able to find it through more traditional sources, please consider checking out other sources. It may well be that you need to extricate yourself from the mind of what is, in effect, a childhood container of spiritual beliefs. That may be, as it was for me, one of the most important motions of self-liberation.

"And, no matter how much help you get from anybody, no matter how profound anyone's Transmission to you, or Blessing of you, or radiating of spiritual energy, and good wisdom and instruction and counsel, my experience and observation is that when it all comes down, you have to somehow dare. Take the leap. Find your own way. The groping is self-empowering as is the despair all through the experience."

Alan -"I would say, 'Hello, Self!' I would say that authenticity is the key to enlightenment. As each of us is true to our own passion and our own inner spirit, we begin to attract experiences that empower us to create miracles.

Raphael - "For most of my life, I was what I would call a great seeker. And I had a really important precept. That was that I would not believe anything that I did not experience directly. I was very lucky to have that precept, because it helped me distinguish between what was real for me and concepts and ideas that came from others which may have been powerful or interesting or intriguing but ultimately not true for me.
"On the other hand, sometimes skepticism comes with a certain sort of rigidity, a kind of, 'prove it to me' attitude that makes it difficult for new experience to arrive in one's life. So I would suggest that it's important to have a healthy skepticism yet at the same time be really open and humble in each moment and to truly understand that we never know what's going to happen next...
"I think that the great miracle of our life here on earth—as well as the

great mystery—is that when we stop making assumptions and when we stop pretending to be God we come to understand that we have absolutely no knowledge about what will happen next. And that lack of any kind of knowing is the very thing which allows us—if we let it seep into every pore of our being—to become available for greater and greater spiritual freedom."

Surya - "I would say this: 'American Buddha—awaken! Throw off your chains, your concepts!'...We need to find a way that resonates with our heart and bring it to our lives day after day and year after year, and not just imitate somebody else.

"We have to be honest, authentic, sincere and genuine. And, you know, [take it] *lightly*, not so seriously, not grimly. Taking it lightly is very important, with a sense of humor, with a sense of the cosmic absurdity of the entire quest.

"...As we practice self-inquiry and other mindful and contemplative practices we gain more insight toward ourselves, we realize that we are not really who we think we are. And that frees us from a lot of delusions. I truly think that that's the direction that spirituality takes beyond the isms and schisms. This is the direction of *dharma*. Not just Buddhism, or Hinduism or *vedanta*.

"This is the convergence point of the *dharma* today—one *dharma*, a *dharma* that realizes the truth of who we are. It realizes the Buddha-light within one's self, which means with the other, also, within our relations, within everyone and everything."

Dasarath - "I think you just trust your own self. You know, there are a million answers. The world is *full* of answers, and they're beautiful answers. But, somehow, we ultimately turn to our self because the self is the answer. If you're willing to turn fully to this beingness that's here, to this silence that's here, it reveals everything to you. So there's nothing you need to know. There's nothing you need to do. Just be you."

Antonio - "I'd like to say, 'Have fun! If you are having fun, you can be sure that you are growing!' You are expanding in Consciousness. Our biggest enemy is fear. So, we have to expand this Awareness that we are all part of the same big, living cell that we call Mother Earth. And if we f--k up Mother Earth, we f--k up ourselves. So let's get a grip and have fun while we're doing it! Be nice, accept others, live and let live. Be and let be. Have fun while growing.

"And you can be sure that all of the power is within. You won't find it outside of yourself. And if you do find it outside, you can be sure that this power has come from inside yourself."

Matthew - "Well, I'd ask them to listen to their hearts. And if the heart has been blessed with either a small opening or a big breakthrough, I'd ask them to realize that this is important work of the spirit that's coming upon them. And they want to pay attention to that, and let the spirit through. That can mean, of course, developing meditation practices, but it can also mean study and learning about traditions, especially their own tradition.

A lot of Westerners think that they have to go East and that's because Western religion has often ignored spirituality. But I think as my work has demonstrated, we have great mystics from the West...but have the same impact, really, as many of the creative teachers of the East. I think that the East has kept to its practices better and so there are a lot of practices that we can invoke such as yoga, for example, and meditation and others.

"Also, of course we can look to the indigenous wisdom...We're all native Americans in the sense that we're on their land and this is where their spirits were honored for centuries. So we can be open to that...So, we should not ignore the beautiful, powerful contribution of the indigenous wisdom.

"Certainly, my writing and the writing of many others has been to recover the treasures of the Western mystical tradition and (especially in my most recent book) to put them into the same pool with the treasures of the Eastern traditions. I think that's where we have to be as a species today.

"We can't be hiding behind our denominational boxes. It's too late for that. We need all the wisdom we can get. So, whenever there's an opening in our hearts and in our souls, that's wisdom trying to pour through so let's give it some attention."

Catherine - "...given the sample of people that will be in this book, I think that any resonance that the reader might have with any of us (or any branches or teachers or books that those people may recommend) is a very useful place to start.

"It's helpful in the beginning to have a teacher, for want of another word, a person, a living presence within whom you can sense both their humanity and their divinity so easily. So, it's very, very helpful and inspiring. And, there's a worldwide *sangha* of fantastic people, not just the teachers but all of the people interested in this, who you immediately plug into when you begin studying this journey. All of that is very helpful and rich."

Wayne - "I wouldn't say anything! But, if they come to me with some question...if they are drawn to me for some reason, then we can sit together. And we'll see what happens. That's all.

"...This teaching, as it has come to me from Ramesh, is one in which there are no prescriptions. It just continually points back to *what* is. But, you keep trying to get *there*, but 'there' is *here*!

"It doesn't get any better than this. I mean it'll change in the next moment but *this is it! This is what you've got! This is what is!*

"And this is the touch-point for God. Right here!"

Nadeen - "Well, the book found them. The shift found them. The search is over. We're just so conditioned by our past that even when we have found what we were looking for, the mind goes crazy trying to figure out 'why and how.' You will go through what I call 'bobbing in and out' when you experience this shift, and you will think you have lost it, but you haven't. It just keeps coming back in waves of understanding, and the contrast that is needed for this understanding is for limitation to seem to come back in. And then understanding seems to return. And it feels like, 'two steps forward, one step back.' That's how this shift goes. Until finally there are no more questions, no more doubt, no more seeking.

"Everyone is Source, and they will get it when they get it. The most one can do now is just be, and enjoy this Freedom."

Neelam - "I would say be absolutely truthful and honest with yourself. If you think you know something, throw it out. Just be totally honest with your heart. That's what really matters. Reading books, you know, doesn't do it. There is such a tendency to pick things up. We often reach out for a book when we are in confusion, when we don't know what's going on. And for us to know what's going on is so much more precious than to know what someone else knows about it. Because then we just adapt everything.

"Be honest with what you really know. Be really truthful. In the heart, we all know the truth. It's not something that is just for a few chosen ones. So be honest with yourself about that."

Akash - "Don't postpone. Look at whatever you are postponing and see how willing you are to give that up. Postponing is suffering. Life is here now. Being here now is the liberation."

Isaac - "I would say for most people, it's useful to be around somebody that they can sense their own Being with. Because this is a big assistance, to get that recognition clear in yourself. And then once that's happened, there's just a natural process that starts to go on, and your attention gets interested in it in a conscious way, you could say. Then there's the usual thing of being around people with like interests.

"Yes, it's a funny thing because in one sense, there's the total recognition that what is needed will manifest no matter what you tell anybody. It's just like it's happening by itself. Whatever Intelligence there is that's taking care will guide them to the right place, the right person and the right circumstance for them to see."

Appendix II

Bibliography of Interviewees

This bibliography is offered as the best possible listing of writings available to the author at the time of publication. Every effort was made to ensure the accuracy and completeness of the list. If you have a particular interest in a certain guest and his or her published work, we highly recommend that you get in touch with that person directly, using the contact information provided at the end of their interview. In this way, you can not only obtain up-to-the-minute and totally accurate lists of books available, but you may find that there are pamphlets, audio/video tapes, newsletters and other pertinent and interesting information available that are not listed here.

Arjuna Nick Ardagh -

The Beloved: Living Essence Tape Series (Self X-Press, 1998)
Relaxing Into Clear Seeing (Self X-Press, 1998)
How About Now? (Self X-Press, 1999—Video, 1999)
The End of Seeking (Video, 1999)
It Is Simple (Video, 1999)
Beyond Flinching (Video, 1999)
Love Bursting Forth (Video, 1999)
Worship The Worshipper (Video, 1999)
Various Audiocassettes (1999, 2000)

Rev. Michael Beckwith -

40 Day Mid Fast Soul Feast (Agape International Spiritual Center, 2001)
Various audiocassettes

Saniel Bonder -

The White-Hot Yoga of the Heart (1995)
Waking Down: Beyond Hypermasculine Dharmas (1998)
While Jesus Weeps: Conversations in the Garden of Gethsemane—A Novel (1998)
The Conscious Principle (1999)
The Incarnation of Mutuality, Volume One (2000).
Waking Down: Beyond Hypermasculine Dharmas—unabridged audio book—(1998)
White-Hot Freedom: An Invitation to the Human SUN Teachings of Saniel Bonder—audiocassette (2001)
Saniel Bonder—Waking Down—a short film (2001)

193

Alan Cohen -

Rising In Love (Dolphin Communications, 1982—Hay House, 1996)
Setting the Seen: Creative Visualizations for Healing
   (Dolphin Comm. 1982)
Peace That You Seek (Dolphin Comm., 1985)
Have You Hugged a Monster Today? (John Seymour Books, 1988)
Joy Is My Compass (Hay House, 1990, 1996)
The Dragon Doesn't Live Here Any More
   (Fawcett Books, 1993—Audio 1996))
Dare To Be Yourself (Fawcett, 1994)
I Had It All the Time (Alan Cohen Productions, 1994—Audio 1996)
Are You As Happy As Your Dog? (ACP, 1996)
A Deep Breath of Life (Hay House, 1996)
Lifestyles of the Rich In Spirit (Hay House, 1996)
A Time To Awaken (Seven Hills Books, 1997)
Handle With Prayer (Hay House, 1999—Audio 1999)
Happily Even After (Hay House, 1999)
My Father's Voice (ACP, 2000)

H. Raphael Cushnir -

Unconditional Bliss: Finding Happiness in the Face of Hardship
   (Quest Books, 2000)

Lama Surya Das -

Schlepping Towards Enlightenment
   (Hay House, 1999—Audio 1999)
Natural Perfection (1999—Audio: Sounds True, 1999)
Tibetan Dream Yoga (2000—Audio: Sounds True, 2000)
Buddhism In America (2000—Audio: Sounds True, 2000)
Awakening The Buddhist Heart (Broadway Books, 2000—Audio
   2000)
Awakening To The Sacred (Broadway Books, 2000)
Natural Meditation (2000—Audio: Sounds True, 2000)

Dasarath (David Davidson) -

*Wisdom at Work: The Awakening of Consciousness
   in the Workplace* (Larson Publications, 1998)

Antonio Duncan -

> *The ABC's of Crystals* (1999)
> *The Path of the Stones* (2000)

Catherine Ingram -

> *In the Footsteps of Gandhi: Conversations with Spiritual/Social Activists* (Parallax Press, 1990)

Wayne Liquorman -

> *Consciousness Speaks* (Advaita Press, 1993)
> *Acceptance of What Is: A Book About Nothing* (Advaita Press, 2000)
>   **as Ram Tzu -**
> *No Way: A Guide for the Spiritually Advanced* (Advaita Press, 1990)

Satyam Nadeen -

> *From Onions To Pearls* (Hay House, 1999)
> *From Seekers To Finders* (Hay House, 2000)

Isaac Shapiro -

> *Outbreak Of Peace* (1998)

Matthew Fox -

> *Meditations with Meister Eckhart* (Bear & Co, 1982)
> *Illuminations of Hildegard of Bingen* (Bear & Co., 1985)
> *Hildegard of Bingen's Book of Divine Works* (Bear & Co., 1987)
> *Coming of the Cosmic Christ* (Harper San Francisco, 1988)
> *Creation Spirituality* (Harper San Francisco, 1991)
> *The Reinvention of Work* (Harper San Francisco, 1995)
> *The Physics of Angels, with Rupert Sheldrake* (Harper San Francisco, 1996)
> *Natural Grace, with Rupert Sheldrake* (Main Street Books, 1997)
> *Confessions: The Making of a Post-Denominational Priest* (Harper San Francisco, 1997)
> *A Spirituality Named Compassion* (Inner Traditions Intl Ltd, 1999)
> *Sins of the Spirit, Blessings of the Flesh* (Three Rivers Press, 2000)
> *Original Blessing* ((Putnam, 2000)

Passion for Creation: The Earth Honoring Spirituality of Meister Eckhart previously titled Breakthrough (Inner Traditions Intl Ltd, 2000)

One River, Many Wells (J.P. Tarcher, 2000)

Glossary

Advaita - nondual understanding of the Divine, from the Hindu tradition

Bhakti - The Hindu path of love and devotion as a means of recognizing one's godliness

Bodhisattva - one who vows to return to embodied form until all sentient beings are Awakened

Chakras - seven psychic energy vortices in the body

Darshan - literally, "sacred seeing"; the sighting of the physical body of an Awakened one. In ancient times this was seen to be a source of potent blessing

Dharma - the Truth, the law of Reality, the teaching of the Way of Liberation; one's personal means of expressing this Truth

Decentralization - Quidam's term for the recognition of Awakening event; he uses this word to indicate that in the moment of first noticing his already-Awakened Condition, he sensed that his Awareness was equally present in *all* that exists, not exclusively in and as his own body-mind

Dzogchen - nondual understanding of the nature of the Divine, in the Buddhist tradition

Jnani - the path of intellectual knowledge, reasoning and discrimination as means of Awakening

Leela (or "lila") - the play of the Divine

Mahayana Buddhism - "Great Vehicle" or "High Way"; an aspect of Buddhism stressing Awakening as a service to all sentient beings

Sadhana - spiritual practice or exercise

Sangha - a spiritual gathering or community

Satori - Awakening (typically, temporary and partial)

Satsang - association with Truth; a gathering dedicated to the revelation and/or celebration of Divine Truth

Seva - selfless service to Truth

Shakti - spiritual force or power

Sila - ethics; character; moral perfection

Sunyata - a Tibetan term meaning "empty fullness"

Tantra - the use of the senses to go beyond the senses; also called the "rapid path"

Vedanta - "end of the Vedas"—one of the six schools of Hindu philosophy originating in the ancient Hindu texts; direct knowledge of Consciousness

Vedas - The four ancient Hindu scriptures; said to be Divinely revealed

197

Yoga - from sanskrit for "yoke"—the science of joining (yoking) body, mind and spirit

Yogi - a male practitioner of yoga, especially hatha yoga (the yoga of *asanas*, or physical postures)

Yogini - a female practitioner of yoga

About the Author

Quidam Green Meyers is an ordained minister and certified spiritual counselor who resides in Los Angeles. He is a spiritually-Awakened being who lives an ordinary Western family life.

From an early age, Quidam (pronounced "key-DAHM") expressed a fascination with spiritual topics and by the age of 12 had developed a deep interest in yoga and meditation. As an adult, he spent a total of seventeen years studying intensely with a number of Eastern and Western-born spiritual teachers.

During this time he was simultaneously engaged in a successful career in the international rock and New Age music industries. He worked as a professional musician, radio station promotions director, record label executive and musical artist manager. During this period, he was awarded rock radio's National Best Marketing Director title and helped guide the careers of several Grammy-winning musical groups.

On March 7, 1997, Quidam experienced a "shift" in consciousness that he now refers to as *decentralization*. In a public talk in 1999, he noted:

"In this shift, which might traditionally be referred to as Awakening or Enlightenment, it was simply noticed that identification with the 'I' which had been felt to be the center of my existence, had relaxed. What remained was, and is, a profound recognition that 'I' have always existed as Consciousness - as a universal sense of Awareness Itself. This is the reality of each of us. We simply need to recognize it."

After this shift, Quidam retired from music and moved into a period of study and writing which led to formal ordination as a minister and to his endorsement as a certified spiritual counselor by the Living Essence Foundation in Northern California.

Quidam has spoken and taught in a number of cities in the U.S. and in Australia. In 2001, he and his wife Diana formed the Spiritual Freedom

Foundation, a non-profit organization dedicated to sharing Awakening world-wide. Spiritual Freedom Foundation offers spiritual training and guidance through lectures, weekend Intensives and other direct contact events. Quidam also offers a unique program of ongoing Awakening training called *Spiritual Mentoring*, which makes use of a non-authoritarian, peer-based sharing model.

Quidam transmits a powerful Awakening energy that is highly effective in gently dislodging habits of separative thought which can obscure our already-Happy nature. He offers spiritual counseling in-person and by phone, gives public talks and weekend seminars, and sponsors other ministerial services.

Spiritual Freedom Foundation can be contacted by phone (310) 915-9167 or by email at BeHappinessNow@aol.com.

A Word from the Cover Artist

Circumstance (or was it intervention?) decreed that the artwork for *Wide Awake* became the project of Lerentia Basson.

With the cutoff date looming, a synopsis and parts of *Wide Awake* were e-mailed to her on the other side of the world—Cape Town, South Africa. And so the writer and artist had a meeting of minds and hearts over a very short, intense period of time and great physical distance.

Lerentia comments, "After reading *Wide Awake* and sharing a telephone conversation or two with Quidam, I tried to visually capture the essence of this truly profound and amazing book. The inspiration to use exploding rays of light became obvious to portray the often dark inner travels and brilliant spiritual breakthroughs, as explained by the people interviewed. I truly believe that the world needs books of this caliber and content."

Lerentia Basson has a BA (Ed) Arts degree and produces graphics for several publishing firms. She also creates and designs websites.

She can be contacted at:　　lerentia@techcare.co.za
http://www.techcare.co.za

"From across time and space yet another Blessing showered forth when the cover art landed in Lerentia's loving care. Her depiction of the brilliant Radiance of the Awakened Heart exploding from its Source and illuminating the darkness of mankind's imagined separation is beyond inspiration. The image is itself a teaching device.

I am in awe of the Grace which Lerentia brought to the artwork and I'll be forever grateful for the 'Divine Accident' which brought her to the project."—Quidam

ALSO FROM THE BOOK TREE

Zen and the Lady
by Claire Myers Owens

Now back in print! When this book was first published in 1979 it was praised by the most respected spiritual researchers and psychologists of the time including Ken Wilbur, Kenneth Ring, Charles Tart, Jack Kornfield and Willis Harmon. Her earlier work was also praised by Abraham Maslow and Aldous Huxley.

Zen and the Lady is the personal story of an American woman's journey into Zen, beginning in her 70th year and continuing into her eighties. In this book Claire Myers Owens brings the reader with her on the path to enlightenment. It is a journey of spiritual development, perfect for those seeking the same type of growth, no matter what background or tradition one is from. Claire is no longer alive today, but her powerful and touching story will live on in the hearts of those who read it. This book is already considered a classic of Western mystical literature.

"All struggles were ended, all seeking forgotten, all dualities abandoned. Every hope fulfilled. Every question answered. Every problem resolved— briefly, if not for all time. I was content..."
—from *Zen and the Lady*

"A beautiful tale, artfully told... I've read a number of spiritual autobiographies, including several within a Zen setting, but ZEN AND THE LADY *is without parallel."*
—Kenneth Ring

"I found it absolutely fascinating and a totally absorbing story, a superb blend of autobiographical remembrance and sophisticated psychological insights."
—Ken Wilbur

"Thank you for being an inspiration to us all."
—Willis Harmon

"It is a treasure trove... of wisdom."
—Sonja Margulies
Journal of Transpersonal Psychology

"Beautiful."
—Jack Kornfield

"Fascinating."
—Charles Tart

ISBN 1-58509-129-4. 192 pages, 6 x 9, trade paper, $17.95. To order with credit card call 1-800-700-TREE (8733), or mail $22.45 to The Book Tree, PO Box 16476, San Diego, CA 92176 (CA residents add 7.75 % sales tax).

Triumph of the Human Spirit:
The Greatest Achievements of the Human Soul
and How Its Power can Change Your Life
by Paul Tice.

This book is about those who changed the entire course of history. They did not start with money, power, or great armies—all they had was an idea, and a passion for the truth. Gandhi, Joan of Arc, Dr. King and others died for their ideas but made the world a better place. This book outlines how an intuitive spiritual knowledge, or "gnosis," provided these people with guidance and helped to create the most incredible spiritual moments that the world has ever known. These events are all part of our spiritual evolution. We have learned from past mistakes, have become more tolerant toward others, and the people in this book have been signposts- —pointing us collectively toward something greater. This book also shows how a spiritual triumph of your own can be achieved. Various exercises will strengthen the soul and reveal its hidden power. Unlike the past, in today's Western world we are free to explore the truth without fear of being tortured or executed. As a result, the rewards are great. This is the perfect book for all those who believe in spiritual freedom and have a passion for the truth.

BT-574 · ISBN 1-885395-57-4 · 295 pages
6 x 9 · trade paper · illustrated · $19.95

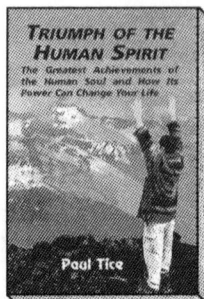

Buddhist Suttas: Major Scriptural
Writings from Early Buddhism
by T.W. Rhys Davids.

These seven scriptural writings are considered by many to be the most important of the Buddhist religion. Originally written in the Pali language, they date to the fourth and third centuries BC. This early date is what makes them so important—they form the very core of Buddhist teachings. The influence of the texts contained in this book upon the entire Buddhist world is enormous. They have been sought after and studied by monks and scholars for centuries, and there could never be a complete understanding of the true meaning of Buddhism without them. This collection of texts was not only translated by the great T.W. Rhys Davids, but edited by the renowned scholar of eastern religions, F. Max Muller, making it clearly the most reliable text of its kind in the English language.

BT-794 · ISBN 1-58509-079-4 · 376 pages
6 x 9 · trade paper · $27.95

CALL FOR A FREE CATALOG 1 800 700-TREE (8733)

Was Jesus Influenced by Buddhism?
A Comparative Study of the Lives and Thoughts of Gautama and Jesus
by Dwight Goddard.

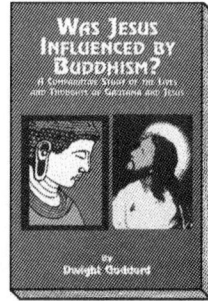

Christianity as we know it today differs from the eastern religions in many ways. There seems to be a huge gap between east and west when comparing religious traditions. Dwight Goddard manages to bridge that gap, however, with this revealing book. Much of what we find in Christianity today had been added to the faith on top of the original teachings of Jesus. What is interesting is that Buddhism has suffered with the same problems of additions and distortions over the centuries as Christianity did, and has also failed to uphold some of the original teachings of its founder. A powerful religion sprung up based on his teachings and flourished half a millennium before Jesus was ever born. Five hundred years is a long time for a religion to spread and flourish, so Jesus could have easily been influenced by Buddhist teachings as proposed by this book. There were many years in the life of Jesus that remain to this day unaccounted for. Goddard also puts forth evidence that the Essenes, of whom Jesus had contact with and may have been a member himself, had strong Buddhist influences. If either (or both) of these scenarios is true, then the parallels between Jesus and the Buddha are more than just a coincidence.

BT-271 · ISBN 1-58509-027-1 · 252 pages
6 x 9 · trade paper · $19.95

Early Buddhism
by T.W. Rhys Davids.

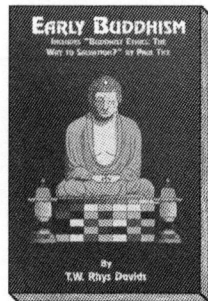

There is no better scholar to have outlined the early formation of Buddhism than T.W. Rhys Davids. This book is short, to the point, and filled with interesting facts. It is a step by step guidebook to what Buddhism really is and was intended to be, and is perfect for providing a complete overview of Buddhist origins. Paul Tice has contributed to this work with a short section entitled *Buddhist Ethics: The Way to Salvation?* In it he explains how Buddhism was not meant to be a form of religious worship, but an important system of ethics. When practiced properly, as the Buddha had done, this ethical system was meant to bring personal salvation.

BT-76X · ISBN 1-58509-076-X · 112 pages
6 x 9 · trade paper · $12.95

www.ingramcontent.com/pod-product-compliance
Lightning Source LLC
Chambersburg PA
CBHW032058080426
42733CB00006B/328